The
Single
Father

—

A Dad's Guide
to Parenting
without a Partner

"And always remember I'm here for you, son,
at Dadman@connect.pop.net.'

The
Single
Father

A Dad's Guide
to Parenting
without a Partner

Armin A. Brott

Abbeville Press • Publishers
New York • London • Paris

To Zippy the Pokadoke and Roodle Doo, who kept me sane and out of jail then, and who keep me proud and laughing now

Excerpt from J. Bigner and F. Bozett, "Parenting and Gay Fathers," *Marriage and Family Review* 14 (1989), reprinted by permission of the Hayworth Press, Binghamton, New York.

Excerpt from Jane Nelsen, Cheryl Erwin, and Carol Delzer, *Positive Discipline for Single Parents* (Rocklin, Calif.: Prima Publishing, 1994), reprinted with permission.

Child Care Aware's guidelines for identifying quality child care, reprinted with permission.

EDITOR: Jacqueline Decter
DESIGNER: Celia Fuller
PRODUCTION DIRECTOR: Hope Koturo

First edition
10 9 8 7 6 5 4 3 2 1

Cover photograph by Jack Deutsch
For cartoon credits, see page 303

Library of Congress Cataloging-in-Publication Data
Brott, Armin A.
    The single father : a dad's guide to parenting without a partner / Armin A. Brott
        p.   cm.
    Includes bibliographical references and index.
    ISBN 0-7892-0518-1 (hardbound). — ISBN 0-7892-0520-3 (pbk.)
    1. Single fathers.   2. Parenting.   I. Title.
HQ759.915.B75   1999
649'.1'0243—dc21   98-49531

Contents

Acknowledgments

Although there's only one name on the cover, it's really amazing how many people contribute to creating a book. I'd like to thank all of the following, without whose help, generosity, wisdom, advice, guidance, encouragement, prodding, and occasional silliness this volume wouldn't have been possible.

Jane Adams at Child Care Aware, for her help on the child-care selection sections; Michael Aiello, for helping with Internet Resources; Eve Aldridge, for reminding me when to tone things down a little and for adding her special perspective to the sections on new relationships; Richard Austin, Jr., for his suggestions on parental alienation and false accusations of abuse; Jimmy Boyd and Ron Henry, who for years have been sharing with me their enormous resources of information on divorced fathers and who have encouraged and supported me throughout much of my writing career; June and Gene Brott, for their continued moral and financial contributions toward my continued mental health; Marilyn Courtot, for sharing her knowledge—and her database of kids' books—and adding to the children's reading lists; Jackie Decter, my encouraging yet firm editor, who always keeps me on track; Celia Fuller, for giving us a look; Amy Handy, who once again did way more than copyedit; Charlotte Hardwick, for her book and for sharing her advice about supervised visitation; Elizabeth Hickey, for her wisdom on mediation and parenting agreements; Grace Lacoursiere, for her advice and for sharing her newsletter for widowers raising children; Mary Lamia, my dear friend, for reviewing every word in every section dealing with fathers' and children's psychology and for trying to straighten out my personal life; Jim Levine, for steering me in the right direction more than once and for getting me into all this trouble in the first place; Ro Logrippo, for her wonderful comments and suggestions on designing and setting up kids' rooms; Stuart Miller, for his hospitality and friendship, as well as for his careful read and fine-tuning of the parts on child support, custody, visitation, and anything else having to do with the law; Ross Parke, for his inspiration and advice and for looking over—and greatly improving—the sections on child development, father involvement, and men's psychology; Jonathan Petruck, who helped a lot with the sections on financial planning and insurance; Jeff Porter and Eric Tyson, for their advice and guidance on just about everything having to do with money; my buddy Janice Tannin, for the tomato soup, the rice pudding, and her kitchen and cooking advice; Kelly Taylor and Charlotte Patterson, for their insight into the concerns of gay dads; and finally, to the dozens of single dads who responded to my Internet posts or let me interview them for this book, who read pieces of the manuscript, and who so willingly shared their own experiences.

*"I've never once demanded resepect from you simply because
I'm your father. You should respect me for that."*

Introduction

Every year a million fathers get divorced. And every year a million men who aren't married become fathers. There are also about a million gay fathers out there, as well as hundreds of thousands of widowers who have children under eighteen. Although each of these categories of fathers is quite different, they share a common bond. They are all single fathers.

Some people might argue that the phrase *single father* should apply only to men who are raising their children on their own, without help from the children's mother. I disagree. As far as I'm concerned, any man who has a child is a father—no exceptions. And any man who isn't living with his child's mother is a single father.

It doesn't matter whether you were once married or never married, whether you are widowed, gay, or in the process of ending a relationship. Nor does it matter whether you have full-time custody of your children, share it equally with your former partner, or hardly get to see your kids at all. What matters is that you want to be—and stay—actively involved in your children's lives any way you can. In that case, this book is for you.

As you may have already found out, though, being and staying involved with your kids is usually a lot harder for single fathers than it sounds. In divorce cases, mothers are given sole custody more than 85 percent of the time, and most fathers are left with every other weekend, alternate holidays, and a couple of weeks in the summer. Never-married men have even fewer legal rights to see their children, and gay fathers suffer widespread social and judicial discrimination. Legally speaking, widowers are the best off, but like almost all other single fathers, they endure the societal suspicion that they aren't capable of taking care of their children by themselves.

In addition to these legal and societal impediments, too many single fathers who are faced with the seemingly daunting task of setting up and running a new household lack the necessary skills, experience, or social support to be as involved with their children as they'd like to be.

What This Book Is . . . and Is Not

The Single Father: A Dad's Guide to Parenting Without a Partner is *not* anti-woman. It's also not about how to win a child-custody battle or how to hurt your children's mother. Those attitudes help no one and end up taking a terrible toll on the children. If you're looking for that kind of information, you'll have to try someplace else.

Instead, *The Single Father* is designed to help you recognize the legal, social, and practical obstacles to being an involved single father and find ways to overcome them. It will also educate you—whether you're divorced, separated, or widowed—about the emotional, psychological, practical, and social aspects of single fatherhood. Finally, it will give you the knowledge, skills, support, and other tools you'll need to preserve and develop your father-child relationship and to make a difference in your children's lives.

The time to start is now. Researchers have found that fathers who don't have much meaningful contact with their children in their first two years as single fathers probably won't have much contact at all. Being an actively involved single dad isn't going to be easy. You may feel lost, alone, helpless, and confused along the way. But it will also be joyous, educational, and uplifting. Guaranteed.

How This Book Is Organized

Although each single father's experience is different, there are many common characteristics. I've organized the book in a way that makes sense for most men, but feel free to skip around. The book is divided into the following major parts:

You

Losing a partner, whether you wanted to or not, is hard. It brings up more feelings and emotions than you could possibly imagine. In this part we'll take an in-depth look at the emotional side of becoming a single father, with a focus on understanding and coping with your feelings. You'll be a far better parent to your children if you've got a grip on your own emotions first.

We'll also talk about some of the practical steps, such as hiring a lawyer and/or finding a mediator, that you'll need to take right away in order to ensure that you and your children have the opportunity to develop and nurture the kind or relationship that's best for all of you.

You and the System

In this part we'll discuss the various obstacles (including your ex) that sometimes make it hard for single fathers to be as involved with their kids as they'd like to be. We'll examine child-custody arrangements, child support, alimony, and access (visitation), all with an emphasis on preserving your mental well-being and your relationship with your children.

You and the Kids

Although becoming a single father will undoubtedly take its toll on you, it will have longer-lasting, more profound effects on your children. And if you're going to be able to help them, you'll need a solid understanding of what they're going through. That's what you'll get in this part. We'll examine the wide range of emotions they'll be experiencing and take a serious look at how you can help them cope.

This part also includes valuable, age-appropriate information and tips on how to stay actively involved with your kids, whether you see them every day, every week, every month, or only once a year.

You and Your Ex

If you aren't a widower, in all likelihood you're going to have an ongoing relationship with the mother of your child(ren), possibly for the rest of your life. The very idea may make you sick, but you'd better start getting used to it. Remember, one of the biggest predictors of how kids fare psychologically and emotionally after their parents break up is how well the parents get along. In this part we'll talk about the importance of getting along with your ex and we'll take a look at some easy (and important) ways to keep your relationship civil.

Unfortunately, your ex might not be as open-minded as you. For that reason, this part also includes a serious discussion and plenty of hard-hitting advice on what to do if she interferes with your relationship with your kids.

Practical Matters

In this part we'll concentrate on the nuts and bolts (and shopping lists) of setting up your new home and your new kitchen. We'll go over some of the finances of fatherhood, such as saving for college, reducing your expenses, saving for retirement, and estate planning. We'll also discuss the ins and outs of finding quality child care.

Starting Over

It may be the farthest thing from your mind right now, but sooner or later you'll want to rekindle your love life. In this part we'll talk about getting back into dating, about how your new relationship(s) will impact you, your kids, and even your new partner. And since she many have kids of her own, we'll get you ready for yet another role: stepfather. Finally, we'll discuss your ex's love life and how it— and her new partner(s)—might affect you and the kids.

A Note on Terminology

He/She/Child/Children

Because you might have a son or a daughter or one (or more than one) of each, I've tried to alternate fairly regularly between "he" and "she," "your child" and "your children," and "your kids." Except where it's obvious, most of these phrases are interchangeable.

Your Ex

Whether the mother of your child has passed away or was your wife, your girlfriend, your lover, your fiancée, or a one-night stand doesn't matter. She's still your child's mother and occupies a special place in your child's heart and mind. Given the number of possible appellations, I decided, in most cases, to go for the most generic term: your ex.

A Small but Important Disclaimer

I'm not a pediatrician, lawyer, financial planner, or accountant, nor do I play one on TV (I do have a radio show, though). I'm also not gay or widowed, although I am single. And even though every sentence you're going to read in this book has been reviewed by real live single (or formerly single) fathers and by experts in the appropriate fields and has been pronounced sound, accurate, and reasonable, each single father's situation is unique. So please check with a professional whenever you're unsure about whether the steps you are taking are in your best interests and in those of your family.

First Feelings

Whatever it was that made you a single father—whether it was the death of your wife or the breakup of your relationship—you're going through an emotional upheaval unlike any you've experienced before, and things are going to be tough for quite a while.

"Fathers encountered marked stresses in practical problems of living, self-concept and emotional adjustment, and interpersonal relations following divorce," say researchers E. Mavis Heatherington and her colleagues Martha Cox and Roger Cox. "Low self-esteem, loneliness, depression, and feelings of hopelessness were characteristic of the divorced couple." Interestingly, a number of other researchers have found that widowed fathers have nearly the same reaction following their loss.

Most of what you're experiencing now and will be going through for the next weeks and months and maybe even years will come under the general heading of "grief." A lot of people believe that grief is a word that applies only to widowers. But the truth is that divorced and separated fathers experience it as well, and what they go through is remarkably similar to what widowed fathers go through.

Another common misconception about grief is that it's a single feeling; on the contrary, it's a rather complex set of emotions that evolve in a fairly predictable way over time. One of the first people to see grief this way was Elisabeth Kubler-Ross, who in the late 1960s identified five distinct stages that people go through when they're told they have a terminal illness.

1. Shock and denial
2. Anger
3. Bargaining

4. Depression
5. Acceptance

In the decades since, many people have come to believe that Kubler-Ross's stages apply equally well to other kinds of grieving, including the breakup of a relationship and the death of a spouse.

Naturally, these stages aren't set in cement and each man experiences them in his own way. You might go through them in a different order, you might get bogged down in one or another for months or years, you might skip one altogether, or you might even return to one three or four times. But one thing is absolutely certain: you will grieve. Even if you have hated your ex for the past five years and only recently summoned up the courage to end your relationship, you're still mourning a major loss—your hopes, your dreams, your plans for the future. So no matter how tough you think you are, don't delude yourself into thinking that you're immune to these feelings.

Let's take a look at these stages in a little more detail.

Shock and Denial

Most relationships don't end by mutual agreement. One of the partners has usually made the decision long before telling the other. This gives her (and because about 70 percent of all divorces are filed by women, it's safe to say "her") the chance to get a little used to the idea, to prepare for the upcoming changes, and maybe even to start a new relationship.

The other partner, usually the guy, is generally stunned. Granted, men could take some of the edge off the shock if they were better at reading signals, but in most men's experience, one day life was going along perfectly; the next, they come home to an empty house. Whether you're widowed or divorced, you're probably in a situation you never imagined you'd be in.

According to Jane Burgess, an expert on widowers, widowers and men whose wives initiated the divorce had similar immediate reactions to their loss: feelings of shock, denial, hopelessness, panic, self-pity, and confusion, as well as insomnia, depression, and an inability to concentrate.

Many men whose partners leave them respond by simply refusing to believe that the relationship is over. You can actually see this kind of denial in action by looking at many newly single or separated men's apartments, says author Stuart Kahan. "It takes an inordinate amount of time to unpack the boxes and put everything away," he writes. "Why? A reluctance to start the new life, to end the old one. It's as if the old life is still in the boxes and unpacking them will make it disappear."

"Repression and denial have always worked for Dad."

Widowers, too, are often reluctant to acknowledge that their old life is over, keeping their wives' voices on answering machines, for example, or their clothes in their closets. Denial can last weeks, months, or longer.

Anger

For most men, being angry is much safer (not to mention socially condoned) than being sad or depressed. There are basically two types of anger:

- **Passive.** You express your anger by doing things designed to get your ex and others angry at you, such as "forgetting" to pick up the kids when you're supposed to, not returning phone calls, or not paying your bills on time.
- **Active.** You express your anger physically, verbally, or by trying to get revenge against whomever you're furious at.

However you express it, being angry feels kind of energizing, filling your head with all sorts of ideas and giving you the motivation to try to do something about your situation. But all that may be something of a mirage. "Angry adults feel they are taking steps to stabilize their out-of-control experience, and this tends to make them stay angry," writes Shirley Thomas, author of *Parents Are Forever*. Accepting and moving beyond your anger is an important part of grieving, but staying angry for too long just because it makes you feel good will interfere with the process and make your recovery even slower.

Anger also has a tendency to become blame, which, even if it's accurate, isn't particularly productive. If you've just gone through a breakup, you've got a hundred things to be angry at your ex about, and she's got the same number of complaints against you. But you also might be angry at your ex's friends or relatives for urging her to get out of her relationship with you, at yourself for getting involved with this woman in the first place, at your own parents for not supporting you unconditionally, at the lawyers and judges you feel screwed you in court, at women in general for making your life miserable, and even at your kids for whatever you think they've done.

Widowers, too, sometimes lash out at everything and everyone around them. You may be furious at your deceased wife for not taking her vitamins, not exercising, staying in the sun too long, driving too fast, killing herself, or for some other reason. Or you may be angry at the doctors, the nurses, and yourself for not having done more, or at God for allowing her to die, or at your friends for not helping out in ways you thought they should have.

Bargaining

Divorced or never-married fathers in this stage of grieving often spend a lot of time running around trying to reconcile with their exes, doing everything they can to make themselves more desirable to the ex and to delay the final breakup.

Another approach some men (and women) use to maintain contact with their exes is what psychologist Richard Austin calls negative intimacy—hassling, fighting, arguing, harassing, spying, calling in the middle of the night, making threats, or any other kind of negative behavior. "What negative intimacy does is keep spouses tied together," says Austin. "A judge can end a marriage externally, by signing a piece of paper. But the couple's negative feelings and hate for each other can keep them together internally in a very powerful way."

Widowers, too, do plenty of bargaining, often making promises or pleading with God or some other higher power to bring their partner back to life, to wake them up from their nightmare, or to give them the strength to make it through.

"Have you forgotten?
We were divorced last week!"

Depression

Anger may be the easiest emotion to express, but depression is by far the most
common, affecting just about every single father at some time or other.

Depression can kind of sneak up on you, suddenly overwhelming you with feelings of hopelessness, helplessness, and sadness. Other symptoms include difficulty
getting out of bed in the morning; bursting into tears virtually without warning;
feelings of futility; loss of appetite; lack of interest in friends, children, or activities
you used to enjoy; an inability to concentrate; no longer paying attention to your
hygiene; and even thoughts of suicide.

As, well, depressing as depression is, it may actually be a positive sign: it means
that you're beyond the denial phase and you're seriously dealing with the reality
of your situation. But knowing that probably won't make you any happier. You may
also be depressed because you're starting to see yourself through your ex's eyes,

as undesirable, unattractive, or unworthy (see the paragraphs on abandonment and rejection on page 19 for more). So if you're feeling depressed, even just a little, I'd strongly suggest that you read the "Getting Some Help" section on pages 23–24 and that when you're done, you actually get some. Now.

Acceptance

One day—and it could be several years from now—you'll get comfortable with the idea that while you can't control what goes on around you, you *can* control how you react to things. In a sense, this realization is like a line separating your old life from your new one. It doesn't mean, of course, that your old one is over, just that you can focus more on the new one now that your anger, depression, and other emotions have slipped into the background and no longer dominate.

But Wait, There's More . . .

The five stages outlined above cover the grieving process from beginning to end, but as you've already started to figure out, grief is far more complex than that. And while you're working your way from initial shock and denial to acceptance, you'll probably experience a lot of other emotions as well:

- **Relief.** If *you* initiated your divorce or breakup, you might be rejoicing at being out of a bad relationship. But even if you didn't initiate your breakup, you may still feel relieved: "If you can step back for a moment and let go of the hurt, chaos, and shame created by the situation, you might just realize that your ex did you a favor by ending things," says psychoanalyst Mary Lamia. And if you're a widower, and your wife was sick and in a lot of pain, you might be relieved that her suffering is finally over. As nice a feeling as this one is, it usually doesn't last long and is often followed by guilt.

- **Paralysis.** You may feel absolutely unable to function—physically or emotionally—in any kind of productive way. You might, for example, not be able to find the energy to get yourself out of bed in the morning. Or you might be so consumed with worries and fears that you can't concentrate on anything else, including your job or your children.

  Keep in mind that feelings of paralysis and worries about your finances, about whether you'll ever be able to see your kids again, about how you can help them cope with what's going on in their lives, about whether you'll be able to take on the responsibilities of being a single parent, or that the world is falling apart are all perfectly normal at this stage. But if you're concerned that they're going on too long or that they're seriously interfering with your ability to manage your life, it's probably time to get some professional help. See pages 23–24 for more.

♦ **Loneliness and isolation.** Not long ago your house was buzzing with activity, but now there's way too much silence. The woman in your life is gone. If you're not a widower, your kids may be gone—at least for a while—as well. "When a man is divorced, he is alone," writes Stuart Kahan. "Unless he has custody, he no longer sees those kids every night at the dinner table or hears them bickering over who has first dibs on the bathroom or feels a basketball bouncing on the outside wall of his bedroom early on a Sunday morning."

If you're like most men, your ex probably took care of managing your social calendar, but now that she's gone, you're on your own. As a result, you may be experiencing a rather drastic change in your social life. Couples tend to hang out with other couples, and as a single guy, you may be left out. Other friends may have dumped you altogether. All of a sudden you may feel as though you're all alone in the world.

At this point you need to spend a little time thinking about whether what you're feeling here is loneliness or just a fear of being alone. There's a big difference, but not enough people make the distinction. If you're really craving human companionship, the best solution is to try to get involved in things that put you in contact with other people—your friends and family, or even strangers. But don't force yourself. Sometimes going to crowded places can make you feel even more alone than before.

Being alone, however, can be a great thing, allowing you to spend time with yourself and think things through—maybe for the first time in years. Many men are grateful for the opportunity, but too many simply can't handle it. I developed a sudden, fanatical interest in square dancing (which I'm fortunately over now). Some men throw themselves just as fanatically into their jobs or their hobbies, while others spend their time pouting or drinking.

♦ **Abandoned and rejected.** When I was in high school there was a Kenny Rogers song about a woman named Lucille who left her husband with four hungry kids and a crop in the fields. If your Lucille left you or if she died suddenly, you might feel exactly like this. In addition, when you lost your wife or girlfriend, you may have lost your best friend and closest confidant, leaving you with the feeling that you haven't got a friend or source of support in the world (whereas your ex's best friend was most likely another woman).

Feelings of abandonment often turn into feelings of rejection—a leap that's easy to understand if your ex was the one who initiated your breakup. Widowers, too, sometimes take their wives' deaths as a personal rejection. In some cases these feelings of rejection start to snowball, and you might find yourself thinking that your ex must have been right to reject you because you're a lousy husband, a lousy man, and a lousy father, and that it's only a matter of time until your children reject you too. If you're finding yourself in this situation, please remember this: your ex may have rejected you, but your children almost never will.

♦ **Like a failure as a man.** You might be thinking that a "real man" would have picked the right partner or known what to do to keep his relationship from failing; a "real man" would have figured out a way to keep his wife from dying; a "real man" would have been able to protect his children from the pain they're feeling right now. This sense of failure can escalate into feelings of doom; you may begin to think that your failings as a man, a husband, or a boyfriend are so great that you'll *never* be able to be happy in a relationship. If you're feeling this way or if that's the direction you think you're heading, it's crucial for you to get some professional help. Ignored, feelings like these can too easily become self-fulfilling prophecies that can undermine your relationship with your children and keep you from getting on with your life.

♦ **Helpless, weak, and out of control.** As men, we're socialized to control our emotions, or at least to think that we can. But that's nearly impossible right now. And it may stay that way for the foreseeable future.

♦ **Guilt.** Just about everyone has something to feel guilty about. If you were having an affair or left your ex for someone new, you're probably feeling at least a little guilty about the pain you caused her. Even if you didn't do anything wrong at all during your relationship, you're probably blaming yourself in some way for hurting your children, especially if you were the one who initiated the end of the relationship.

Be careful not to let your guilt cloud your judgment. Too many men try to ease their internal pain by giving up money, assets, or even a decent relationship with their children. Try taking some responsibility and telling your ex you're sorry instead.

If you're a widower, you may have completely different reasons for feeling guilty. You may second-guess yourself for not having done enough to save your wife's life. You might feel guilty for feeling angry at her or, if she was sick for a long time, for feeling relieved that she died. You might feel guilty if you've had any fun or even laughed since your wife died. And you might even feel guilty that you never had a chance to say good-bye or that there was some other issue between you that didn't get resolved.

At this point there's not much you can do to ease your guilt. But Amy Hillyard Jensen, author of *Healing Grief,* offers one suggestion that seems to have helped a lot of widowers, if only a little. Write your wife a letter and tell her everything you have to say, in as much detail as you can. When you're done, leave the letter on her grave or burn it and scatter the ashes there.

♦ **Frustration with other people.** If you're lucky, you'll always have someone around who can comfort you. But you'll be amazed at how unintentionally insensitive some people can be. Friends and family were constantly asking me whether I'd heard anything from my ex or telling me that they'd just seen her, apparently not bothering to consider that I really didn't want to think—let alone talk— about her at all and that doing so was terribly painful.

I was also stunned by how many intelligent people tried to fix me up with other women just weeks (or, in a few cases, days) after they found out I was getting divorced. I think they honestly believed that I should just "be strong" and "move on." If you're a widower, this can be especially hard to deal with. Here's how one man in Jane Burgess's study summed it up: "The way my friends and colleagues treated me, it was as though I was expected to bury Anne on Saturday, return to work in a week, and then in another week be out looking for a date."

Coping with Your Feelings

Men and women live in very different worlds. Men are brought up to be tough, strong, competent, knowledgeable, and in control of their emotions. "Weakness"—especially tears—is discouraged. Anger and frustration are okay, but sadness and pain are not. This kind of socialization is very effective in a lot of ways. But when we face some kind of emotional upheaval, such as the breakup of a relationship or the death of a spouse, we many of us have no idea how to react.

Instead of acknowledging our grief and dealing with it, we ignore it. Instead of getting help, we pull away from the people closest to us. The results can be dangerous. "If feelings are left buried, they cause prolonged turmoil, bitterness, family problems, and even ill health," writes William Schatz, author of *Healing a Father's Grief.*

Like a lot of men, you may try to deal with your grief by diving headlong into your job and spending as much time as you can there. The rationale, says Schatz, is that since you've failed in your other societally approved roles, you can at least succeed at being a breadwinner. Unfortunately, this isn't an effective way of coping with your grief—in either the short or the long term. "Grief will change you," adds Jensen. "But you have some control over whether the changes are for better or worse." Here are some things you can do to cope with the many different feelings you're experiencing as a newly single father:

♦ **Let it happen.** "Surviving grief does not mean escaping from it," says Jensen. "Grief itself is the healing process and you must go through it."

♦ **Get out of the house and see other people.** Loneliness is a major problem for newly single fathers, many of whom simply drop out socially. But try to get together with your friends and family. Ideally, of course, they'd be reaching out to you, but the truth is that many of them don't know how to react to your new situation and have chosen, by default, not to react at all.

♦ **Streamline your schedule.** Besides burying yourself in work you may try to escape your grief by accepting every single social invitation that comes along. Don't. Give yourself time to be alone. You've got a lot on your mind, and you can use the time just to think.

♦ **Express your anger.** If you feel comfortable talking to your friends or family about your anger (and you think you can do so without upsetting them), great. If not, there are plenty of other ways to express it: buy a bunch of dishes at a flea market and smash them up, run until you drop, go to the batting cages (from certain angles softballs look a lot like human heads). If you want something a little quieter, try venting in a journal. All these things will help your anger fade. But however you choose to express your anger, be absolutely sure your kids aren't anywhere nearby and make sure no one else could possibly get hurt.

Another effective way to deal with anger is to consciously rearrange your thinking. If your ex was late dropping your child off last week, does that *really* mean she's going to be late every time? And if she happens to call you just as you're stepping, naked, into bed with your new girlfriend, do you *really* think she's spying on you?

♦ **Get professional help.** There's nothing to be embarrassed about. See pages 23–24 for more.

♦ **Don't try to get back at your ex**—or anyone else you feel has wronged you—physically, psychologically, or legally. It might make you feel better for a little while, but it will hurt your children in the long run.

♦ **Take good care of yourself.** Research has found that depression and all its symptoms (see pages 17–18) can actually reduce your body's natural resistance to disease. So be sure to eat right and get plenty of exercise. Keeping in shape can also help you get comfortable with the idea that you're a good and worthwhile person, a feeling you may not have had for a while.

♦ **Give yourself a treat once in a while.** Take yourself out to a movie or go camping for a weekend when you don't have the kids. Do it for making it through a tough day without falling apart. Or do it just because. Widowers often feel that having fun is in some way a betrayal of their wives' memories or that it's somehow undignified. But it isn't. Having fun is a critical part of your recovery. And since your children will be modeling their behavior after yours, it's important for them to get your "permission" to laugh and play and enjoy life again.

♦ **Don't make any major decisions.** Don't sell your house, unload any stocks, quit your job, or have major surgery unless it's absolutely unavoidable. Depression and the other emotions associated with grief can take their toll on your ability to make sound decisions.

♦ **Prepare yourself.** Special days such as birthdays, holidays, and anniversaries can bring up feelings you may have thought were long gone. So be sure you're booked on those days. Do something fun, something that will keep your mind off the memories they might bring up.

♦ **Be patient.** As the months and years go by, your feelings and emotions will evolve. Some will pass, others will crop up. Some may even get worse before they get better. E. Mavis Heatherington found that most couples actually felt worse a year after their divorce than they had during the first few months. Basically, the novelty had worn off and the harsh reality had begun to set in. But remember, ultimately, you will get through this.

♦ **Take people up on their offers to help.** If someone offers to cook you a meal, take care of your kids for a few hours while you go to a movie, or virtually anything else, accept immediately. You may be thinking that you can handle everything by yourself and you might actually be right. But at what cost? Trying to be a hero or a martyr right now isn't a good idea and will only put additional—and completely unnecessary—stress on yourself and your kids.

Getting Some Help

Let me start off by saying that I'm a big believer in getting therapy and that I think you should seek professional help immediately after your breakup or the death of your wife—events that can trigger all sorts of serious emotional, sexual, economic, and social problems.

I realize, of course, that not everyone agrees with me. Some guys think they can handle things on their own and that getting therapy is an admission of some kind of weakness. Others might consider getting professional help, but only if things get really, really bad.

If you're in the macho category, all I can do is urge you to reconsider—if not for you, then for your kids. If you're in the second category, here are some red flags that indicate that it's time to pick up the phone and make an appointment:

♦ If you're overwhelmed by simple decisions, such as whether to buy 1 percent or 2 percent milk at the grocery store, you should be getting some help.

♦ If you're having trouble making sense of your life, if you're letting your responsibilities slip (at home and at the office), or if you feel that your kids are just too much to handle.

♦ If you are suffering any of the symptoms described in the section on depression (see pages 17–18).

Therapy doesn't have to be a long-term commitment. In fact, if you start at an early stage, your therapist may be able to help you quickly identify your feelings and figure out ways of dealing with them that might be effective in preventing a long-term depression.

If you decide to go this route, interview several candidates before making your final decision. The therapist you choose should have a lot of experience dealing with relationships or the death of a partner. Friends, relatives, your clergy person, and even the clinical psychology department at a nearby university can all provide referrals. If you're too embarrassed to ask someone yourself, try the therapy referral Web site at www.psychology.com/therapy.htm.

Special Considerations If Your Wife Committed Suicide

The death of the woman you love is always going to be hard to deal with. But according to Jane Burgess, "Emotions are more intense when death is unexpected and sudden."

Most of the emotions discussed on pages 18–20 will apply here, but some may be exaggerated, such as denial, anger, guilt, self-blame, and rejection. You may be spending a lot of time trying to convince yourself that her suicide was really an accident. You may be absolutely furious that your wife did such a completely selfish thing—abandoning her children and scarring them so deeply and so permanently. You may be looking around for someone to blame: her employer for making her so stressed, yourself for not knowing how much help she needed. And you may even think that her suicide was a deliberate attempt to reject you as a husband, a father, and a man.

While all these things may contain a kernel of truth, ultimately your wife and no one else was responsible for her own actions. People rarely commit suicide in order to punish or get away from a single individual. So unless you were a truly horrible person (and if you were you wouldn't be reading this book), try to get that thought out of your mind.

If your wife did kill herself, it's extremely important that you get some professional help immediately. Read the section on getting help (pages 23–24), but don't wait for any symptoms to appear. Go now. You really need it. In addition, you might want to find a suicide survivors' support group in your area. It may be hard to go, but it's important. Finding out that you're not alone in what you're feeling and getting help from people who have been through a similar experience will help more than you know. And finally, I'd suggest that you read Harold Kushner's *When Bad Things Happen to Good People*. It's nearly twenty years old, but just as powerful and helpful today as ever.

In addition to getting professional help, it's important to build a strong support system around you. Getting in touch with people who are going through what you're going through can make things a lot easier for you. Divorced fathers' groups can sometimes be a good source of support, but some are so bitter and angry that you should stay far, far away. If you're a widower, find a local chapter of the Compassionate Friends, a group of widows and widowers. If you're not already actively involved in your church or synagogue, this might be a good time to get back in touch.

Individual friends can also be invaluable sources of solace. But one word of caution: you might want to stay away from sharing your grief with your close female friends—especially if you're a widower. Vulnerability, comfort, support, and tears can often develop into other things and this isn't the right time for you to be starting a new relationship.

Your Kids as Therapy

You're going to be spending a lot of time comforting your children, but they can be a great help to you too—sometimes without even knowing it. For example, just having your kids around can help you keep your mind off your own grief, says Jane Burgess. "Men who have their children readily available to them seem to cope better with their feelings of loneliness and despair than those without children."

They can also do wonders for your self-confidence. "Once a man finds that he can meet the practical as well as the emotional needs of his children, he begins to feel confident in himself not only as a parent but as a person," writes Burgess.

"Push me, Dad. Mozart was pushed."

Support for Gay Dads

Even if your ex is okay with your being gay, you'll still have to deal with society's biases, with the legal system's discrimination, and, perhaps, with the lack of support from the gay community. As a result, you may find yourself feeling lonely and depressed. If you do, it's critical that you seek some support immediately. The Family Pride Coalition and COLAGE (Children of Lesbians and Gays Every-where) are good places to start. Contact information for both can be found in the Resources section (pages 287–88).

Getting a Lawyer*

The minute you get served with divorce papers—or the minute you suspect you might be—get yourself a lawyer. "Being your own lawyer is the surest path to disaster," says Timothy J. Horgan, author of *Winning Your Divorce*. "So don't even consider representing yourself unless you have no possessions, no income, and no interest in the outcome of your case." Get the point?

Hiring a lawyer doesn't mean that you're heading for the courtroom; if you're lucky, you'll never even meet a judge. Nor does hiring a lawyer mean that you're expecting a confrontation with your soon-to-be-ex. What it does mean, though, is that you're involving someone who, without any unpleasant emotional attachments, will protect your interests and make sure that your concerns are properly addressed. Most divorce attorneys have seen dozens of cases like yours and know exactly what to look out for. Do you? Finally, your lawyer can also help you draft fair property settlements and custody arrangements that will hopefully avoid conflict in the future.

There are several reasons why it's critical for you to act quickly:

♦ **You're a man.** The simple truth about the divorce system in this country is that it is designed to protect and defend women and their interests. When it comes to the children, for example, women are given sole or primary custody about 85 percent of the time. Having a lawyer can help you even the playing field just a little (though far from completely). One recent study found that fathers who were awarded sole custody had been represented by lawyers 92 percent of the time, and those who won joint custody had lawyers 90 percent of the time.

---

*In this chapter we're assuming that your marriage or relationship with the mother of your children is ending or over. If you're a widower, you can skip to the next chapter.

In contrast, among fathers who failed to win any type of custody, only 60 percent had hired lawyers.

♦ **You're playing catch-up.** About 70 percent of divorces are filed by women, and about the same percentage of nonmarital relationships are ended by women. There's a lot of dispute about what, exactly, these statistics mean. For example, if a man is having an affair and his wife files for divorce, who really ended the relationship? But what is absolutely clear is that the person who files the papers has a significant element-of-surprise advantage over the other spouse. Thus, by the time you get the news, your wife has probably already seen a lawyer and has had a lot of time to put together a plan for why she should have the kids, the house, and all your joint assets.

♦ **Things change.** Even if you're having the most amicable breakup in the world, you'd be foolish to assume all the good will you and your partner have for each other right now will last forever. "Once the word 'divorce' rears its ugly head, your relationship with your wife automatically becomes an adversarial one, even if it was not before," says Horgan. Ending relationships does strange things to people, and even the most mild-mannered individuals can suddenly and inexplicably become mean and vindictive—especially if they're shown how by a mean and vindictive lawyer. So if you let your guard down and she goes out and gets herself a hard-liner whose mission in life is to take you for everything you've got, you're in serious trouble.

A Short Course in How to Find a Lawyer

If a friend of yours was recently divorced (and ended up with what he wanted), get a reference. Or check with men's or fathers' rights groups. But beware: while support groups can be a valuable source of contacts and comfort, they also can be a hunting ground for unscrupulous lawyers who prey on men who are at their most vulnerable.

Two excellent (and safe) resources are the Children's Rights Council in Washington, D.C. ([202] 547-6227); and Fathers' Rights & Equality Exchange, headquartered in San Jose, California ([500] FOR-DADS). Both these organizations are nonprofit and have chapters in every state. Whatever you do, don't let recommendations substitute for face-to-face interviews with the top prospects. Although it may cost you a little up front, finding the right lawyer can make the difference between feeling helpless and being in control.

Here are a few things to keep in mind when interviewing attorneys:

♦ Ask a lot of questions and be completely honest about your situation—financial and emotional. If you aren't, you're just going to complicate your own case. And don't worry: any conversation you have while interviewing an attorney—even if you don't ultimately hire him or her—is completely confidential.

♦ Be ready to answer a lot of personal questions about you and your wife. The more your attorney knows about your wife's character, the better he'll be able to protect you.

♦ Ask each candidate about the strengths and weaknesses of your case and get a good-faith estimate of whether you're going to end up with whatever it is that you want. Stay far, far away from any attorney who tells you that he can "get you everything you want, no problem," or that she can "get the judge to see things your way."

♦ Don't worry about gender. Despite what you may have heard ("judges are more sympathetic to women lawyers" or "men are tougher"), the gender of your attorney probably won't affect your case in any way.

♦ Ask yourself whether the attorney is really interested in you and your children and try to gauge his or her views on the importance of fathers. Many lawyers— of both genders—believe that mothers should get custody of the children and that fathers should be little more than visitors.

♦ Find out how well the attorney knows local judges and other divorce attorneys. Each judge has his or her own prejudices, and having a lawyer who can maneuver within the system may be critical to your case.

♦ Find out whether he or she is particularly sensitive to men's feelings and concerns. Hopefully you'll never end up in court, but if you do, the odds are very much against you.

♦ If you're a gay father, it's essential to find out whether the attorney has represented gay clients in the past and how he or she feels about gay fathers wanting to take an active parenting role.

♦ Find out what it will cost. Most attorneys will charge you an up-front retainer— a flat, usually nonrefundable fee that covers a certain number of hours of work. Retainers can range from $500 to over $5,000. My lawyer was willing to take $1,500 up front, and since my case didn't take her long, she ended up giving me most of it back.

♦ Hire the best attorney you feel you can realistically afford. Someone fresh out of law school might be able to do the job for half the money, but if things go wrong, you'll wish you'd gone with the more experienced—and more expensive— lawyer. It's better to invest some money now to get things right than to spend a lot more to get them fixed (or try to) later.

♦ Don't even think about sharing a lawyer with your ex, no matter how well you're getting along. "It's unrealistic to think that an attorney can simply shift from side to side and represent each of you with equal vigor," writes Harriet Newman Cohen, coauthor of *The Divorce Book for Men and Women.*

♦ Don't be shy or embarrassed about your needs and wants. If, for example, your wife makes more money than you do, and/or if you've been the primary caretaker of your children, ask for alimony and child support. You know she would. Taking money from your wife is neither a comment about your masculinity nor an insult

If You Need to Make a Change

What you're looking for in a lawyer is someone who will keep your best interests at heart all the time and who will do everything reasonably possible to help you. If you follow the steps outlined on pages 27–29, that's exactly what you should get. Sometimes, though, things between you and your attorney might get a little tense. Most of the time the two of you will be able to work things out; remember, you're not looking for a friend here. But if your current attorney does any of the following, you should seriously consider making a change.

♦ He never contacts you—unless he's looking for money.

♦ She's been taking your money but doesn't seem to be producing any results.

♦ He won't give you an itemized bill.

♦ She doesn't return your phone calls.

♦ He's a little too cozy with your wife's attorney.

♦ She completely ignores your instructions and refuses to tell you why.

♦ He tries to talk you out of the custody arrangement you want.

♦ She doesn't seem to be spending enough time on your case.

If you aren't sure whether you should change attorneys or not, call your state's bar association. They'll help you to evaluate what you're seeing. And given that most of the points above are violations of attorneys' codes of ethics, the bar association will probably take your complaints very seriously. Whatever you do, keep in mind that changing attorneys is a serious and potentially very expensive decision. At the very least, you may not be able to get the unused portion of your retainer back, and it'll take you quite a few billable hours to get the new guy (or gal) up to speed.

to your abilities as a parent. The money is for your kids and they shouldn't have to suffer because of your ego.

After you've made your decision, prepare yourself for your first appointment by sitting down and making a detailed list of all your assets and debts (including account numbers), real estate, full names and social security numbers of everyone in the family (kids, too), and your wife's and your birthdays, driver's license numbers, and dates of marriage and separation. Also bring along your tax returns for the last four or five years. You're going to need all this information soon anyway, and there's no point in paying someone $100 or $200 per hour to sift through your wallet, tax records, and other documents.

Finally, never, never confuse your attorney's interest in your case with friendship. Sure, she'll interrupt her day to let you stop by and cry on her shoulder. She'll also charge you for it. And with many attorneys billing in quarters of an hour, that thirty-second plea for sympathy could set you back $50.

Don't Move Out

In the old days, men facing a divorce would move out of the house—it was considered quite the chivalrous thing to do. Today, however, moving out may be the dumbest thing you could possibly do. Depending on the state, "If you move out of your house, you're essentially abandoning any possibility of getting custody of (or even any sort of meaningful visitation with) your children," says Timothy Horgan. In some states, your wife's attorney may be able to argue that since you left your children with your wife, you aren't interested in having a relationship with them, and your custodial rights should be severely limited.

"Wait a minute! When we decided to separate,
I thought I was leaving home!"

Unfortunately, the judge is likely to agree. Most divorce attorneys find that the courts are generally quite reluctant to make any changes to the status quo in custody cases. This means that the one who's living in the marital home has a great advantage.

If there's no alternative to moving out, however (for example, if the judge orders you to), keep these things in mind:

♦ Get a place as close as possible to your former home so you'll be able to see the kids every day.

♦ Explain the situation to the children yourself, stressing that it's not their fault. (You may want to check with a mental health professional about the best way to broach this topic.)

♦ Be alert to what your wife is saying about you to the children. If she's badmouthing you, you'll need to make doubly sure that the children understand what your leaving does—and doesn't—mean. One important warning: never respond to anything your ex is saying about you in front of the children. You never want to put your kids in the middle.

♦ Consider taking your valuables with you. "If you move out and leave your possessions behind, don't count on seeing them again," writes Harriet Newman Cohen. If there are things you can't take, make a written or videotaped inventory of everything that stays.

A word of caution: try not to let your refusal to move out escalate into a huge confrontation between you and your wife (She: "Get out!" You: "Screw you!"). Your anger may later be used as the basis for your wife getting a court order to throw you out.

Don't Leave Your Kids

Whether you move to a new place or stay in your old one, make absolutely sure that you maintain regular and frequent contact with your children from the moment you and your partner stop living together. "If you leave the house to 'get your head together,' you risk creating a situation where it's easy for a judge to give custody to the parent who's taking care of the kids," writes attorney Hayden Curry and his colleagues. "Courts don't like to disrupt the status quo and often put a high value on keeping kids with whomever they've been living." In other words, if you stop seeing your kids—even if it's only for a few weeks or months, you may have a tough time later on explaining why you should be able to spend any more time with them.

Get Control of Your Finances

In most states, assets that have both your names on them (particularly things like checking accounts and money-market accounts) are assumed to be owned equally by you and your wife. But since it's tough to tell whose half is whose, there's nothing to stop your wife from completely cleaning out the entire checking account, leaving you penniless. Every divorce lawyer I've ever spoken with had literally dozens of stories about divorcing men who came home one day to houses that had been stripped bare and to checking accounts that were in much the same condition.

To protect yourself (and to make sure you've got enough to live on and to pay your attorney with) do the following immediately:

- Close all your joint credit card accounts: bank cards, ATMs, department stores, gas stations, and so on. Do this in writing and mention the fact that you're getting a divorce—that usually speeds things up. Until you close these accounts, *you*'ll be responsible for half of any debts your *wife* incurs until the divorce is final. Actually, according to the law in most states, after the date of your legal separation you are responsible only for anything *you* charge; your wife is responsible for her own charges. Unfortunately, most creditors don't really care about the law; all they want is their money, and they're perfectly willing to trash your credit rating if that's what it takes to collect.
- Change the beneficiaries on your insurance policies, retirement accounts, and especially your will.
- Postpone any extraordinary income you can (royalties, bonuses, salary increases). Any money that comes in before your wife's financial affairs are separate from yours are half hers.
- Get all your important financial records out of the house as soon as possible. Before doing this, however, make a complete copy for your wife; she's entitled to one and making her (or her lawyer) ask for it later will cost you. Documents such as bank and credit card statements, tax returns, and life insurance policies can be stored in a safety deposit box or at your lawyer's office. And don't forget to change the account address, so future statements don't go to your wife.
- Make a list (a videotape is better) of everything in your home (or elsewhere) that's of any value: artwork, cars, jewelry, exercise equipment, furniture, rare books, and the like. Get copies of bills of sale and appraisals if you have them. If you can't prove you owned that Rembrandt, you'll have a tough time getting your share of the proceeds.
- Transfer *half* the money and liquid assets you can put your hands on out of the joint accounts, including the contents of your joint safety deposit boxes, into a separate account—in your name only. If you don't already know which accounts are liquid, have your accountant or your lawyer help you figure it out.
- Before taking anything out of any joint accounts, however, be sure to check with your lawyer. In some states, doing so without the permission of your wife can get you in serious hot water. And beware: taking more than half can put you in the uncomfortable position of having to explain to a judge why you cut your wife off without enough money to live on.
- Switch your automatic payroll deposits and put all new deposits into your new

account—any money that comes into the old, joint account may be lost forever. But be sure to leave enough money in your joint account to cover joint expenses: mortgage and credit card payments, food, insurance, tuition, and so forth.

♦ Keep an extremely accurate, written account of every cent coming out of or going into the old, joint accounts or your new, individual accounts. The last thing you want is to be accused of having stolen money from your wife.

♦ Check with your accountant or financial advisor. He or she may be able to come up with other strategies to protect your share of the family's assets.

Mediation: A Good Alternative to Litigation

If you and your ex are at a point where you can still be civil to each other, I'd strongly urge you to consider adding mediation to your divorce proceeding. In the overwhelming majority of cases mediation is cheaper, takes less time, and is a lot less psychologically and emotionally damaging for everyone involved, including the kids, than going to court. (In some states, though, including California, Maryland, and Oregon, you won't have a choice: mediation is mandatory for parents who can't agree on custody.)

Even if you and your ex are committed to beating each other up through your lawyers in front of a judge, mediation can be quite successful in reducing tension and increasing the chance of a successful resolution.

And if you're a never-married father—whether you and your ex are on good terms or not—mediation may be the *only* chance you have of getting a fair child-custody arrangement.

Overall, mediation will be successful "if both spouses are willing to put aside their emotional differences and focus on settlement options that make the most sense under the circumstances and allow everyone to win, especially the children," write Elizabeth Hickey and Elizabeth Dalton, authors of *Healing Hearts*.

Community Property

In some states (California, for example) *everything* acquired from the day you got married until the day you get separated is considered "community property." Even if you have a bank or stock account in your name alone, your wife may still be entitled to half and vice versa. Just about the only exception to the community property rules is for money or assets you or your wife owned *prior* to the marriage, or inheritances left solely to either one of you even during the marriage. Things like a personal stereo or an inheritance might fit into this category. This is pretty complicated stuff, so if you live in one of the nine community-property states (Arizona, California, Idaho, Louisiana, Nevada, New Mexico, Texas, Washington, and Wisconsin), check with your lawyer.

What Is It, Really?

Basically, "Mediation is a voluntary settlement process that gives a divorcing [or separating] couple the opportunity to sit together at the bargaining table to design a settlement with the assistance of a neutral intermediary," write Hickey and Dalton. You'll probably be limiting yourselves to three main issues: child custody and visitation; property and asset (or debt) division; and alimony.

There's really nothing magical about the process; it consists mostly of getting you and your ex to listen to each other carefully and to respect each other's point of view. But as you know, that's not an easy job; if you could have done it by yourself, you and your ex might still be together.

Your mediator will probably start off your first session by laying out some ground rules that may make you feel that you're back in the first grade: no name calling, no yelling, listen respectfully, no cutting in line (just kidding), and so forth. After you've both agreed to follow the rules, the mediator will start with one issue and ask each of you to explain your position. She may ask you to address each other and she may use "clarifying statements" such as, "Sally, it seems that you really want . . ." If you and/or your ex can't do this like grown-ups, the mediator may need to speak with you separately. But at some point the three of you will be together and you'll start working on some solutions.

One of a mediator's most important skills is to set goals and keep the two of you focused on them. He won't let either of you get sidetracked by your anger and he won't let either of you intimidate the other. The mediator's goal in all this is to get the two of you to better understand each other's position.

Once she feels the two of you understand each other (at least a little bit) and have identified the areas of common ground, the mediator will begin to offer suggestions that are designed to make everyone—including your kids—come out whole, or as close to it as possible. Since she has no stake in the outcome, the mediator can be more creative in her problem-solving approach than either you or your ex might be.

Unless you and your ex agree, the mediator's suggestions aren't binding on either one of you. You're free to argue with the mediator or, if you must, disregard his suggestions completely. Before accepting or rejecting his proposals, have your lawyer review them.

So Why Should You Consider Mediation?

Mostly because it works. A recent report by California's Statewide Office of Family Court Services found tremendous satisfaction with mediation: 90 percent of all clients said that mediation was a good way to come up with a parenting plan. If that doesn't convince you, try these reasons:

- ◆ It will probably keep you out of court. In one study, researcher Robert Emery found that only 11 percent of families who had gone through mediation later ended up in court. In contrast, 72 percent of families in the litigation control group (those who didn't go through mediation) proceeded to court.

♦ You get a chance to be heard. Judges are notorious for making their decisions without taking the father's needs into consideration. Mediators tend to listen better. In the California Family Court Services study, 85 percent of parents reported that they did not feel intimidated and freely said what they really felt; and 86 percent said they felt no pressure to go along with things they did not want.

♦ You'll probably get a more favorable custody arrangement. Robert Emery found that mediated couples end up with more balance in the time children spend with mothers and fathers. And in another study, researchers Jessica Pearson and Nancy Thoennes found that mediation resulted in more joint-custody arrangements than did nonmediated disputes.

♦ You have more control over the process. With mediation, you and your ex schedule the sessions. With court proceedings, you show up when the judge tells you to.

♦ It's easier on your children. The divorce is traumatic enough for them. Knowing that the two of you are working together toward a common solution will help them cope.

♦ It can improve your relationship with your ex. If you pay attention, the mediation process can teach you some conflict-resolution skills that you'll need in your future dealings with each other—and you'll have a lot of them in the years to come.

♦ You can always change your mind. If you or your ex decide that you'd rather go back to being adversaries, there's nothing to stop you from duking it out in front of a judge.

♦ It's more private and more confidential than going to court. Nothing you or the mediator says can be used (without your permission) in front of a judge.

♦ It's a lot less adversarial than the courtroom. It focuses on the needs of the parties rather than on their wants and their extreme positions. This is especially true when it comes to the children. The mediator will probably be especially interested in the children and won't propose solutions that would harm them. Lawyers, on the other hand, in the interest of helping their clients, sometimes forget about the kids and end up doing things that hurt them.

Finding a Mediator

In states where mediation is required, the court may appoint a mediator for you. But in most cases, you and your ex will select one yourselves. You can get recommendations from your lawyers, from friends, from your local Yellow Pages, or from the Academy of Family Mediators ([781] 674-2663; for more information on this organization see the Resources section, page 291). As with finding a lawyer, recommendations are no substitute for an interview. In this case, though, because both you and your ex have to agree on the final choice, the selection procedure may take a little longer than you expect.

*"When we divorced, my ex and I reached an agreement.
It was our first."*

Here are a few factors to take into consideration as you screen mediator candidates:

- Cost. Most mediators charge by the hour—probably close to $200. You and your ex should split the cost equally.
- Time. Expect to need two to six sessions, but since each case is different, a firm estimate is impossible.
- Their views on fathers and fathers' involvement with their children. Although they're supposed to be neutral, many mediators still believe that mothers are the primary parent and that fathers should do little more than visit their children. If this isn't what you want, keep looking.
- Professional background. Most mediators are either therapists or lawyers and thus have training in social work or the law. In addition, however, a mediator should have completed special training in mediation techniques.
- Mediation services offered. Not all mediators are trained or interested in mediating every issue that comes up. Many specialize only in certain areas and augment their own expertise by working closely with other professionals (accountants and custody evaluators, for example).
- Experience. Consider only mediators with significant experience in the areas you and your ex have agreed to mediate. A mediator who has handled only "one or two" cases like yours is probably not the right choice.
- Do not hire your own lawyer or your ex's. There's no way either of them, no matter how nice they are, can possibly be objective.
- For the same reasons, don't hire a friend or anyone who knows either you or your ex.

When Mediation Won't Work

Although mediation offers many advantages to many people, it isn't for everyone. You and your ex are probably wasting your time and money on mediation if one of you:

♦ Can't or won't work together in a civil, cooperative way.

♦ Can't or won't compromise on important issues.

♦ Has some power—intellectual, financial, social—over the other.

♦ Is more interested in revenge and causing emotional pain than in resolving the issues at hand.

♦ Has serious psychological problems.

♦ Has falsely accused the other of child abuse or spousal abuse.

♦ Can't accept that the relationship is over and still wants to reconcile (the danger here is that this person will give up everything to get the other to take him or her back).

What If Your Ex Doesn't Want to Mediate?

If your ex doesn't want to mediate, it simply won't happen. But if you're interested, there are some ways you may be able to overcome her resistance.

♦ If you're able to communicate with each other, have her read the sections in this book on the benefits on mediation.

♦ Reassure her that you're trying to work toward equitable solutions for all of you.

♦ Encourage her to get involved in interviewing, checking references, evaluating qualifications, and selecting the mediator.

♦ If you aren't able to communicate with each other and you still want to give mediation a try, have your lawyer recommend it to hers. If that doesn't work, ask your lawyer about asking the court to order it. Like most people in the family-law system, judges are overburdened, and they tend to be supportive of attempts to reduce the conflict in their courtrooms.

Why Your Ex May Not Want to Mediate

Despite the overwhelming evidence that mediation can go a long way toward helping even high-conflict couples work out their differences like grown-ups, many women's groups and "feminist" lawyers are adamantly opposed to the idea. The reason seems to be the simple fact that, as mentioned above, couples who mediate agree on joint custody more often than couples who don't mediate. In other words, they don't like mediation because it just might give fathers a fairer shake and just might reduce women's dominance in the parenting sphere.

Custody

Without a doubt, the most common questions newly single fathers ask have to do with child custody: where are the kids going to live, with whom, and how much time will they be able to spend with each parent? If you're a widower, the answers to these questions are usually straightforward: the kids will live with you. But for every other kind of single father, child custody is an incredibly complicated—and stressful—issue.

Before we get to the intricate details, let's go over two important terms that you'll be hearing a lot of in the near future: *legal custody* and *physical custody*. In the simplest terms, the parent with legal custody is the one who's legally responsible for making decisions about anything that affects the health, education, and welfare of the children. The parent with physical custody is the one with whom the child lives. Unfortunately, too few fathers make a distinction between the legal and physical custody and, as a result, too many end up with an unfair settlement.

Within the two broad categories of legal and physical custody, there are a variety of different alternatives. Here are the most common:

♦ **Sole or primary.** One parent has complete or nearly complete physical and legal custody of the children. The noncustodial parent will have limited access to the children. (Access is more commonly called visitation, but because noncustodial parents are parents, not visitors, I try to stay away from that term.)

♦ **Joint.** This one is a real hodgepodge. Parents can have joint physical custody, legal custody, or both. Theoretically, the word *joint* means equal rights and responsibilities, but in most cases children have a primary residence where they live more than half the time. We'll talk about joint custody in greater detail below.

- **Alternating or divided.** Kids switch back and forth between you and your ex, usually staying for a minimum of three or four months at a time. This option is fairly rare and probably works best if you and your ex live near each other so that the kids' school and social schedules don't get too disrupted.
- **Split.** One or more of the kids lives with you, the other(s) live with your ex. In addition, you'll probably have some kind of schedule giving each of you access to the child who doesn't live with you. You should consider this option only if it is truly best for your children. Separating your kids from each other just because you and your ex can't work things out like grown-ups is nothing less than cruel.
- **Bird's nest.** The kids stay put while you and your ex move in and out of the house. You and your ex will have to find someplace else to live when you're not in the house. Again, this is a rare option. It takes a lot of cooperation, and you'll need some clear ground rules (like meeting your respective lovers someplace else). It can also be expensive—the two of you will have to maintain a total of three residences. When my wife and I split up we did this quite successfully while our house was on the market and until we got settled into our new places.
- **Other options.** Serial custody gives primary legal and/or physical custody to you or your ex for a certain number of years; then you switch. This may work if

you decide you want your teenagers to live with the same-sex parent (for more on boys and girls, see pages 122–24 and 132–33). But it's generally not a good idea, because children need an ongoing relationship with both parents, not just with one at a time. Third-party custody gives custody of your kids to someone other than you or their mother, such as the grandparents or one of your ex's or your siblings. This usually comes up only if a judge decides that you and your wife are incompetent, abusive, or a danger to the children.

♦ **Combinations.** Just about anything's possible: joint legal custody but sole physical custody; sole legal and fifty-fifty physical, and so on.

Joint Custody, or Coparenting: The Best Alternative

Since you're reading this book, I'm assuming that you're doing so because you want to maintain a strong relationship with your children. The best way to do this, of course, is to spend as much time with them as you possibly can. If you live far away from them, that's going to be hard (see pages 153–58 for tips on long-distance fathering). But if you and your ex live close to each other, joint custody provides the best guarantee of regular contact with your kids.

But what, exactly, is joint custody? (Don't be embarrassed; most people think they know, but they really don't.) In many states, it's already the norm. In California, for example, about 70 percent of splitting couples have it. But this figure is highly deceptive because it refers to joint *legal* and not joint *physical* custody. If you have joint legal custody you'll get to sign your children's report cards, but when it comes to actually seeing them, you may be limited to almost the same visitation schedule as a noncustodial father. This, by the way, effectively renders your share of legal custody useless, what with possession being nine-tenths of the law.

The kind of joint custody I'm recommending here is joint *physical.* But even that term doesn't mean what you might think. In most states, joint physical custody is defined simply as "frequent and continuing contact," which covers everything from equally splitting expenses, decision making, and time with the kids to arrangements that are basically indistinguishable from sole mother custody with occasional visitation by the father.

Pursue as much physical custody as you can reasonably manage, which is probably going to be somewhere between 30 and 50 percent. Unless there are extenuating circumstances (some of which we discuss on pages 56–57), don't shoot for more than 50 percent: your children need their mother just as much as they need you, and your ex needs them just as much as you do.

Because the terms *joint legal* and *joint physical* custody are so confusing and have so many different meanings, let's use another term altogether to describe this type of custody arrangement: coparenting.

The Advantages of Coparenting

So why go for coparenting? Simply put, because it's the best thing for everyone.

- **Parents like it.** Former couples who share physical custody of their children are happier with their custody arrangements than those who don't. They fight less and are generally more satisfied with the overall outcome of their breakup.
- **Fathers like it, too.** Coparenting dads are "more likely than nonresidential fathers to share in decision making about their children and to be satisfied with the legal and physical custody arrangements," says researcher Margaret Little.
- **Judges like it.** Parents who coparent are half as likely to go back to court to settle their disputes as sole-custody parents.
- **Kids feel more secure.** Seeing their parents break up can make children feel frightened, out of control, and perhaps unloved. And if one parent disappears— or almost disappears—these feelings can get worse.
- **Everyone wins.** "At its best joint custody presents the possibility that each family member can 'win' in post-divorce life rather than insisting that a custody decision identify 'winners and losers,'" writes social policy expert Ross Thompson. "Mothers and fathers each win a significant role in the lives of their offspring and children win as a consequence."
- **It increases father-child contact.** Fathers who share physical custody of their children have far better visitation records and keep in much closer contact with their children than dads who don't have as much time with their kids.
- **It nearly eliminates child-support default.** The U.S. Census Bureau found that over 90 percent of men with joint physical custody pay their entire child-support obligation on time. Compliance goes up even further when adjusted for unemployment, underemployment, disability, or other legitimate inability to pay.
- **It promotes flexibility.** In the early stages of coparenting, some kids may find it a little confusing. But it usually doesn't take them long to get used to the idea. Coparented children quickly learn to cope with and accept the different ways their parents do things. My ex, for example, is quite religious; I'm not. When the kids are with her, they do what she does; when they're with me, they do what I do.

Despite all these advantages, there is still a heated debate about whether coparenting is actually a good option or not. A lot of the debate has been more concerned with politics than with what's actually best for the children. Here are some of the common misconceptions—political and otherwise—that you're likely to hear about joint custody and coparenting, and the truth, which is far less commonly available:

MISCONCEPTIONS	TRUTH
- **It works only when parents actively cooperate**	- You don't have to see or interact with your ex very much in order to coparent your children.

MISCONCEPTIONS	TRUTH
♦ **It's bad for women**	♦ "The maternal custody preference ... can coerce today's 'liberated' women into becoming or remaining fully responsible for raising the children of our society," writes attorney Anne Mitchell. According to Mitchell, sole or primary mother custody—which is what most women have—is so limiting to women that they may not be able to "break free to pursue other objectives." By giving women time to have a life away from the children, joint custody is good for women.
♦ **It's bad for kids**	♦ Critics claim that kids need consistency and that coparenting undermines kids' sense of security and stability. But custody experts such as Richard Warshak say that it is sole custody—not joint custody—that creates inconsistency, "because it disrupts the relationship between child and noncustodial parent."
♦ **It promotes conflict between ex-spouses**	♦ Researchers Jessica Pearson and Nancy Thoennes tracked more than nine hundred divorced parents with a wide variety of custody arrangements and found that the conflict between divorced parents "did not appear to worsen as a result of the increased demand for interparental cooperation and communication in joint legal or joint residential custody arrangements. On the contrary, parents with sole maternal custody reported the greatest deterioration in the relationships over time."

MISCONCEPTIONS	TRUTH
♦ **It fuels children's hopes for reconciliation**	♦ In some rare cases this may be true. Usually, though, spending time with both parents and watching them move on with their lives makes it easier for children to let go of the fantasy that Mom and Dad will get back together. But if they never see one of their parents, they can keep that unrealistic hope alive.

When It Works and When It Doesn't

Most experts now agree that coparenting is the best option. They also agree that there are times when it just won't work and shouldn't be implemented.

COPARENTING WORKS BEST IF YOU AND YOUR EX . . .

- **Live near each other.** Even though they're moving back and forth between two homes, your children should be able to keep going to the same school and participate in the same extracurricular activities.
- **See each other's value to the children.** You and she must recognize how important it is for the other to have a healthy relationship with your children, and how important those relationships are to the kids themselves.
- **Can cooperate.** You need to be willing to shelve your personal differences in the interests of working together. This means trying to come up with a set of common rules for behavior, discipline, and parenting style. And if you can't agree completely, it means accepting and respecting each other's choices.
- **Don't fight in front of the children.** Experts have found that the single most accurate predictor of children's long-term adjustment and well-being after divorce is the level of conflict between the parents.

MAKING COPARENTING WORK

The most important thing to remember about trying to coparent with your ex is that you don't need to like each other to do it. "The secret of successful co-parenting is putting the needs of your children ahead of your own," write Elizabeth Hickey and Elizabeth Dalton. "Learn how to separate your needs from your child's, and when interacting with your co-parent, focus specifically on your child's needs."

Here are some steps you can take that can help you build a successful, long-lasting coparenting relationship with your ex.

- **Treat her like a business partner.** "Many business partners are not good friends," writes family therapist and mediation expert M. Gary Neuman. "Yet their common goal allows them to respect each other's strengths and overlook each other's shortcomings." Your children, of course, are your business.
- **Write a parenting agreement.** The worksheet on pages 271–74 covers all the bases. If you and your ex can't sit down together, have a mediator help you.
- **Respect her relationship with the children.** Unless she's doing something dangerous or damaging to the kids, let her parent them the way she wants to. Hopefully she'll do the same for you.
- **Keep her informed.** Let her know about anything important happening in your children's lives that she might not know about. She'll appreciate the effort—guaranteed.
- **Come up with some ground rules for resolving conflicts.** You're going to have plenty of disagreements, so you should have a plan—probably including mediation—for how to handle them from the very beginning.
- **Be flexible.** Emergency trips, illnesses, out-of-town guests, weddings, and other impossible-to-foresee events can mean asking your ex to keep, or to let you keep, the kids a few extra days. Whether you're asking for help or offering it, be nice and she'll probably return the favor.
- **Know your limitations.** "Differences in your parenting styles tend to become more pronounced—and the incentives to compromise less compelling—after divorce," writes Neuman. "Recognize the control you have over your child while at the same time learning to accept what you cannot control."
- **Agree on a fair custody schedule.** If the kids are going to be living with one of you more than the other, there are dozens of scheduling options and you'll have to pick the one that works best for you. If you're dividing custody fifty-fifty, two options are especially good. A week at your place followed by a week at Mom's is fine for kids over eight. But for smaller kids, a week away from either parent is too long. So try dividing each week up. My ex and I came up with a two-week rotation that works extremely well—so well, in fact, that it's fine for kids of any age. Here's how it works (it's a lot less complicated than it looks):

WEEK 1							WEEK 2						
M	T	W	Th	F	Sa	Su	M	T	W	Th	F	Sa	Su
me	me	ex	ex	me	me	me	ex	ex	me	me	ex	ex	ex

Please also check out the section on age-appropriate visitations on pages 77–82.

- **Have regular meetings.** These can be formal, informal, in person, or on the phone. For more on parenting meetings, see pages 169–73.
- **Respect each other's privacy.** You don't want her asking lots of nosy questions about your private life, so don't ask her any about hers.

◆ **Keep up your end of the bargain.** If you make promises, keep them. If you agree to be somewhere, be there. And expect the same from her.

COPARENTING WON'T WORK IF YOU AND YOUR EX . . .
◆ **Are constantly at each other's throats.** Even supporters of coparenting agree that it's not a good idea in cases where the parents are verbally, emotionally, or physically abusive to each other in front of the children. Realistically, though, this is pretty rare. Although about 25 percent of divorces fall into the "high-conflict" category, only 10 percent of them—2.5 percent of all divorces involving children—show any kind of correlation between joint custody or frequent visitation arrangements and poor child adjustment, says John Guidubaldi, a commissioner on the United States Commission on Child and Family Welfare.
◆ **Put your kids in the middle.** Too many parents use their children to carry messages back and forth and to inform them of the other parent's activities. Researcher Christy Buchanan and her colleagues found that adolescents with a higher likelihood of being caught in the middle were more apt to experience depression and anxiety and engage in deviant behavior, such as smoking, drugs, fighting, and stealing, than adolescents who experienced more cooperation between their parents.
◆Live too far apart.

Who Decides How Custody Is Allocated?

Somewhere between 75 percent and 90 percent of the time, splitting couples do the smart thing and agree on a workable custody arrangement. Sometimes they get some help from their lawyers, sometimes from a mediator, and sometimes they just put it together themselves.

The rest of the time—when couples can't work things out for themselves—the decision is made by a judge, and the results for fathers are devastating. As we've said before, mothers get sole or primary physical custody about 85 percent of the time and fathers are usually left with every other weekend, an evening during the week, some holidays, and perhaps a week or two in the summer—a total of about one-fifth of the child's time.

What If You Really Don't Want Any More Custody Than the Minimal Amount You Already Have?

In some cases fathers are actually perfectly happy with minimal custody and visitation arrangements and see no reason to change them. If that's true for you, great—just as long as you're happy for the right reasons.

"While we've got the chance, Dad, we'd like to thank you for these little glimpses of you we've had through the years!"

Here are some of the most common reasons given by the men I interviewed who chose not to pursue any more than minimal visitation with their children. Whether they're right or wrong is, of course, up to you.

- ♦ **Work.** If you travel a lot, put in a lot of overtime, or have a very long commute, you may not be able to take on any additional responsibilities. But is there any way you can change your schedule to accommodate your children?
- ♦ **New relationships.** Having your children live with you—even part-time—will probably have an impact on your love life. But if you plan ahead, you can always get a baby-sitter, and if you're involved with a woman who doesn't like children, you may be involved with the wrong woman.
- ♦ **Your ex.** Sharing custody with your ex might bring you into closer and more continual contact with her than you'd like to have. But things don't have to be that way. You can exchange your kids at school and do your communicating in writing (for more strategies on getting along with your ex, see pages 172–73).

- **Lack of confidence.** You may think that you aren't a good enough father, that you don't know what to do with children, or that your ex is naturally better at parenting than you are. See pages 48–49 for an explanation of the motherhood mystique and read the activities sections on pages 135–49.
- **Emotions.** Ending a relationship is a traumatic experience and you may not feel emotionally or physically ready to take on the additional responsibilities of parenting. But have you checked out all the opportunities for help? Your parents, friends, or other relatives might be able to help out until you feel up to the task.

If you're opting for not spending as much time with your children as you reasonably could, I'd strongly urge you to reconsider, for the following reasons.
- **Your children need you.** The rejection they'll feel if you step out of their lives will hurt them badly and limit the type of relationship you'll be able to have with them. Please also take a look at pages 128–29.
- **Most of these situations are temporary.** If things resolve themselves or you change your mind later, it may be too late. Routines are hard to break and judges are extremely reluctant to change custody and access schedules after they've been in place for a while.

A Few Additions to Your Parenting Agreement

You'll find all the ingredients for a fair, healthy, and mutually satisfying parenting agreement on pages 271–74. Here are a few other important points to keep in mind before you get started:
- **Keep your kids out of it.** Asking your kids to tell you which parent they'd prefer to live with is basically asking them to tell you which one of you they love best. It puts them in a horrible spot. They may, of course, give you their preference anyway, even if you don't ask for it. If this happens, listen to what they say, but clearly let them know that the final decision will be made by you and your ex.
- **No trades.** It's not uncommon for fathers to agree not to seek custody or to very limited visitation in exchange for their exes' agreeing not to ask for child support. This kind of I'll-give-up-anything-just-to-get-you-out-of-my-life agreement is incredibly damaging to your children.
- **Be honest with yourselves.** "If you are interested in protecting your children, honestly attempt to decide where the best future home for them would be, and make sure that is where the children end up," writes child-custody expert Charlotte Hardwick.
- **Be flexible.** As your kids grow and as your ex's and your life situations change, so will your custody needs.

How Judges Make Their Decisions

For at least the past fifty years, judges have heavily favored mothers in awarding child custody in divorce cases and based their decisions, in part, on what used to be called "the tender years doctrine." In 1978 West Virginia Judge Richard Neely summed up this doctrine in a ruling against a father who wanted to share custody of his children: "We are clearly justified in resolving certain custody questions on the basis of the prevailing cultural attitudes which give preference to the mother . . . of young children."

In the 1980s legislators gradually started eliminating such blatantly discriminatory gender-based custody determinations, and today most states have some kind of "gender-blind" legislation specifically barring judges from considering the gender of the parents when making custody decisions. Instead, judges—often assisted by special custody evaluators and other experts—are supposed to base their decisions on other factors, including:

♦ The level of involvement of the parents: who takes the kids to the doctor or dentist, goes to PTA meetings, helps with homework, coaches the baseball team, supervises the kids' religious training, and so on.
♦ The parents' wishes.
♦ The children's wishes.
♦ Family unity: siblings will generally be kept together.
♦ Stability: which parent will be best able to maintain the children's routines—school, friends, extracurricular activities.

♦ **Keep trying to work things out.** If you need help, get yourselves into mediation ASAP. (See pages 33–37 for more on mediation.)

Heads Up

Before you sign any parenting agreement, take a long, hard look at how you're thinking and feeling. Even though most separating couples reach custody agreements without going to court, most of those agreements don't reflect what fathers actually want or what's truly best for the children. In fact, the agreements reached by couples themselves look uncannily like the ones handed down by judges. So why do fathers agree to these arrangements? There are three simple reasons:

♦ **The motherhood mystique.** According to psychologist Richard Warshak, who coined the phrase, the "motherhood mystique" is the prevailing societal wisdom that tells us in no uncertain terms that (a) mothers, by nature, make better parents than men, and (b) mothers are more important to children than fathers. Many women have bought into this dangerous myth completely—and so have a lot of

♦ Other criteria: judges tend to frown on a history of criminal activity, drug or alcohol abuse, promiscuity, spousal or child abuse, and homosexuality.

Sadly, while judges take all these factors into consideration, they still ultimately base their decision on the one thing they're not supposed to: gender. Study after study of state divorce and custody proceedings shows an overwhelming, automatic preference for mothers. And in one study in Colorado, the mother had to be "nearly dysfunctional" not to win custody.

One way judges and legislators justify their antifather bias is by claiming that they're giving primary custody to the child(ren)'s "primary caretaker." At first blush, that sounds almost reasonable. But when you look at what they mean by "primary caretaker" you'll immediately see that the definition includes only the types of tasks mothers traditionally perform and completely skips the things fathers do to nurture their children. In one case, for example, a judge ruled that the primary caretaker is the parent, regardless of gender, "who has devoted significantly greater time and effort than the other to [among other things] . . . breast-feeding."

Under the primary caretaker rule, the mother who spends money on her children's food and clothes is rewarded, but the father who earned the money to pay for those purchases is punished. The mother who washes the little league uniform gets custody of the child, while the father who developed and nurtured his child's interest in sports gets every other weekend. In short, they dole out child custody like a prize "for vacuuming the floors but not for cutting the grass, and for chauffeuring the children, but not for driving to work," writes attorney Ron Henry.

men who too often conclude that their children belong with the mother. "As much as these fathers might genuinely want their children to live with them, they believe they would be hurting their children by removing them from their mother," writes fathers' rights attorney Anne Mitchell. As a result, about a third of fathers routinely ask for less custody than they admit they really want.

♦ **Men and women have different views about custody.** In one recent study, fathers and mothers were asked to rate their feelings about custody on a 1 to 10 scale, with 1 indicating they didn't care how it turned out, and 10 being a willingness to fight for exactly the "right" kind of custody arrangement. Women's and men's answers were nearly identical. The difference, however, was in what men and women identified as the "right" kind of custody. Women typically want sole custody and tend to view joint custody as losing. Men, on the other hand, generally want joint custody and tend to view that as a victory.

♦ **Men are lousy negotiators.** In an "ordinary" negotiation, the two parties involved ultimately end up somewhere in the middle, at around 50 percent. But in this case, where women want sole (100 percent) custody and men want joint

"You're not real experienced at this father business, are you?"

"We got custody of the cat."

(50 percent) custody, the compromise position ends up being 75 percent in favor of women. And that's just about exactly what the typical custody arrangement ends up being.

Should You Ever Fight for More Time with Your Children?

Let's just cut to the chase: a custody battle—even if all you want is joint custody—is an extremely unpleasant and painful ordeal for everyone involved, especially your children. But if you've tried everything you can—civil discussions with your ex, mediation, communication through your lawyers—and you've run into a brick wall, going to court may be the only option you have left. You simply cannot allow your ex or a judge to deny you and your children a reasonable amount of time together or to cut you out of their lives altogether. The more you're in their lives, the better off all of you will be—emotionally, physically, and psychologically. (For a look at the ill effects on kids of growing up without regular contact with their fathers, see pages 128–29.)

If you're thinking of taking your custody or visitation battle to court, here's what you'll need:

♦ **A lot of money.** Expect to spend a minimum of $5,000, and there really is no maximum. I've spoken with a number of fathers who have spent well over $100,000 on their custody cases. And that doesn't even include your ex's attorney's fees, which you'll probably have to pay in addition to your own.

♦ **A thick skin.** "When a woman seeks custody of her children, it seems natural and we don't think twice about it," writes Warshak. "But when a man seeks custody, we are filled with doubts and questions. Why does he want custody? How does he handle the job? How are his children affected?" There's little or no social support out there for men who want more time with their children, and a lot of people will think you're fighting for all the wrong reasons. Besides money, a custody battle will cost you a lot in terms of privacy, self-confidence, reputation, and maybe even friends.

♦ **A realistic understanding of your chances.** In a study conducted at Stanford University, psychologist Eleanor Maccoby and law professor Robert Mnookin found that when mothers asked for sole custody and fathers asked for joint, the mother got sole custody 68 percent of the time. When both parents asked for sole custody, the mother got sole custody 46 percent of the time, the father less than 10 percent, and joint custody was ordered the rest of the time.

Most important of all, you'll need to have a clear idea in mind of why, exactly, you're doing what you're doing. Besides the fact that your being involved in your

Talking to Your Children about the Custody Fight

"A custody or visitation dispute that ends up in court provides the ultimate test in parenting," writes M. Gary Neuman. "Whatever issue brings you to court, no matter who's right or who's wrong, it is never a happy occasion." And it can become even more unpleasant if your kids get caught in the middle—a scenario that happens all too often in these situations.

Here are some ways you can keep your children up to date on what's happening without hurting them:

♦ **Give simple, calm explanations.** Tell them what's happening every step of the way and how it will affect them. Explain who the judges and lawyers are and what their roles are (stay away from lawyer jokes, though). It's best to start with something like, "Your mother and I have tried to figure out on our own where you're going to live, but we haven't been able to, so we asked a judge to help us decide."

♦ **Be honest.** If there's a chance that they'll be asked to testify, let them know. If necessary, small children will talk privately with the judge. Older kids, however, may have to testify in court.

♦ **Reassure them.** A custody battle can bring out the worst between you and your ex, and your children need to know that no matter what happens you and their mother will never stop loving them and that you'll both be there to care for them.

children's lives is the best thing for all of you, there are really only three other reasons to fight for more custody:

1. It will keep you from dropping out of your children's lives. Fathers (and mothers) with little or no court-ordered access to their children tend to disappear over time. We'll talk more about this on pages 127–29.
2. You know your ex is an incompetent mother.
3. You're afraid that she poses a serious emotional, physical, or sexual danger to the kids.

The last two reasons are actually serious grounds for seeking sole or primary custody, which we'll talk about a little later in this chapter.

In contrast, there are a slew of truly rotten reasons to try to increase your visitation or seek a more favorable custody arrangement. The following were suggested by Richard Warshak:

♦ To extract a better financial settlement from your ex.
♦ To avoid child-support payments.
♦ To force your ex to stay in a relationship with you.

♦ **Don't put them in the middle.** That means no asking them to take sides, no comments like, "Your mother is trying to keep me away from you," and no coaching on what to say to the judge. Finally, don't ever tell your children, directly or indirectly, that your happiness depends on their being with you. These kinds of things put your kids in a horrible loyalty bind and are extremely damaging to them.

"So what's your custody deal?"

♦ To increase the amount of contact you'll have with her.
♦ To punish her.
♦ To prove your worth to the world and to show what a great parent you are
♦ To alleviate your guilt about the divorce.
♦ To relieve your loneliness.

In addition, the following factors may or may not affect your decision to go to court, but you should be aware of them anyway:

♦ If you had any hope of maintaining a civil relationship with your ex, taking her to court is the surest way to kill it. The whole litigation procedure sometimes causes bigger problems and communication breakdowns than the ones that led to the divorce.

♦ If your kids are older than about six, they may have to testify in court, where they could be severely traumatized by a couple of hard-nosed lawyers (yours and your ex's) who think they're looking out for their clients' interests.

♦ Although men in our society are supposed to be aggressive, when it comes to family law they're supposed to be docile. I've spoken with a number of fathers who lost their courtroom bids for joint or sole custody and who ended up with less time with their kids and higher child-support obligations than they would have had if they hadn't gone to court at all.

Improving Your Chances of Getting a More Favorable Outcome

The odds that your custody dispute will actually reach a courtroom are pretty slim— nine to one against, says attorney Jeffrey Leving. "You, your spouse, or both of you will run out of money or patience. The need to move on will overwhelm the desire for vindication and validation."

If you're one of the "lucky" ones who does get to court, you'll need every advantage you can get. And very few things can destroy your case more quickly than showing the judge that you don't know anything about your children or that you're not involved in caring for them. Here are a few important things you should be doing with your kids (if you aren't already):

♦ Get up early and make their breakfast and lunch. Take them to day care or drive them to school.

♦ Get to know your children's day-care provider, teachers, soccer coaches, doctors, friends (and their friends' parents)—and make sure they know you. They will be crucial ammunition if your ex's attorney tries to demonstrate what an uninvolved father you are.

♦ Get involved in arranging birthday parties, organizing play dates, and other extra-curricular activities, such as sports and scouting.

♦ Volunteer in your child's school. Reading stories to the kindergarteners or teaching the third graders about computers for even an hour a week shows a judge that you're a committed parent.

♦ Take a parenting education class. Nearly all local community colleges offer low-cost parenting classes; take the ones that cover your children's ages.

♦ Be concerned with safety. Learning CPR and first aid will show the judge that you care about the safety and well-being of your children. So will child-proofing the house and posting emergency numbers on your refrigerator.

♦ Schedule some quality time with the kids *every day*—no matter how long your workdays are. Get up early if you have to, but you've got to demonstrate a deep and continuing interest in, and commitment to, the kids.

Whatever you do, be predictable. "People who do custody evaluations (and who pass their recommendations on to the judges, who in turn usually rubber-stamp them) believe that schedule and stability are the two key ingredients for raising children," says attorney Tom Railsback. Maintain a written schedule of everything you do with your children, and keep receipts (with your signature on them) of doc-

If You're a Gay Father Contesting Custody

The odds are stacked against you even more than against straight fathers. Gay fathers are routinely denied custody of their children (and, presumably, visitation) for no other reason than their homosexual orientation, writes researcher Jerry Bigner. Whether this happens to you really depends on whether your ex and her lawyers want to drag you through the mud or not and, more important, on the prejudices of the judge deciding your case. Even though most states have no-fault divorces, meaning that morality—however one chooses to define it—is supposed to be irrelevant to the divorce, judges routinely take morality into account, and to many, homosexuality is a big, big fault.

The best thing you can do is try to stay as far away from a courtroom as you can. Even if you and your ex have lost your voices from talking to each other, even if your mediator has thrown you both out, try again. If you can't come up with something satisfactory, you'll be leaving the custody decision in the hands of someone who may hold your lifestyle against you in determining the "best interests of the child."

In one case, a divorced gay man's teenage daughters told the judge they preferred to live with their father and his partner rather than move out of state with their mother. But the judge gave custody to the mother, writing, "The Husband has embarked upon a new lifestyle and a new location with a new significant other and his future is unpredictable." In reality, the husband had stayed in the same community where his daughters had been living, whereas the ex-wife moved across country six days after the custody decision, apparently without any idea where she would live or what school the kids would attend.

If your neighbors down the street are homophobic or suffer from some of the common misconceptions about gay parents, that probably won't affect your life very much. But what a judge believes can have a significant, long-term impact on your relationship with your children. Unfortunately, you probably won't have much luck changing your judge's—or anyone else's—mind about gay fathers. But if the discrimination you're facing is blatant, you may have some legal recourse.

If you absolutely have to go to court to contest custody, these two things may help:

+ **Get a lawyer who knows what he's doing.** Yours may, but if he doesn't, don't be shy about getting another one. Make sure your lawyer knows exactly what you want and that he has plenty of experience.
+ **Get some support.** It's going to be a long, hard process and you'll need all the help you can get. The National Gay and Lesbian Task Force in Washington, D.C., (202) 332-6483, can refer you to a gay parents' support group near you.

tor visits, clothing purchases, and so forth. You should also keep track (in writing is best) of the things the kids do when they *aren't* with you. This shows you're interested in them all the time. And pay attention to the details: know their clothing sizes, favorite foods, and all the other telling details that can demonstrate that your role in your kids' upbringing is critical. Remember, whether or not your ex knows the answers to these questions is irrelevant. The judge will *assume* she does, but you'll have to prove you do.

Be sure to keep your wife completely up to date on anything pertinent that happens while you've got the kids: if you bought clothes, tell her; if your child was injured and you took him to the doctor, tell her. Besides being the right thing to do, keeping your wife informed shows that you're trying to keep open the lines of communication. It's a good idea to do at least some of this in writing (and keep a copy for yourself), just in case someone accuses you later of trying to keep your ex in the dark.

Finally, if you weren't particularly involved with your kids during your relationship with their mother don't go overboard now. Some people—your ex and your judge in particular—will be quite suspicious of your new Superdad image and will think that you're only doing what you're doing to hurt your ex or to lower your child-support payments.

In some unfortunate cases this is true. But a lot of newly single fathers, to paraphrase Joni Mitchell, don't realize what they've got 'til it's gone and react accordingly. Fortunately, it's never too late to start building a close bond with your children. So even if you don't end up getting the exact custody arrangement you wanted, you can still take pride in having done the next best thing: having gotten to know your kids better and improved your relationship with them.

Fighting for Primary or Sole Custody

Trying to get sole custody of your children—either right from the beginning or after your ex has had them for a while—is infinitely harder than trying to increase your visitation or even get joint physical custody. Unless your ex is a true danger to the children, judges look for almost any excuse to keep the kids with her. Even under the best of circumstances, where both the mother and father say they want the father to be the primary or sole custodian, judges often award custody to the mother anyway.

That means that if you're fighting for primary or sole custody you've got quite a struggle ahead of you. Knowing about your kids will certainly help you. But you're going to have to demonstrate not just that you're an adequate parent but that you are the superior one, and that's going to be hard. It may be easier, instead, to prove that your ex is an inferior parent. Here are a few things, some of which were suggested by M. Gary Neuman in his book *Helping Your Kids Cope with Divorce*, that might convince a judge to rule in your favor:

- Your ex refuses to allow you access to your children. Document this every time it happens and read pages 181–84.
- Your ex actively attempts to alienate your child from you, physically or emotionally. Again, document this as well as you can and read pages 184–87.
- Your ex wants to move the child far from you or has already done so. This may be a violation of your parenting agreement or a court order and is pretty much the same as refusing to allow you access.
- Since being under you ex's care, your children have begun suffering from major emotional or behavioral problems, their academic performance has dropped significantly, or they've gotten involved with drugs, alcohol, or sex at too young an age.
- Your ex is a lesbian. But this is a nasty and completely unfair card to play; your ex's lifestyle has absolutely nothing to do with her abilities as a mother.
- Your ex, or anyone who has access to your kids while they're under her care, is emotionally, physically, or sexually abusing your children.
- Your ex abandoned the kids and refuses to visit them or does so inconsistently.

As mentioned above, men who seek joint custody often get a lot of suspicious looks from people. Well, if you're trying to get primary or sole custody, it's even worse. The "motherhood mystique" is so strong in this country that even if your ex is a convicted ax murderer, people are going to think that your children should be with their mother and that you're only fighting for custody so you won't have to pay child support. Okay, the ax murderer stuff isn't really true, but you get the point.

Generally speaking, says Warshak, men who seek custody feel strong bonds with their children and cherish those bonds. "They take their child-rearing responsibilities seriously and want to provide a good home for their kids."

All the other reasons for pursuing or not pursuing joint custody that we discussed earlier apply here as well. In addition, there are a number of interesting advantages and disadvantages to being a sole or primary custodial father that you might want to consider.

Advantages of Sole or Primary Custody
- **You'll have a strong relationship with your children.** Seeing and spending time with them every day will make you all closer to one another.
- **You'll be a major presence in their lives.** You'll have a far greater chance to influence your children and pass on your values than if you see them every other weekend.
- **Your self-esteem will grow.** Learning that you really can handle the responsibilities of raising children on your own will make you feel more confident in other areas of your life as well.

♦ **You won't feel as lonely and cut off from your family.**
♦ **You may develop a sense of empathy and understanding for all those single mothers** out there and how difficult it is to do what they do.

Disadvantages of Sole or Primary Custody

♦ **You may take a lot of flak from people.** Some of the men you work with may accuse you of not being serious about your job. And if they're divorced and don't have custody of their kids they may resent you for getting what they really wanted. In addition, "Women with traditional attitudes about sex roles, or divorcées whose ex-husbands have threatened or actually initiated challenges to the custody of their children, often resent fathers with custody and have a psychological stake in proving that the father-custody life style is not viable," says Richard Warshak.
♦ **There aren't enough hours in the day to do what needs to be done.** It's extremely difficult to find the right balance between being with the kids, taking care of their physical and emotional needs, and earning enough money to keep everyone fed and happy.
♦ **You're on your own.** All the parenting decisions that you and your ex made together you have to make yourself. In one study (cited in Warshak) custodial fathers ranked "feeling totally responsible" for their children as more stressful than the problem of combining work and child care.
♦ **It's expensive.** Now there's a big surprise.
♦ **It can mess with your social life.** No more spur-of-the-moment movies or late nights drinking with your buddies. And then there's the issue of meeting women. Not everyone wants to go out with a guy who has kids.

What If You Don't Get the Custody Arrangement You Want?

The sad truth is that your chances of getting joint custody—let alone sole or primary custody—are fairly slim. Nationwide, only about 15 percent of single-parent families are headed by fathers, about 10 percent of whom are widowers. And only about 8 percent of fathers have any kind of shared physical custody. Worse yet, nearly 40 percent of noncustodial fathers have *no* legal access or custody rights at all.

If you end up with limited access to your children, there's not much you can do to improve the situation. Here are a few options:

♦ **Work on improving your relationship with your ex.** The more comfortable she is with you, the more likely she is to agree to let you spend more time with your children.
♦ **Go back to court.** But you'll need the money, the emotional strength, and the

---

"Winning" Custody

In case you were thinking that you could "win" a custody battle, better think again. The fact is that everyone loses, especially the kids. If your wife gets sole or primary custody, your relationship with your children will suffer greatly, and your children will bear the many negative consequences associated with father absence (see pages 128–29). But if *you* get sole or primary custody, your ex will miss out on having a relationship with the kids. And while this may sound like the perfect way to hurt her, keep in mind that the negative consequences of mother absence are just as significant as those of father absence. The bottom line is that the best parent is both parents.

---

willingness to put your children through the whole thing again. Most people are missing one or more of these ingredients.

♦ **Try to make the best of it.** That may sound trite, but it is possible to have a good relationship with your children even if you can see them only infrequently (see pages 153–58 for more on this). The same is true if you suddenly find yourself doing your fathering from hundreds or thousands of miles away.

♦ **Be aware of—and manage—your feelings.** It's hard not to get depressed: the constant good-byes are going to be deeply painful, and in some cases, seeing the kids may be a stinging reminder of the loss of your marriage. According to several studies, these two factors are among the major reasons divorced fathers taper off contact with their kids.

♦ **Don't drop out.** As in most things, try to think of your kids before deciding you can't deal with seeing them. Seeing them may be painful to you, but *not* seeing *you* will be much more painful to them. Be sure to read the chapter on staying involved with your kids (pages 127–50).

What If You Do Get the Custody Arrangement You Want?

If you've managed to beat the odds and have gotten what you were fighting for, don't relax just yet. You still have a lot to do:

♦ **Be gracious.** Don't rub your ex's face in it, and don't tell your children that you "won."

♦ **Be understanding.** It's not easy in this country to be a single mother and not have custody. A lot of people are going to think there's something wrong with her.

♦ **Be prepared.** Noncustodial mothers are more likely to take their former partners back to court to contest custody than noncustodial fathers. If your ex is hostile or vindictive, this is a real possibility.

♦ **Reassure your ex.** She needs to know that the reason you fought for custody—joint, primary, or sole—was not to hurt her but because it was the best thing for the children. You may have a very tough time convincing her that you're being sincere, but keep trying.

♦ **Encourage your ex to participate as much as possible** (unless, of course, she poses a danger to your children). If you have joint custody, this probably won't be much of an issue. But if you have sole custody, she may gradually fade out of their lives. Keep reminding her, and yourself, that your kids need you both.

♦ **Encourage your children's relationships with their mother.** You'd want your ex to do the same if the situation were reversed.

♦ **If your ex is out of the picture, try to have some positive female role models around.** Girls will learn a lot from them about how adult women behave and they'll learn from you how they can expect to be treated by men when they grow up. At the same time, boys will be learning about how to treat women and how they can expect to be treated by them.

♦ **Spend time with your children every day.** It's going to be hard finding a balance between work and family (see pages 195–200), but don't think that having your kids live with you is a substitute for spending quality—and quantity—time with them.

♦ **Take care of yourself.** Try to get some time to yourself a few hours a week just to unwind. The frustrations of parenting are building all the time; left to fester, they easily turn into resentments that can undermine your relationship with your kids. Try some of the stress-reduction suggestions on pages 21–23.

Gay Fathers

According to most estimates, about 10 percent of the adult male population is gay. For a variety of reasons, about 20 to 25 percent of those men have been married at least once and about a quarter of those men—500,000 to 600,000—are fathers. But despite that fairly large number, many Americans are still quite uncomfortable with the idea of a gay man being a parent. According to a 1996 poll done by *Newsweek* magazine, while 57 percent of adults said they think gay people can be as good at parenting as straight people, nearly a third disagreed. The top reasons were religious concerns, concern for the welfare of the children, or a general antigay bias.

Perhaps because these myths have gone unchallenged for so long, a lot of people believe that gay men can't be good fathers. Nothing could be further from the truth. Researchers Jerry Bigner and Brook Jacobsen did a major comparison of gay and straight fathers and found that gay fathers:

Some Popular Misconceptions about Gay Fathers

THE MYTHS	THE TRUTH
◆ Gay males are sexually attracted to male children and want to molest them.	◆ Sure, some gay males are child molesters, but no more so than straight males.
◆ Because they can't reproduce on their own, they recruit little boys to swell their ranks.	◆ There is absolutely no evidence to support this.
◆ Children of gay fathers will become gay or suffer from some kind of sexual confusion.	◆ Only about 10 percent of children of gay fathers later identify themselves as gay—the same percentage as in the general population, says University of Virginia researcher Charlotte Patterson. In addition, a number of studies have shown that the kids of gay parents play with the same toys, have the same interests, and grow up to enter the same professions as kids of straight parents.
◆ A father's homosexuality will psychologically scar his children.	◆ Children of gay fathers have just as many (or as few, depending on your perspective) psychological problems and do as well in school as kids of heterosexual parents. In fact, the psychological problems most kids face have more to do with the breakup of their parents' relationships than with their parents' sexuality.

◆ Tend to be more strict than nongay fathers and consistently emphasize the importance of setting and enforcing limits.

◆ Seem to go to greater lengths than nongay fathers in promoting cognitive skills of children by explaining rules and regulations to them.

◆ May place greater emphasis on verbal communication with children compared to nongay fathers.

◆ Are more responsive to perceived needs of their children than nongay fathers.

Bigner and Jacobsen believe that some of this greater strictness and responsiveness probably has to do with gay dads' fears that they're under greater scrutiny from judges, lawyers, and society in general. In short, gay fathers are, as a rule, nurturing, caring, actively involved with their children, and try to create a stable environment for them.

Notes:

Child Support

Just a few years ago researchers Peter Benson, Judy Galbraith, and Pamela Espeland did a study of 273,000 children and uncovered thirty "assets" kids need in order to succeed. They divided the assets into two categories, internal and external. Of the sixteen external assets critical to children's success in life, not one concerned finances. In the public's mind (and in the minds of most legislators and family law judges), however, money, a.k.a. child support, is number one.

If you're a widower or you have full-time custody of your children, you won't have to worry about paying child support. But if you're any kind of noncustodial single father, you'd better listen up.

What Is It?

In the simplest terms, child support is the court's way of making sure that your children will be provided for, whether you and your ex hate each other or not. In theory, the law recognizes that parents have a joint responsibility to provide for the financial needs of their children at least until they're eighteen (longer in some special circumstances). But in reality, that responsibility falls far more heavily on fathers.

What this means is that the noncustodial parent (probably you) will be ordered to pay the custodial parent (probably your ex) a certain amount every month to keep the children fed, clothed, educated, and healthy. Child support also covers more than just the basic needs. The paying parent (which we'll assume throughout most of this chapter is you) will also have to kick in enough so that the children can maintain the same standard of living—including the ballet lessons, the private schools, and the summers in Italy—they had before you and your ex split up.

Calculating Child Support

Each state has its own elaborate formulas for coming up with support payments that take into consideration both parents' incomes, ages of the children, amount of time each parent has with them, income taxes paid, and much more. Just to give you an idea of how elaborate these calculations are, family judges in California calculate all their support awards using a computer program called Dissomaster, which comes with a two-hundred-page instruction manual.

But roughly speaking, for a typical single father who earns $500 to $1,000 a week, the formula looks something like this:

NUMBER OF CHILDREN	PERCENTAGE OF NET INCOME PAID
1	25%
2	32%
3	37%
4	45%

A couple of things to remember about these numbers. First, "net income" isn't exactly what you might think it is. For child-support calculations, net income is net of federal and state withholdings (including unemployment and Social Security) and that's just about all. It *isn't* net of your rent, car payments, or credit card payments.

Second, these figures are based on your having custody of your children 20 percent of the time (that's the standard every-other-weekend-and-a-few-weeks-in-the-summer arrangement most fathers get). If you have them more, the percentage you pay theoretically drops, but probably not by as much as you might think. Even if you have your kids 50 percent of the time, if you make more than their mother does, you'll probably still be writing checks.

And finally, in some states, some or all of your new wife's earnings may be used in calculating your net income. This has been the subject of protests and proposed legislation by fathers' rights groups and second wives' groups across the country, but the practice still continues.

Unfortunately, state-mandated guidelines don't give judges much flexibility in setting child-support awards. Say you bring home $150,000 per year after taxes. If you have one child, your child-support order would be around $37,500—more than most adults make in a year and way, way more than is necessary to meet the needs of the child. You, the judge, and your ex all know that a lot of your child-support payment will be spent by the ex on herself. But since that's what the formula calls for, there's nothing you can do about it.

"If it's all right with your mother and her attorney, then it's all right with me and my attorney."

Or say you bring home only $25,000 a year. After paying your rent and buying your food, you probably won't have much left over to pay the $6,250 annual support award. But you'd better or you could wind up in jail.

Fortunately, there's another way: in most states, if you and your ex are on fairly civil terms, you can bypass the guidelines completely and write your own child-support agreement. As long as the needs of the children are being met, the courts will approve pretty much anything the two of you come up with. And since no one knows your kids, their needs, and your own individual financial situations better than you and your ex, your agreement will undoubtedly be a lot more reasonable for everyone.

If you and she aren't able to communicate, consider mediation (see pages 33–37 for more on that). Otherwise, plan on spending a ton of money so that some guy in a black dress can order a settlement neither you nor your ex will be happy with.

Coming Up with Your Own Plan

Before you start working on your own child-support agreement, ask your attorney or mediator to tell you what the state guidelines would be in your case—sometimes they actually work out okay.

If you're not happy with the guideline figure, the two of you should put together an accurate list of your individual incomes and expenses, as well as a complete list of child-related expenses. Once you've done that, you'll have to figure out a way of dividing your children's expenses fairly—and that isn't always easy.

One particularly good way is to split the child-related expenses according to the percentage of your combined income that each of you earns. So if together the two of you make $65,000 and you bring in $40,000 of that, your share of the expenses is 62 percent. Each month, then, you would write her a check for 62 percent of the budgeted amount, minus, of course, any expenses you pay for directly, such as school tuition and medical insurance.

Here are some things to keep in mind when you and your ex are drafting a child-support agreement:

+ **Limit the agreement to child support.** Any other non-child-related financial business each of you has with the other should not be included in this arrangement.
+ **Be honest.** Don't lie about your income or do anything to deliberately lower it, and don't overestimate your expenses.
+ **Be fair.** Any agreement you and your ex come up with will have to be approved by a judge.
+ **Be understanding.** If you're making a lot of money, your ex may resent you for it.
+ **Neither of you can waive support completely.** You can, however, set each other's child support payments at zero. The judge can then approve your proposal but leave the door open for change later on if either of your circumstances change.
+ **Be flexible.** Renegotiate your agreement every year or more often if the situation calls for it. Any change in your ex's or your financial situation can have a dramatic effect on your children.
+ **Allow for contingencies.** If you lose your job or get injured or incapacitated, your support payments should be adjusted accordingly. If you win the lottery, they should go up.
+ **Try to keep payments in percentage terms rather than flat dollar amounts.** This is especially important if your income fluctuates. (Say, for example, you're a carpenter and you don't get much work in the winter.) "Some claim this is unfair to the mother because she can never predict when she is going to receive money," writes Tim Horgan. "Agreed, but if she had remained married . . . she would have lived with this uncertainty."
+ **Avoid automatic cost-of-living escalator clauses in your agreement.** Discuss actual changes in expenses and income in your annual review.
+ **Ask for a complete accounting.** If you're paying for support, you have a right to know how it's being spent.
+ **Don't agree to pay more in support than is fair because it will help you feel less guilty about having left your wife and children.**

A Few Notes on Paying Child Support

♦ Pay it. On time and in full. Paying late or not at all can make your children feel as though you've abandoned them. Pay it even if you're struggling to make ends meet and your ex has moved into a mansion with her new, millionaire husband.

♦ If you can't afford to pay what you've been ordered or have agreed to, pay as much as you can and see page 68.

♦ Be generous. Pay as much as you can possibly afford to. If your ex needs help and you're in a position to do something for her, do it. Your kids will benefit in the long run.

♦ Never pay in cash. There's just too much risk of the money "disappearing."

♦ Pay by check only. In the memo section, write "Child Support," and the month and year. Putting your ex's name on a check every month may bring up all sorts of feelings. You can avoid those feelings by paying your support through your county district attorney's office. But that has always struck me as absolutely humiliating.

♦ Keep meticulous records of every check you write, when you mailed (or delivered) it, and when it cleared.

♦ Never use child support as a weapon. Yes, it's tempting to withhold money to punish your ex for something she's done to you, such as interfering with your access to your children. But in lashing out at her, you'll be hurting yourself. In addition, as far as the courts are concerned, child support and visitation are two completely separate issues and they will not back you up if don't pay. If you're having problems with access interference, see pages 181–83.

♦ No, you can't deduct child-support payment on your taxes.

Concerns about Support and How It's Being Spent

Child support is for children, not for your ex. That sounds simple, but you'd be surprised to learn how many people aren't quite clear on this concept.

In perhaps the most public example of misspent child support, Los Angeles County prosecutor Marcia Clark took off some time during the O. J. Simpson trial to ask a judge to increase her husband's support payments. He wasn't delinquent, and he wasn't paying less than he could afford (she was actually making twice as much as he was). Her excuse? "Because of the notoriety of the trial with press and television coverage, I have purchased five new suits and shoes at a cost of $1,500," she wrote in court papers. "I am under constant scrutiny and on public display. It has been necessary for me to have my hair styled . . . and to spend more money on my personal care and grooming. As I am a county employee, none of these expenses are reimbursed."

Knowing that your ex is spending some or all of your child-support money on herself can be absolutely infuriating. But it's so commonly accepted among custodial mothers and family law judges, that there are really only a few things you can do:

♦ Document that she's misspending the money and report it to the court. But proof is almost impossible to come by. Even if you can, if your child support was set by the mandated guidelines, there's basically nothing the judge will be able to do.

♦ Ask the court to let you make some or all of your support payments directly to third parties such as day-care providers, insurance carriers, and others.

♦ Ignore it. As angry as you feel, the fact is that unless your ex has some kind of substance-abuse problem, the money she spends on herself will, in some small way, make your children's lives better.

What to Do If You Have Trouble Paying Your Support

As unfeeling as the legal system appears to be, it does (theoretically, at least) allow fathers who are legitimately unable to pay their child support to have their payments reduced or waived altogether. Unfortunately, few men ever find out—until it's too late—that such options exist.

If you lose your job or become disabled and can no longer afford to pay, you're pretty much on your own. You'll have to pay your lawyer—which you probably can't afford to do—to go to court and ask that your payments be lowered or suspended until you're back on your feet. Even if you can afford the legal fees, there's no guarantee that you'll be successful. Judges are extremely reluctant to "reduce child support orders on the assumption that incomes will eventually improve, but in the meantime arrears accumulate," says Elaine Sorensen, a senior researcher with the Urban Institute, a well-respected Washington, D.C., think tank. According to Sorensen's research, only 4 percent of noncustodial fathers who were paying court-ordered child support received a downward adjustment when their earnings fell by more than 15 percent from one year to the next.

While you're waiting for the judge's decision, you'll be getting farther and farther behind on your payments. And if your arrearage gets bad enough, you could lose your driver's and/or professional license or even end up in jail.

Sadly, there are some jerks out there who are so intent on hurting their exes that they quit their jobs or do other ridiculous things in order to avoid paying child support. Their arrearage starts piling up as well. The problem is that the legal system doesn't make much of a distinction between the jerks and those who really need some relief.

The Truth about "Deadbeat Dads"

One of the things I hate most about being divorced is that there are so many misconceptions about single fathers. And perhaps the most widespread—and the most painful and frustrating to deal with—is the idea that single fathers are, almost by definition, "deadbeats," delinquent on their child-support payments.

Fathers who don't pay child support are being blamed for everything from poverty and crime to the breakdown in family values. They've been on the cover of *Newsweek* and featured in every newspaper and on just about every television news program in the country. And in political campaigns across the nation—from small-town mayor to president of the United States—one of the only issues candidates will agree on is that deadbeat dads should be chased down and jailed. But the truth is that *real* deadbeat dads are few and far between.

Sixty-six percent of mothers who receive less child support than they are entitled to say the fathers are simply financially unable to pay—for a number of legitimate reasons. One major government study found that 81 percent of men consistently employed over a given year made all their support payments, while only 45 percent of men who experienced employment problems did. In addition, a recent GAO study found that as many as 14 percent of men who were delinquent on their child support were actually dead.

*"Dead*head *Dad, honey, not dead*beat."

Sometimes just being alive and having a job isn't enough. A recent list of the top ten most wanted support evaders in the state of Virginia included a construction worker, a mechanic, a health-care assistant, a few laborers, several truck drivers, a painter, and a roofer. Not a lawyer, doctor, commodities trader, or software developer in the bunch.

Money, of course, is certainly important. But as University of Maryland sociologist Jay Teachman argues, "Simply making child-support payments only partially fulfills the more general role of fathering." There are plenty of ways that you can contribute to your children's social, cognitive, and emotional well-being. One of the best is simply to share in their daily lives. This means investing time, taking an interest in their school, getting to know their friends, or taking them to the doctor.

Unfortunately, discussions about deadbeat dads never include any mention of these important nonmonetary contributions. But research has shown that when child support is defined broadly enough to include *time* investments, such as homework and school events, as well as other contributions, such as clothes or gifts, almost all noncustodial fathers provide some form of assistance to their children— a clear demonstration that single fathers are interested in making our children's lives better any way we can.

What If You're the One Collecting Child Support?

Men collecting child support? It's rare—so rare that it often ends up as headline material—but it does happen. While about 58 percent of custodial mothers receive some kind of child-support award, only 40 percent of custodial fathers do. In addition, custodial mothers' awards are a third higher than those awarded to custodial fathers.

But just because it's rare doesn't mean you shouldn't pursue it. If you have your children any more than 50 percent of the time and/or your ex makes more money than you do, talk to your lawyer about getting a support order (or talk to your ex about a writing a voluntary one).

A Few Notes on Collecting Support

- Don't use the kids as a weapon to help you collect money. It's tempting, but it will backfire. Your kids need their mother just as much as they need you.
- Be nice. You may resent your ex's money and the freedom it buys her, but all her money can't buy the kind of relationship you're developing with your kids.
- Don't refuse the money out of guilt for something you did or didn't do during your relationship. Child support is to help you provide for your kids, not yourself.
- Keep good records. Record the amount and date of every check that comes in.

♦ Keep an accurate log of how you spend the child-support money. You'd want her to do the same for you.
♦ No, you don't have to declare it as income on your taxes.

If You Need Help Collecting What's Due You

With all the talk about deadbeat dads, you wouldn't expect that noncustodial mothers ever get behind or refuse to pay their child support. But here's the truth: according to recent U.S. Census Bureau data, only 20 percent of noncustodial mothers with child-support orders pay at least some part of their obligation, compared to 61 percent of noncustodial fathers. Nearly half (46.9 percent) totally default on support, compared to 26.9 percent of noncustodial fathers.

If your ex isn't paying you what she owes, here's what you should do:
♦ Go to your county district attorney. They're required by law to help—for free—custodial parents collect child support. But because you're a man, they may just flatly refuse to help you.
♦ Talk to your lawyer.
♦ Call the Federal Office of Child Support Enforcement, (202) 401-9373, or one of the other public and private agencies listed in the Resources section on page 292. But be prepared for some hassles: most of these places aren't used to dealing with men (except to get money out of them).
♦ If you need public assistance, such as food stamps or subsidized housing, get it.
♦ Don't be shy or embarrassed. Asking for help doesn't mean you're not a man or that you can't take care of your family by yourself. Your children are being hurt by someone and you need to do whatever you can to help them.

Spousal Support

If you were married, you may be ordered to pay your ex spousal support (it used to be called alimony) in addition to or instead of child support. Spousal support used to be automatic in divorce cases, but today it's getting somewhat rarer. There are two basic types:
♦ Short-term spousal support is designed to allow your ex to get career retraining, go to school, or find a job. After that she's on her own. Generally speaking, this type of support won't last any longer than the marriage did. And if the marriage lasted less than two years or if you're both young, educated, and employable, there probably won't be any alimony at all.
♦ Long-term support may be awarded when the marriage lasted a long time (usually more than ten years) and when the two of you have very different employment prospects and earning abilities.

Because spousal support is designed to correct for financial inequities, you may be entitled to support if your ex makes a lot more money than you do. But even if this is true, don't get your hopes up. Unless your ex is making millions, it's unlikely that you'll get any kind of spousal support. Because you're a man, a judge is far more likely to assume that you can just get out there and make more money on your own.

How much and how long spousal support will last depends on a number of factors, including your ages, the assets each of you brought into the marriage, the assets the two of you accumulated during the marriage, how long the marriage lasted, what each of you gave up for it, your current income and your long-term employment prospects, the lifestyle you had during the marriage, your mental health, and the ages of your kids.

Years ago, alimony was used as a financial slap on the wrist with the intent of punishing people—especially husbands—for their faults during the marriage. But today no-fault divorce is the standard, so no matter how horribly you behaved while you were together, it won't cost you any more. Conversely, her horrible behavior won't save you a nickel.

As with child support, you and your ex can work out your own spousal-support agreement on your own, in mediation, or through your attorneys. If you do, be sure to specify the amount, the duration of the obligation, and the factors that could result in stopping or suspending payments. And don't sign anything without your lawyer's okay.

Whether you work out your own agreement or a judge makes an order, be sure to pay what you owe. As with failure to pay child support, the consequences can be severe.

Making Changes

Spousal support usually ends when the receiving spouse dies or gets remarried. But what if she just moves in with someone? You may be able to reduce or eliminate your support payments if her new relationship lasts for a while—more than a year —or if you can prove that your ex is being supported by the new guy.

Your spousal-support payments can also end or be suspended if you lose your job, get disabled, or are unable to pay for some other legitimate reason. But if you're paying support—especially long-term support—and your ex is hospitalized or disabled, your payments may actually increase.

Taxes and Spousal Support

Unlike child support, spousal-support payments are tax deductible, and receipts are taxable as income. It may be to your benefit, then, to try to get a higher spousal-support award and a lower child-support award. But there are exceptions: if you were ordered or agreed to pay spousal support as a lump sum, the IRS may classify it as a property settlement—which is *not* deductible. So talk to your accountant before you start writing out your checks.

Access (Visitation)

If your children's primary residence is anywhere else but your home (or both homes, if you have fifty-fifty joint physical custody), you'll be allowed some visitation—either by the courts or by agreement with your ex. Legally speaking, visitation is simply the right of the parent who doesn't have physical custody of the children to spend time with them. But a lot of people, including me, feel that the term is a little demeaning; it seems to imply that you're some kind of distant relative from out of town and not your children's father. For that reason I prefer the term *access*.

The Access Agreement

Generally speaking, your access schedule will either be included in your parenting agreement or specified in a court order. You shouldn't be surprised that I'm suggesting that you and your ex try to work out your own access agreement rather than leaving it up to a judge. Access schedules are supposed to take into account the best interests of the children, and many judges know or care far too little about that.

The typical pattern for noncustodial fathers is every other weekend (Friday afternoon through Sunday afternoon or Monday morning), an additional two to four hours on a weekday afternoon, some holidays, and a larger block—a month, maybe—in the summer. To be perfectly blunt, this schedule is simply inadequate. It doesn't give you or your kids enough time with each other to develop or even maintain a close relationship. In effect, it's almost encouraging you to abandon them (see the section on fatherlessness on pages 127–29).

Some of the basic points necessary to establish a good access schedule are covered on pages 43–45. But there are quite a few additional items to keep in mind as you're going through the process.

- **Get it done ASAP.** Fathers with clearly outlined access schedules are much more likely to spend time with their children than those without them. Establishing the pattern now will get your new relationship with your kids started right and will help you maintain it over the long haul.
- **Be nice to your ex.** As the primary custodian, she has nearly complete control over your access to your children. This means that she can either allow you a lot more time with the kids than your agreement provides, which can strengthen your relationship with them, or make you stick to the schedule.
- **Make sure you get a good amount of time with the kids.** If you and your partner had stayed together, your children would have been able to see both of you every day. While continuing that pattern isn't very practical now, your plan should allow your child regular contact with both of you.
- **Take into account the ages of the children.** Generally speaking, visits should be as frequent as practical. But what this mean varies with the children's ages. Younger children, for example, do better with frequent, shorter visits. Two weeks is far too long to be away from either parent. We'll talk about age-specific schedules in more detail on pages 77–82.
- **Do not, under any circumstances, agree to "reasonable visitation."** You might think that seeing your children every day is reasonable, whereas for your ex, once a month would be just fine. And even if the two of you do agree now, what happens if she changes her mind later?
- **Specify the schedule in excruciating detail.** Most experts agree that regular access is at least as important as frequent access. Include specific days and times for pick-ups and drop-offs (such as the first and third Fridays at 4:00 P.M.); where transfers are to take place (you pick the kids up at their mother's to start the visit, she picks them up at the end, for example); which holidays are yours with the kids (try to include at least Father's Day and your birthday) and which are hers; plans for how to handle emergencies or other unforeseen events that might change the schedule; the procedure for scheduling make-up visits; agreements on phone calls in between visits; and so on.
- **If you can, incorporate penalties for violating the agreement.** If your ex, for example, interferes with your access, alienates the children, or kidnaps them, there should be some serious consequences: an immediate change in custody or a fine are two possibilities. And to be fair, include a provision fining you for being late or delinquent on your child support (unless you can document that you're unemployed, injured, or otherwise legitimately unable to work). Remember, though, that child support and access are two completely separate issues and that the penalty for not paying support should never, never be a reduction in visitation.

♦ **Think about your skills.** Be honest with yourself. Do you have the skills to have the kids stay with you for two or three days at a time? If you do, great. If you don't, it's not too late to learn them. Community centers, church groups, and other organizations offer parenting classes—if you need one, take it.

Time: The Mechanics of Access

The central question in your access agreement is how much time your children will be able to spend with you, the noncustodial parent. In trying to come up with a fair schedule, you and your ex will have to strike a balance between your children's needs and your own.

Obviously, the children's needs should come first. They not only need, but have a right to, strong, healthy, productive relationships with both their parents. The purpose of coming up with a time-sharing arrangement is not to restrict their access to either parent but to ensure that they have enough time with both of you to meet their needs.

Your needs are important too, but not as important as your kids'. Still, you should think long and hard about this one. Mothers usually do an excellent job of figuring out what they need and communicating it to others. But fathers don't (see pages 48–50 for more on why). So don't be afraid to express, and stand up for, your needs.

So How Much Time Is Enough?
The basic rule is to try to get the most liberal access you can. Schedules are very difficult to change once they're in place. If you start off seeing your children every other weekend and then you want to add two full days a week, you'll have a tough time doing so.

However much time you end up with (and we'll talk about some specific guidelines below), the most important consideration is to make sure your visits are regular. Your kids need to have a sense of consistency in their relationship with you. They need to know they can count on you and that you'll always be in their lives. These are things they just can't get from random visits (more about this on pages 76–77).

Regularity, however, is nothing without frequency. (Once a year obviously just won't cut it.) Most experts agree that frequent visits—even short ones—are better for your children than infrequent ones, even if they're long. What, exactly, the words *frequent, short,* and *long* mean depends on a lot of factors, including your kids' ages and on how far apart you and your ex live from each other.

We'll discuss some age-appropriate schedules below. But overall, visits should be:
♦ **Frequent enough** to allow you and the kids the continuing contact they need from you and to allow you to keep up with the changes going on in their lives. A week is a huge gap for children under six or seven, but it may be okay (though far from ideal) for a teenager.

The closer you and your ex live to each other, the more frequently you can see your children. So live as close as you can. You and your ex don't have to get along with each other, you just have to agree that the children need an ongoing relationship with you.

♦ **Long enough** to maintain and develop a relationship with your kids. If your baby is a year or younger, three or four hours a day is fine to get you started. But for an eight-year-old, that's nowhere near enough.

Richard Gatley and David Koulack, authors of *The Single Father's Handbook,* say that parent-child visits have three distinct parts:

1. Acquaintance renewal (hello again)
2. Middle (living together again)
3. Separation (good-bye again)

If Your Visits Are Too Infrequent . . .

♦ There'll be so much to catch up on that the hello stage will overshadow your time together. Spending so much time catching up, and then having to turn around and say good-bye is tough on everyone. Sometimes fathers begin questioning whether it's really worth it to put everyone through the exercise and they cut back their visits even more.

♦ You'll miss out on having a relationship with your children. They won't get the feeling of consistency they need so much and you'll really be able to play only a

"Marsha, I can't take the kids—I've got my mutual funds this weekend."

limited role in their lives. You can, of course, take the edge off this by staying in touch in other ways (see pages 153–58 for more on this).

♦ You'll be pretty much out of the loop when it comes to keeping track of what's going on in their lives, including their physical development, their homework, their friends, their after-school activities, their health, and even their teeth.

♦ You'll suffer too. "Everyday spats, for example, that arise in the course of a visit may have to wait a week or more for resolution," write Richard Gatley and David Koulack. "Children generally forget about these incidents right away, but newly separated fathers often keep themselves on tenterhooks worrying about what their kids think of them after a blowup. These and other kinds of emotional problems that would normally be resolved by everyday contacts within the family can easily get blown out of proportion when they have to wait too long, causing great distress for the separated father."

If Your Visits Are Too Short . . .

♦ You'll spend all your time catching up with each other and saying good-bye, leaving little time, if any, to actually settle into a nice, comfortable routine. This will probably upset your kids, who will want to do something with you, not sit around talking about what they had for lunch every day since they saw you last. The more frequent your visits, though, the less likely this is to be a problem.

♦ It limits what you can do with them. If you have only a few hours or maybe a day together, you can't take trips or work on any long projects.

♦ You'll be under a lot of pressure to fill every second of every visit with fun and excitement. This, too, may upset your kids, who sometimes need to spend as much time with you quietly doing puzzles as riding roller coasters.

Although you and your ex are going to have to come up with a schedule that meets everyone's needs, use the following age-appropriate guidelines to help you establish the *minimum* time you should have with your children:

Infants and Toddlers

Although most noncustodial fathers have some variation on the traditional every-other-weekend access schedule, fathers of children under two usually have even less time with their children. Most experts agree that children, especially very young ones, need consistency and routine. Unfortunately, too many of these people, relying on outmoded stereotypes about men and women, believe that infants and toddlers should live almost exclusively with their "primary parent" (the mother) and that the father should be allowed to visit only two or three hours every other weekend with no overnights. This kind of schedule, however, is "absolutely inappropriate for infant contact," writes pediatrician Robert Fay. "It is almost as damaging as total denial of any contact and explains the sole mother's frequent claim that 'the baby doesn't even want to see his father.'"

The bottom line is that your children need daily contact with you. It will be years until they develop enough of a grasp of time and space to understand that you exist between visits and that if you go away you'll be back sometime soon. If they don't see you every day when they're infants—or at least pretty darn close to every day—they'll never really know who you are.

Here's an idea of the kind of visitation schedule that a number of experts, including Dr. Fay, think your infant or toddler really needs. We'll assume, for the sake of this discussion, that your child is living primarily with your ex and that you'll be visiting:

- **The first month.** If she's being breastfed, you should have one or two visits each day for an hour or two each time. If she's being bottle-fed you can spend even more time; Fay recommends a minimum of four hours each day and eight on weekends. You can divide these hours up into two shifts if you need to. At this age there's not much to do but hold the baby, feed her, and change her. But as boring as they sound, these activities are laying the foundation for your future relationship together.

- **1–3 months.** For breastfed babies, a minimum of one three-hour session each day, plus more—perhaps eight to twelve hours—on the weekends. Even at this age, your baby can tell the difference between you and her mother and she knows to expect different things from each of you. For bottle-fed babies, more time is fine.

- **3–6 months.** Breastfed: at least four hours a day, twice as much on weekends. Bottle-fed: two full days each week, including overnights. Go easy with the first few overnights at your house. Start off with a single night the first two or three times, then go to two nights in a row after that.

- **6–12 months.** Eight to twelve hours twice a week plus at least four hours on other days, if being breastfed. If your baby is being bottle-fed, overnights are important and it's fine for your baby to spend the whole weekend, three nights in a row, with you. Try to fit in four hours on other days as well.

- **1–2 years.** After the first year, a less intensive schedule is okay. Your baby will have gotten used to being cared for by two people with two different styles. But don't cut the schedule back too far. You should still spend three or four hours with your toddler three times a week, plus a two- or three-night overnight every other weekend. Children this age still don't understand time very well and a few days, let alone a week, without you might as well be forever. They'll feel abandoned and rejected and will soon start resenting you.

SOME PROBLEMS THAT MIGHT COME UP

- **Breastfeeding too long.** As we discussed in *The New Father: A Dad's Guide to the First Year*, the benefits of breastfeeding are well known, and your ex should breastfeed your baby for at least a year, if at all possible. Sometimes, though, says

Dr. Fay, "breastfeeding has been prolonged . . . for the purpose primarily of pro-longing mother-child contact to the exclusion of father contact." If you have a sense that this is happening, talk it over with your ex in a nonaccusing way. If you can't come to an agreement about it, ask your mediator or your attorney to step in.

♦ **Adjustment.** In the early months after their parents split up, infants and toddlers can have some problems adjusting to all the transitions. They may be especially tearful, fussy, clingy, or have some problems eating or sleeping with either you or your ex. These symptoms are absolutely normal—the baby is getting used to his new situation and everything will be fine soon. "When loved and secure and bonded, children can and do adapt well to changing environments," says Fay. Unfortunately, too many people who really should know better try to "treat" these problems by cutting back on the children's time with the nonprimary parent (you). This is exactly the wrong approach and will lead to even more adjustment problems later. Of course, if the problems go on for more than a month (less, of course, for the eating and sleeping problems), or if they seem especially severe, contact your pediatrician.

"Older" Children

Regular, frequent contact with "older" children is still important, with your goal being the more the better.

♦ **Preschoolers (3–6 years old).** Kids this age still need consistency and routine. Visits of three or four hours three times a week plus the every-other-weekend overnights is a good place to start. You should also have daily phone contact. Vacations: You should have a large block of time—anywhere from a week straight to half the summer—with the kids. But if you're going to be keep-ing the child with you for any more than two weeks at a stretch, make sure your ex has some regular visitation. Being away from her for a long time is just as bad for the kids as being away from you.

♦ **Early school years (6–8 years).** Now that the kids are in school, three- or four-hour blocks of time are going to be hard to find. So shoot for two afternoons a week (pick them up at school, give them dinner, and help them with their home-work). Also, add a night to your every-other-weekend sleepovers (make them from Thursday after school through dropping off on Monday morning). And don't forget the daily phone calls. But remember, kids this age are developing interests and needs outside of the family: friends, sports, homework. So be flexible and allow your child plenty of time to get everything done. You and your ex should alternate vacations during the school year and split the summers. If possible, allow for some visitation, especially if the children are going to be away from either of you for more than a few weeks.

♦ **Middle school years (9–12 years).** The early-school-years schedule (above) is okay as a minimum. But it may start getting harder to get in your daily phone

"During the next stage of my developement, Dad, I'll be drawing closer to my mother—I'll get back to you in my teens."

call. And when the kids are with you, you'll need even more flexibility than before to deal with their expanding school, social, and extracurricular activities. The kids may be sleeping at your house as much as before, but they'll probably be spending less actual time with you. Vacations and holidays should be split between you and your ex, and anytime the kids are in camp should be split as well, with part of the time counting as "yours" and part as your ex's.

SOME PROBLEMS THAT MIGHT COME UP

♦ **Adjustment.** Your preschooler may be weepy, clingy, or sad, and may act out or even show some regressed behavior (a potty-trained child might start having accidents again; a child might start or resume sucking his thumb). And your grade-school child might become withdrawn or depressed, start having problems with friends, or behave unusually aggressively. These are all very common—and usually completely normal—ways that kids react to the stress of their parents' breakup and to the change in their living situation. If you and your ex keep showing them that you love them and that their world is still secure, they'll gradually get used to things. The solution is *not* to reduce the amount of time you spend together. If these problems persist or seem truly severe, consider counseling.

If your children are exhibiting any kind of adjustment problems, resist the urge to blame the symptoms on your ex. She probably has the same concerns you do. In some cases, though, children's behavioral and emotional problems are the result of one parent's attempts to alienate the children from the other parent. If you're concerned that this might be happening in your case, please read pages 184–87.

♦ **Preferences.** It's really best not to ask your kids when they want to visit you. But that probably won't stop them from telling you. "When children do express preferences, either in words or in their behavior, caring co-parents will take these wishes into account," says Shirley Thomas. "But they will not give the burden of absolute choice to a child of any age." This is especially important if you have preschoolers. Kids are remarkably fickle, and every single time you or your ex disciplines the child or disagrees with her she'll demand never to see the offending parent again.

Teens (13–18 Years)

Like younger kids, your teenager needs regular, frequent contact with both her parents. But with her busy schedule and ever-expanding world, you'll have to be more flexible than ever.

Some of your weekday afternoons together may be preempted by softball or band practice, by rehearsals for the school play, or by a trip to the mall. And weekend time together may be reduced by sleepovers at friends' houses. It's critical to let your teenager know that you support her friendships and other outside interests. But be firm. She has to know that her freedom is contingent, in part, on finishing her homework, doing her chores, coming home when she's supposed to, showing up for meals, and allowing some time just to hang out as a family.

Your teenager may look like an adult, but she still needs a lot of support and encouragement from both parents. Boys typically start wanting to spend more time with their fathers; girls, with their mothers. In addition, teens of both genders often develop a sudden interest in spending time with the parent they spent less time with growing up. Try to take these and other preferences into account, but remind your child that the final schedule is up to you and your ex.

POTENTIAL PROBLEM AREAS

♦ **Adjustment.** If you're a fairly recent single father, don't be surprised if your teenager becomes rude or uncooperative, has difficulties making or keeping friends, tries to play you and your ex off each other, shows a sudden interest in people of the opposite sex, or starts getting involved with drugs or alcohol. These are all rather common teen reactions to their family's breaking up. Some are fairly minor, but some have extremely serious consequences, and if you see them you should consider family counseling immediately.

"Gee, I'd love to, but that's the weekend my father gets me."

♦ **Your ex overbooks your kids.** Finding time to spend with your children is hard these days. And in order to get more, your ex may book all the kids' extracurricular activities on days when you have them, leaving you to spend your time with them working as a chauffeur. This, of course, is wrong: she can book every activity in the world on her days with the kids, but she has no right to obligate you.

Your ex may do this without even realizing it, in which case mentioning the problem will probably take care of it immediately. But she may be doing it deliberately, trying to cut into the time you have with the kids or make you into the bad guy for not letting them do what they want when they want to. If so, read pages 184–87 on parental alienation.

Holidays and Other Special Occasions

You and your ex will probably alternate most of the major religious (Christmas, Passover, and so on) and secular (July Fourth, Thanksgiving, and so on) holidays. In some cases you might even split them (Christmas Eve or the first seder with

Mom, Christmas Day or the second seder with you). Either way, you'll need to plan ahead and be as flexible as you can.

If Mother's Day falls on one of your days with the kids, offer to trade your ex for Father's Day or your birthday or some other day that's special for you. And if you're scheduled to have the kids on Thanksgiving but your ex is having a huge family reunion, let the kids go there. Hopefully your ex will do the same for you sometime.

If there are going to be changes, tell the kids in advance. Their routine may be upset somewhat, but they'll learn a valuable lesson by watching you and their mother work together.

And when the kids come back from spending a special time with their mother, let them talk about it as much as they want to. Encouraging them with questions like, "What did you do that was the most fun?" is fine, but stay away from asking too many questions about your ex, the new man in her life, or any of her personal business.

Birthdays

Because they last only one day, birthdays can raise some unique issues. If at all possible, have joint birthday celebrations. This avoids birthday overkill: one party that your side of the family comes to, another attended by your ex's side, and a third for your child's friends. That's way too many parties for one child.

The other advantage of a joint party is that it's probably what your child wants anyway. But it won't work, of course, if the two sides of the family can't stand each other.

What You May Be Feeling

• **Cut off.** Before my divorce I was very involved with my kids. I spent hours every day with them playing, doing homework, running errands, reading books, and just hanging out. I had a lot of control and influence over their lives, and just knowing that I could tiptoe into their room and listen to their breathing as they slept made me feel important and powerful and secure in the knowledge that I would always be there to protect them. Whether or not you were deeply involved with your kids before your breakup isn't important. You still probably had some kind of contact with them every day—even if it was for only a few minutes—and you played a major role in their lives. And if there was any part of their lives that you missed, chances are your partner would fill you in.

But after your breakup things change rather suddenly and dramatically. For me, it meant having my kids only half the time. For millions of other men, it's having them only 15 percent of the time, or even less. We can't see them every day, no matter how much we want to. We don't have nearly the same amount of influence, we certainly can't watch them sleep every night, and we have no way to keep up to date on what's going on with them when we're not there.

♦ **Guilty.** After a few months of feeling cut off from my kids and missing them nearly every minute I wasn't with them, something changed—and I remember the day it happened. I had started writing at 8:30 that morning and kept going until midnight, when I finally quit, exhausted and nearly blind from having stared at my computer for such a long time. As I sat alone in my living room, drinking a beer and listening to Bach, I thought about how much work I'd done that day and how wonderful it had been not to have any kids around. Those thoughts had barely entered my mind when I was overcome with guilt. How could I possibly call myself a loving father and be glad that my kids were someplace else?

Over the following weeks I realized that there were plenty of other times when I was perfectly glad not to be with the kids—when I was on dates, for example, or hanging out with my friends. And sometimes, after spending a few days feuding with the kids, I actually remember wishing, just for a second, that they'd just go away and never come back.

Yes, I felt guilty, sometimes very guilty. But after torturing myself for a while, I came to the conclusion that I didn't have to be pouty and miserable when my kids weren't around to prove that I was a good father and that I loved them. That was a hard lesson to learn, but it was one that all single fathers can benefit from.

Your having fun or enjoying being alone is not a betrayal of your children. In fact, just the opposite is true. You can't make anyone else happy if you're not happy yourself. Having a life of your own will make you appreciate your visits with your kids all the more and will make your days together more enjoyable for everyone.

♦ **Afraid of losing their love.** How your ex feels about you has nothing to do with how your kids feel about you. But that doesn't prevent many, many single fathers from thinking that since their exes don't love them anymore, their kids can't be far behind. As a result, too many noncustodial fathers end up trying to buy their children's love by showering them with gifts, treats, and trips, and forgoing discipline. We discuss the dangers of this "Disneyland Dad" syndrome on pages 90–91.

Interestingly, your kids are probably worried about nearly the same thing you are: if you and their mother stopped loving each other, what's to prevent one or both of you from not loving them anymore?

What Your Children Might Be Going Through

In the next two chapters we will discuss what your children might go through during the early stages of your single fatherhood; here are some typical access-related feelings you may encounter.

♦ **Depression and loneliness.** "Children who have few outlets for their emotions don't know what to do and are easily caught between their parents; they feel helpless about making things better," writes Shirley Thomas. Children who are depressed and lonely frequently have problems in school, develop learning difficulties, find it hard to concentrate, and can even develop real or imagined physical problems.

♦ **Anger.** This can be directed at you and/or your ex and is usually an expression of "See how your breakup ruined my life?" See pages 15–16 for suggestions on how to handle this.

♦ **Resentment.** Your kids may have had some big activity planned that they'll have to miss to be with you. They may use the opportunity to try to manipulate you into doing something special for them "in exchange." Don't fall for this one or get too angry at the I'd-rather-be-doing-something-else-instead-of-being-with-you attitude that's directed at you.

♦ **Happy.** Yes, they'll have some ups and downs, but overall your children are going to be quite happy to see you and will look forward to it.

♦ **Sad.** Each transition between your house and their mother's is a new reminder of the breakup.

♦ **Cautious or distant.** It can take them a little while to get reacquainted with you, especially if they haven't seen you for a while. See page 96 for some ideas on how to overcome these problems.

♦ **Overly empathetic.** If your children are blaming themselves for your breakup, they may also be feeling responsible for your emotional difficulties and may end up trying to "parent" you. You may not notice the symptoms at first, but if your child starts turning down opportunities to get together with friends or inexplicably stops showing interest in a heretofore favorite activity and decides to spend time with you instead, you should deal with this problem right away, says Thomas. The simple cure is to let your children be children. If you need a shoulder to cry on, talk to your friends or get yourself some professional help.

Potential Access-Related Problems

Transitions

One particularly touchy area for many former couples is the transition from mom's house to dad's and back again. If your kids are in day care or school, the easiest way to make your exchange—and the best way to avoid any problems with your ex—is to do it there. If you have the kids for the weekend, for example, your ex drops them off at day care or school on Friday morning as usual and you pick them up when they're done that afternoon; they spend the weekend with you and you drop them off wherever they're supposed to be on Monday morning. You and your ex never see each other.

That approach, of course, works only on school days. If your children aren't in school when the exchange is supposed to happen, if they're too young to be in school, or if using the school as a buffer won't work with your access schedule, there are other solutions.

If you and your ex are on good terms, the easiest way is to work out some kind of pick-up and drop-off schedule at (or in front of, if you'd rather not go inside) each other's houses. But if things aren't going too smoothly, you can minimize potential flare-ups by making your exchanges at some neutral, preferably public, place, such as a restaurant. Having all those people around will probably keep the two of you from biting each other's heads off.

For kids, transitions—especially the kind that happen at one or the other parent's house—can be especially stressful. Here's how you can help make them smoother:

♦ **Keep your child current.** Let him know at least half an hour in advance that he's going back to his mother's house. Tell him you'll be dropping him off (or that his mother will be picking him up), and tell him exactly when you'll be seeing him again. If he brought anything from her house, help him pack. All this will help him start mentally preparing for the transition. Ask your ex to do the same kind of prep work just before his visits with you.

♦ **Have a routine.** I almost always take the kids grocery shopping on the first day of our times together. It gives us a chance to do some catching up and get used to each other again. But ease into things; don't schedule a major activity immediately after the transition.

♦ **Don't use the transition as a time to discuss tough issues with your ex.** Schedule another time to talk.

♦ **Be understanding at the beginnings—and ends—of your visits.** Your child may be angry, tearful, or seem particularly distant just after you pick her up or just before you drop her off. These are natural and common ways for kids to react to the process of separating from one parent and rejoining the other. Your ex is probably dealing with the very same behavior when your child comes back to her house or is getting ready to leave.

Besides the potential conflicts with your ex, transitions can be hard in other ways as well.

♦ **You're a dad, you're single, you're a dad, you're single . . .** Sometimes it can take a few hours to switch from one role to the other. Having some routines of your own often helps. Go for a run, check your e-mail, pay some bills—whatever it takes.

♦ **You may withdraw.** For more than a year my kids and I would have some kind of fight just a few hours before the end of our times together. I finally realized that it was mostly my fault; in order to reduce the pain I felt at having to say goodbye, I began to withdraw from them. That hurt their feelings and made them feel that I didn't want to be with them. So they would do all sorts of annoying things to get my attention, which invariably led to some kind of squabble. Things have been a lot better since I figured this out.

Supervised Visitation

If there was a history of drug, alcohol, or physical abuse in your relationship with
your ex, if she's accused you of having abused her or the kids, or even if she says—
without any justification—that she's afraid of you, a judge may order that any contact you have with your children be supervised. This usually means that another
adult (not your ex) approved by the court will have to be present every minute of
every visit. The supervisor can be either someone you know or an employee of one
of the growing number of facilities that offer supervised visitation services.

Having someone watching everything you do with your child is nothing less than
humiliating. But in most cases it's a temporary solution that allows you to keep in
contact with your children while you're fighting the charges against you, going through
rehab, taking parenting classes, or doing whatever it is you have to do to satisfy
the judge. But no matter how demeaning it may seem, remember that it's far better
for your children to have their time with you supervised than to have no time with
you at all.

If you are ordered to have supervised visitation, try to follow the guidelines
suggested by child custody expert Charlotte Hardwick:

♦ **Don't feel like a criminal.** Eighty-five percent of the charges of abuse or
   dangerous behavior that come up in divorces are dropped or disproved.
♦ **Adjust your attitude to turn this into a positive experience.** This will
   allow you to make the best impression on everyone connected with the supervised-
   visitation experience.
♦ **As soon as you know where the visitation is to take place, visit the
   facility and meet the director.** Ask about rules and get some suggestions for
   how to make the whole experience easier for your children.
♦ **On the days of your visits, arrive early and meet with the observer.**
   The observer's reports—especially if they're positive—can have a major impact
   on how long your access will have to be supervised. Keep notes about when you
   arrived, who the observer was, when the children arrived, how they looked and
   acted, what time they were picked up by your ex, and anything the observer
   said to you.
♦ **Never speak negatively about the other parent.**
♦ **Bring activities to do with your children during the visit.** Make things
   you want them to take home with them. This gives your children a way to stay
   connected with you when you're not with them.

What if the situation is reversed? If *you're* the custodial parent and your ex was
or is now a danger to the kids, or if you think she might kidnap them, you have a
moral obligation (in my view) to go to court to request that her visits with the kids
be supervised.

Other Tough Issues

What If Your Child Doesn't Want to See You?

No matter how great your relationship is with your children, someday they're going to tell you they don't want to be with you. And whether it's because you didn't let them stay up to watch videos the last time they were with you, because the visit with you conflicts with some other activity, or because your ex is trying to turn them against you, it's going to hurt like hell. Especially when they say things like "I hate you," or "I never want to see you again."

When (not if) this happens, it's important not to take it personally even though it's hard to take it any other way. If your ex really is responsible, read pages 184–87 on parental alienation. Otherwise, try to remember that outbursts like these are perfectly normal. Kids see the world as black or white, good or evil, and sometimes you're going to be the bad guy. Here are some steps you can take to reduce the chances that your getting rejected by your kids, even temporarily, will become a regular thing:

♦ Give the kids extra transition time. If you're picking them up at your ex's, spend a few minutes there talking or reading a story before leaving. If she's dropping them off, ask her to help ease the transition by following some of the steps outlined on pages 85–86.

♦ Offer to come back in half an hour. But check with your ex first to make sure you don't upset her plans for the rest of the day. Do this only once. Let your kids

"Is everything all right, Jeffrey? You never call me 'dude' anymore."

know that you respect their feelings but that you and your ex have the final say over when and how visits happen.

♦ Discuss the problem privately with the children. Take them out for a hot chocolate or go for a quiet walk around the block and ask them to explain why they don't want to see you. Listen respectfully and understandingly and don't argue with them.

♦ Tell them the things you've got planned for the day and how much you're looking forward to spending time together as a family. But don't beg and *do not* bribe them. You don't want them to come with you because they feel sorry for you or because they want a chocolate shake.

♦ If your kids' reluctance to see you happens fairly frequently, consider getting family counseling.

When You're the "Good" Parent and the Kid Doesn't Want to Spend Time with Mom

At some point the situation will probably change: you'll be the good guy and your ex will be the bad one. While this may feel like some kind of karmic revenge, don't get too thrilled. Your kids need their mother just as much as they need you, and you have to encourage and foster their relationship with her—even if your ex hasn't done the same for you.

Ask the children to explain as much as they can about why they don't want to see their mother. If there's really something to worry about (say your ex or her new boyfriend is drinking, abusing drugs, or hurting the kids), back them up—but make sure you're right.

But assuming that they're not in any danger—and they probably aren't—explain to your children that not seeing their mother isn't an option. Tell them that you and your ex have worked out a schedule that you feel is best for everyone and that all of you, including them, have to follow the rules. Help them through the transition between you and your ex any way you can and tell them exactly when you'll be in touch next, either in person or on the phone.

What If Your Ex Doesn't Want to See Your Children?

If you have primary custody of your children, your ex is probably feeling a lot of the things that so many noncustodial fathers feel: excluded from their kids' lives, unloved, unneeded, and useless. And, just like some noncustodial fathers, she may simply drop out of her children's lives. Alternatively, she might never have been particularly involved at all. Either way, your kids are going to take her refusal to see then as a personal rejection, and they'll suffer greatly.

Since the courts can't legislate good behavior and can't force people to spend time with each other if they don't want to, explaining to your kids what's happened

On Not Being a Disneyland Dad

Whether it's guilt, the fear of losing their children's love, trying to make up for lost time, a desire to compete with the ex, or something else, noncustodial fathers—especially those with fairly infrequent visitation—often feel obligated to make every second of every visit with their children "count." They buy them extravagant gifts, eat out every meal, take them on expensive trips, give into their every whim, forget about discipline, and generally treat them like visiting royalty instead of children. It's no wonder that a lot of people refer to this kind of father as the "Disneyland Dad."

Falling into this trap is easy, but you won't be able to keep it up for very long; sooner or later you'll run out of money or ideas. And when that happens, your kids will have gotten so spoiled that they'll do one of two things (maybe even both):

♦ Resent you for not giving them "their due."

♦ Think you don't love them any more.

Your goal as a noncustodial father, even if your time with your children is limited, is to have as normal a relationship with them as possible. There's no need to compete with your ex and you don't need to buy their love. If you genuinely love your children and are interested in being with them, they'll know. And they'll love you and want to be with you in exchange.

Here are some simple steps you can take to keep yourself from turning into a Disneyland Dad:

♦ **Plan ahead.** Don't schedule every minute of every day, but over the course of the visit try to devote some time to each of the following areas: fun, food, private time for you with each child, and time for the kids to be by themselves.

♦ **Don't go overboard.** You do not have to amuse your children every second. Don't even try. There's no way you'll be able to keep up the pace. And if you get them used to nonstop entertainment, treats, and gifts, they'll resent the hell out of you if you break the pattern.

♦ **Don't try to make up for lost time.** You can't.

♦ **Vary your activities.** Yes, as we know, kids love routines. But if you go to the movies and take a tour of the chocolate factory every weekend, they'll be bored out of their minds. The weekend newspapers and those free, local

is up to you. Here are a few things you can do to help your children through this tough experience:

♦ **Be sympathetic.** Tell them you know how much it hurts and remind them that it is absolutely not their fault. If you feel you can explain what really happened without being critical of your ex, do so. If you can't, you might simply say that people sometimes go through very tough times and make mistakes.

parenting publications are full of great things to do in your area. Groups such as Parents Without Partners (see the Resources section for contact info) often have activities planned that can help add some variety to your times with your children.

♦ **Treat your kids like they live there (they do), not like visiting VIPs.** This means giving them some chores and making sure they practice the violin and do their homework. It also means having—and enforcing—rules in your house (see pages 159–62).

♦ **Give them some choice in what you do.** Let them tell you what they want to do. Ask them to put together a list of possibilities or give them some options of your own to choose from. You don't have to do everything on their list; the fact that you've asked for their input will reinforce the idea that you genuinely care about what's important to them.

♦ **Allow plenty of down time.** Some of your weekends are going to be packed to the gills with great activities. But don't make them all that way. Cramming too much fun into your time together can cause a lot of stress. Kids of all ages need to spend some time entertaining themselves—even if it means being bored. This can include writing in a journal, doing a crossword puzzle, drawing, or just hanging out in the living room listening to a CD.

♦ **Don't put too much pressure on yourself.** There will be times when you'll have enough energy to run around doing things all day and other times when you'll feel like a slug—just like everyone else in the world. Your kids will understand. You and the kids will occasionally have fights, too. If you do fight, don't spend a lot of time worrying about it; they won't stop loving you. Fights are perfectly normal in intact families, and just as normal in broken ones.

♦ **Be normal.** Of course you'll try not to spend your time with your kids working on some project you brought home from the office. But sometimes things come up that you just have to take care of—household repairs, for instance. Having your kids help out—even if it's only holding one end of the tape measure or handing you nails—can be a wonderful way to spend time together and make them feel a part of your life. It will also tone down any unrealistic expectations your kids might have about you by showing them that you're human and that you have obligations and responsibilities.

♦ **Be honest.** If you know your ex will be back in her children's lives soon, tell them. If not, don't. Giving them false hope will make their feelings of rejection even worse.

♦ **Encourage your kids to talk about how they feel, even if their feelings aren't very nice.** If they don't want to talk, encourage them to write or draw.

♦ **Try to keep in contact with your ex.** Remind her that the children need her

What to Do When the Kids Aren't with You

One of the few advantages of being a noncustodial father is that you can do anything you want to on the days when you aren't with your kids. For many newly single fathers, this kind of total freedom can be hard to deal with. On the one hand, you might feel guilty about doing anything purely for yourself (see page 20 for more on this). On the other, it's probably been a long time since you had this much freedom, and you might not know what to do with it. Here are a few suggestions:

♦ **Keep up to date with what's going on with your kids.** If you and your ex are getting along, this won't be much of a problem: just ask her for regular updates about what they're doing, how they're doing, and any problems or successes they're having. If you're not getting along, this will take some work. Make contact with your children's teachers, coaches, and mentors and ask them to let you know about anything that concerns your child: concerts, ballet recitals, soccer matches, art exhibitions, school fund-raisers, and so forth. Regular phone calls to your kids in between visits are a great way to stay current on their lives, and writing letters might be even better (see pages 153–58 for more on this).

♦ **Have a good time.** There are probably all sorts of things you used to do before you got involved with your ex that you haven't done for years. And there are probably all sorts of new things you've been wanting to try for a while or places you've wanted to go but couldn't because of your family obligations. Well, now you can. . . .

♦ **Don't sit around feeling sorry for yourself.** Not taking advantage of your new opportunities to have fun can actually cause big problems. Denying yourself the enjoyable things in life in the interests of being a "good" father can lead to "resenting the kids, feeling that they're somehow responsible for [y]our loss," say Richard Gatley and David Koulack.

and miss her. If you really can't stand your ex, this might make you gag, but do it anyway. Kids who grow up without their mothers suffer just as much as those who grow up without fathers. So you might want to read (and share with your ex) the information on pages 127–29, replacing the word *father* with *mother*.

♦ **If your ex does resurface at some later date, be supportive.** Unless she poses a danger to the children, encourage their relationship with her. You may be suspicious that she'll leave again and hurt your kids again, but don't let this get in the way. No matter how *you* feel, your kids are going to be elated to have their mother back.

What to Do—and What Not to Do— When the Kids Are with You

Here are some important dos and don'ts to keep in mind for your visits with your children, a few of which were suggested by M. Gary Newman in *Helping Kids Cope with Divorce:*

DO	DON'T
♦ Do be consistent. Show up on time, every time. A lot of research has shown that when it comes to visits, regularity is at least as important as frequency. Children rely on routines and if you aren't there when you're supposed to be they're likely to feel abandoned and rejected. And if your ex is looking for ways to damage your relationship with the kids, your being inconsistent with visitation gives her the perfect opportunity to tell them you don't love them. One nice way to show the kids how important they are to you is to have a large calendar at home with special stickers on the days they're with you. You might even let smaller kids decorate those days themselves.	♦ Don't be irresponsible. Emergencies happen, of course, and you might be late sometimes or have to reschedule (*never* cancel) a visit. When this happens, try to give everyone as much warning as possible. Talk to your child on the phone and explain exactly what's happening and when you'll see each other next. Remind her that you're making this change because you have to— not because you don't want to see her. And be especially nice to your ex. If she's made plans for the time you're supposed to be with the kids, she may be, understandably, more than a little upset if she has to change them at the last minute.
♦ Do have a plan	♦ Don't overbook (see pages 90–91 for more).
♦ Do make visits as normal as possible. Try to make your children feel that your home is their home, even if they're there for only a few days a month. They should have chores to do, even if they're as simple as making their beds in the morning and setting the table for dinner. And there should be house rules. If they pull the old "But mom lets us do . . ."	♦ Never, never, never make visitation contingent on anything else. Your time together is a right—for all of you—not a privilege, and it can't be taken away for any reason. So don't threaten to punish them by not visiting or by not allowing them to visit. Getting angry at them is perfectly normal, but if they're already feeling that their bad behavior drove you away

(continued on page 94)

(continued from page 93)

DO	DON'T
the answer is, "In her house you follow her rules, in this house you follow mine."	from the family (this is extremely common), they're probably petrified that even the slightest bit of anger on your part will make you abandon them forever. So if you do get angry, be sure to tell them that you'll always love them no matter what they do, and that you want to see them every chance you get.
◆ Do respect your ex's parenting. This means making sure the kids do their homework and backing her up on bedtimes and discipline issues (assuming they're reasonable).	◆ Don't tell your ex how to parent. Unless she's doing something truly dangerous or stupid, leave her alone.
◆ Do respect the children's relationship with their mother. Your kids are probably going to want to talk about the things they do at their mother's house. Let them; you might even ask a few non-nosy questions. In most cases, they aren't really trying to cause you any pain; they just want to share their lives with you and they need to know that they're not going to lose your love if they love their mother. Listening to things you don't want to hear about can be harder than it sounds. For the first few months after my divorce, my kids kept telling me about all the things their mother and her live-in boyfriend were doing. I thought I was being good about listening, but one day my older daughter put an end to my little fantasy when she asked, "How come whenever we talk about Mommy and Matt you look like you're going to throw up?"	◆ Don't get your children involved in your problems with your ex. Don't criticize her in front of them, don't ask them to relay messages back and forth, don't try to get them to take sides (or imply that they have to), and don't pump them for information on what goes on at her house—who she sees, where they go, and so on. Sometimes, in an attempt to curry favor with you, the children might start talking about how much they hate their mother. If this happens, try to get them to talk about what they don't like, but do not agree with them. On the contrary, try, as much as you can, to defend your ex and to talk about her finer qualities.

DO	DON'T
◆ Do support your kids' relationships with other adults. It's natural for you to want to keep the kids to yourself the whole time they're with you, but it's also important for them to maintain good, strong relationships with other people as well. Having dinner, going to the park, or just hanging out with your friends and relatives is great if they live nearby. If not, phone calls, letters, and e-mail are good ways to stay in touch.	◆ Don't go overboard. Being with friends or relatives is great, but make sure you set aside plenty of time just for you and the kids. Don't leave the children with friends for hours—or days—at a time while you go off and do other things. And don't forget about the other side of the family. Don't make your children think that loving someone on their mother's side is somehow betraying you or your side.
◆ Do make transitions smooth and pleasant for everyone. When you're picking them up (or if someone else is dropping them off), don't rush off to do anything right away; give the kids a few minutes to get used to being with you again. (An exception here is if you're getting the kids right after school, which is a natural buffer.) The same applies at the end of the visit: don't rush directly from the amusement park to their mother's house. Give them half an hour or so to unwind.	◆ Don't use transition times as a chance to fight with your ex. Keep all of your contacts with her as civil—or as minimal—as possible. If you have some kind of disagreement or something you need to talk about that you think could get either of you upset, schedule a time to discuss it later (see pages 85–86 for more on transitions).
◆ Do keep your visitation and your new love life separate—at least for a while (see page 246 for more on this).	◆ Don't drag your kids along on your vacations or trips with your new girlfriend. Unless you're already one big, happy family, visitation time should be spent with the kids alone. See your new love when the kids aren't around, unless, of course, you're planning a long summer or school-break holiday when there'll be plenty of time for everyone.

(continued on page 96)

(continued from page 95)

DO	**DON'T**
♦ Do have clear boundaries. This means being a grown-up and knowing what's appropriate to talk about and what isn't.	♦ Don't cry on your children's shoulders. This makes them feel responsible for your happiness— a responsibility that is far too much for a child of almost any age to handle. And even if they ask, don't tell them too many details about why you and their mother split up. Hearing too much dirt about either of you will put your child in an uncomfortable loyalty bind.
♦ Do allow them to have some input. Ask them to tell you the kinds of things they'd like to do when they're with you, what they'd like to eat, and so on.	♦ Don't confuse input with control. Children can be master manipulators, especially when they sense vulnerability. So don't give in if they ask for more than you think is reasonable or healthy (cherry pie à la mode for breakfast is fine once in a while but not every day). And never allow them to control or alter the visitation schedule. If they try to, listen to what they're saying, but tell them clearly that you and your ex have agreed to this schedule and that that's the way it's going to be until further notice. Period.
♦ Do set a good example.	♦ Don't drink, do drugs, or flip off anyone who cuts you off in traffic while the kids are with you. Unless, of course, you want them to behave the same way.

Breaking the News to Your Children

As soon as it's obvious that your relationship with your soon-to-be ex is over, you should tell your children. This, of course, is easier said than done; the prospect of having to tell your children that you're breaking up with their mother is enough to fill any man with dread. As a result, far too many people put it off for as long as they can, thinking that that will spare the kids some pain and anguish. In one study, 80 percent of preschool-age children of divorced parents "had neither been forewarned about the departure nor told why it took place," writes parenting guru Vicki Lansky. But the truth is that the longer you delay telling your kids, the worse it will be for everyone.

Before we get into the really scary part (the actual breaking-the-news part), let's discuss a few other important issues:

♦ **Try to do it with your ex.** According to the folks at the Aring Institute in Cincinnati, Ohio, "When parents can tell children together about divorce, several things are more likely to happen":

◊ There is less focus on a "bad guy."

◊ Parents are modeling their ability to cooperate.

◊ There is less pressure for the child to take sides.

◊ Children may adjust more readily.

♦ **Do it at home.** You won't be able to soften the blow by letting the news slip over ice cream or in the middle of an exciting roller coaster ride.

♦ **Pick a time when the children are fully awake and likely to be thinking relatively clearly.** Some Saturday morning after brunch is good; when you're putting the kids to bed isn't.

"Your father and I want to explain why we've decided to live apart."

- ♦ **Leave plenty of time.** You and/or your ex may be crying so much that getting through what you have to say will take longer than you thought. And the kids will probably have a lot of questions. Either way, try not to schedule any important activities for the rest of the day; none of you will be in any condition for it.
- ♦ **Prepare in advance.** You and your ex should jointly come up with a list of things you want to say to the kids (see below for more on this).
- ♦ **Agree in advance** that neither of you will use the time that's supposed to be devoted to your children to argue or blame each other for what's happened.

Now that you've got the when, where, and with whom part down, we can talk about what to say and how. "The best rule is to tell your children enough so they are prepared for the change to come in their lives but not so much as to frighten them," writes Shirley Thomas. "The key to talking to children about divorce is to use neutral terms while describing the truth and avoiding the assignment of blame." That's a daunting prospect, but it can be done. Let's take a detailed look at how:

- ♦ Start off by telling them that you and their mother aren't going to be together anymore. If it's appropriate, tell them what divorce means. If there's any chance that you'll end up in court, you may have to explain what lawyers and judges and psychologists are too, but don't say anything about that yet.

♦ Tell them how their lives are going to change. The most important things to cover are where they'll be living and with whom, and how often they'll get to see each of you and for how long.

♦ Let them know they can always talk to you about what's happening and that you'll always tell them if something's going to change.

♦ Reassure them that although everyone's living arrangements are going to be different, they still have two parents and those two parents will always love them. "The greatest fear that most children have is that when some things change, all things will change," writes Lansky.

♦ Don't lie to them. Don't tell them that they're really lucky to have two houses—they aren't. And don't make promises you can't keep (I'll call you three times a day).

♦ Tell them straight out that none of this is their fault, that you know how much this will hurt them, and that you're truly sorry.

♦ Have some answers ready for their tough questions. You're likely to hear things like: "Is it my fault?" "Will you stop loving me?" "Why don't you love Mommy anymore?" (Or, "Why doesn't she love you anymore?") "When are you and Mommy going to be a family again?" and "Is Mommy in love with that man who lives across the street?"

♦ Tell them the truth about why. If you or your partner was emotionally or physically abusive or if either of you was an alcoholic or a drug addict, tell them in the most nonblaming way you can. Your kids have a right to know that bad behavior has consequences—even for adults. If it applies in your case, it's fine to explain that sexual attachments sometimes change. In certain circumstances, however (if one of you was cheating on the other, or if one of you has come out of the closet), you and your ex might want to agree to tell the kids that some things are private.

What If You Have to Tell Them Yourself?

Naturally, it's not always possible for splitting couples to be together when they break the news to their kids. If your ex has already moved out, has left without telling the children, or simply refuses to be in the same room with you, you'll have to do the job yourself. If so, reread the section above on what to say to your kids and how. And remember, be very careful not to say anything that's even close to blaming your soon-to-be ex.

If, on the other hand, you're the one who left or was thrown out or who can't stand being with your partner for one more hour, you need to set up a time to talk with your children as soon as possible. They might take the fact that you weren't there for the initial announcement as an indication that you don't care about them. They need to know that you do and that certain circumstances made it impossible for you to be there.

When you do get together, the kids will be over the initial shock. But you should still go through the steps outlined below, with a special emphasis on reminding them that you'll always be there for them.

How They Might React to What You're Telling Them

Every child will react to the breakup of his parents' relationship differently. Some kids won't have any outward reaction at all or may even laugh, while others will scream, cry, or try to hit you. Some will be relieved that the fighting is finally over, while others will be genuinely surprised that anything was wrong. Some may want to talk to you about it, while others will run away to be by themselves. Some may want you to hold and comfort them, while others will hold and comfort you instead.

These are all typical reactions to the first hours and days after you first tell your kids. For a detailed look at how kids will react as the news sinks in, see below.

Helping Them Through the First Few Days

The way your children begin coping with the monumental changes in their young lives will set the tone for how they'll adjust in the long term. Here's how you can help them at this crucial time:

♦ **Make sure they really understand what you're saying.** Asking them to tell you, in their own words, what they heard can clear up any confusion.

♦ **Let them react any way they want to.** As discussed above, kids react in different ways, and in most cases they're reacting in the manner that's right for them at that moment. Expecting them—or putting pressure on them—to react in a way you think they should will interfere with their natural adjustment. Let them know it's okay to have angry feelings and give them some safe outlets to express them. And don't tell them not to cry.

♦ **Don't change their routines.** Younger kids in particular need to maintain the same bedtimes, homework periods, piano practice schedules. And older kids, even teens, need reasonable, firm limits.

♦ **Remind them—again—that they can talk to you anytime.** Ask them if they have any questions or anything they want to discuss. If they don't, leave them alone for a while. Trying to force them to talk about it when they don't want to will only make them less likely to do so. You might gently encourage them to talk to their good friends.

♦ **It at any point you don't know what to say, don't say anything.** Sometimes a hug is better than an answer. Sometimes it is an answer.

♦ **If they won't or can't talk to you, encourage them to express themselves in other ways, such as play-acting, drawing a picture, or writing a story.** If your child isn't old enough to write, offer to take dictation. But whatever you do, do not correct anything they write or draw. This isn't a grammar exercise or a writing workshop or an art lesson. It's an emotional exercise designed to let them express what they feel. And whether it sounds silly or idiotic or inaccurate to you is completely irrelevant.

♦ **Read them stories about divorce or give them books to read.** See the list below for some age-appropriate suggestions.

♦ **Let them see you cry.** Showing your kids that you're affected by your breakup will give them permission to have and express their own emotions. But be careful not to go overboard (see page 119 for more on this).

♦ **Don't move in with a new lover right away.** It gives the impression that relationships are completely interchangeable and they'll worry that if you replaced their mother so easily you might replace them next.

Books on Divorce and Separation

UNDER AGE 7

Always My Dad, Sharon Dennis Wyeth
At Daddy's on Saturdays, Linda Walvoord Girard
Daddy, Daddy, Be There, Candy Dawson Boyd
Dear Daddy, John Schindel
Dinosaurs Divorce: A Guide for Changing Families, Marc Tolon Brown,
    Laurene Karsny Brown
Good-bye, Daddy, Brigitte Weninger
I Live With Daddy, Judith Vigna
It's Not Your Fault, Koko Bear, Vicki Lansky
Let's Talk About It: Divorce, Fred Rogers
Let's Talk About It: Stepfamilies, Fred Rogers
Mom and Dad Don't Live Together Anymore, Nancy Lou Reynolds
My Mother's House, My Father's House, C. Christensen
Not So Wicked Stepmother, Lizi Boyd
Starry Night, David Spohn
Why Are We Getting a Divorce?, Peter Mayle

AGES 8–12

Alias Madame Doubtfire, Ann Fine
Always, Always, Crescent Dragonwagon
Amber Brown (and others in the series), Paula Danziger
The Boys and Girls Book about Divorce, with an Introduction for Parents,
    Richard A. Gardner

Dear Dad, Love Laurie, Susan Beth Pfeffer
Dear Mr. Henshaw, Beverly Clearly
The Divorce Express, Paula Danziger
The Divorce Workbook: A Guide for Kids and Families, Sally Ives, David Fassler,
    Michele Lash
The Formerly Great Alexander Family, Susan Shreve
In the Wings, Katie Goldman
Rope Burn, Jan Siebold
Split Sisters, C. S. Adler
Sport, Louise Fitzhugh
Step by Wicked Step, Anne Fine
When Mom and Dad Separate: Children Learn to Cope with Divorce,
    Marge E. Heegaard

OVER AGE 12
The Animal, the Vegetable, and John D. Jones, Betsy Byars
Divorce Is Not the End of the World, Zoe Stern, Evan Stern
Gateway, Lee Robinson
How It Feels When Parents Divorce, Jill Krementz
It's Not the End of the World, Judy Blume
Living with a Single Parent, Maxine Rosenberg
Next Stop: Nowhere, Sheila Solomon Klass
Teens are Non-Divorceable: A Workbook for Divorced Parents and Their Teens,
    Sara Bonkowsky

Breaking the News to Other People: Family, Friends, and Everyone Else

Your children aren't the only ones you need to tell about your breakup. Parents, in-laws, other relatives, teachers, baby-sitters, doctors, dentists, coaches, and friends should also be kept up to date. Since some or all of these people have contact with your children, they may be able to keep you informed about how your child is adjusting and let you know about anything that you should worry about.

Tell anyone whom either you or your child sees on a regular (daily or weekly) basis in person. You can let people you see less regularly know by phone or in writing. You can even let people know in your annual holiday letter (or something similar), if you don't feel like writing out an individual note to everyone. For some, your news won't come as much of a surprise—they'll have suspected something for a long time. But whether it's a surprise or not, it's better that they hear the news from you rather than from someone who doesn't have all the facts.

Fortunately, telling all these other people will be a lot easier than telling your children because you aren't going to feel nearly as responsible for their feelings and because it won't be up to you to help them cope. A few things to think about:

- **Don't go into the gory details with anyone who really doesn't need to know them.** Rumors will be flying and the less people know, the less there is to distort.
- **Be prepared for a variety of reactions.** Some people, such as teachers, baby-sitters, and doctors, will probably appreciate knowing; they might have been wondering what was bothering your child. Relatives will probably align themselves along family lines (see pages 174–78 for more on your post-breakup relationship with your relatives). But friends' reactions can be the most problematic. Some may have no idea what to say; some will congratulate you and others will tell you it's all your fault. I was shocked and hurt by the way some of my friends (and former friends) took sides—some took mine, some took my ex's and have never spoken to me since. Only a few had the class to stay neutral.

Telling Your Children about Death

One of the most difficult things you'll probably ever have to do as a father is to tell your children about their mother's death. And because it's so difficult—and because you most likely haven't come to terms with it yourself—you may be tempted to put the whole discussion off for a while or even to skip it altogether. Don't. As an adult, no matter how much you're grieving, you have some idea what's going on, but your children are relying on you for information and guidance. And if they don't get it soon, they'll begin to make up their own explanations to their questions and fears, explanations that could do them more harm than good. "Don't fool yourself into thinking that you are protecting your child by shutting her off from reality or by telling her things that are untrue," writes Helen Fitzgerald, author of *The Grieving Child.* "The price for that could be years of needless anguish."

Here are some suggestions, several of which were offered by grief expert Amy Hillyard Jensen, to help you discuss this incredibly sensitive topic with your kids:

- **Be straightforward and tell the truth.** Kids need to know that death is final and that although their mother will always be with them in spirit, her body won't be coming back. They also need to know that death is natural and not a punishment or something that happens only to some people.
- **Answer their questions honestly,** including questions about where the body is and what's going to happen to it. If you don't know, say so.
- **Keep things simple.** Your child can process only a limited amount of information at a time. So just answer the questions he asks and don't go on and on. When he wants to know more, he'll be back.
- **Watch your language.** Saying that your wife has "gone to sleep" may give your kids insomnia, and telling them that "God took her" or that "it's all part of

God's plan," may make them anti-religion. Also be careful how you talk about hospitals. The fact that your wife may have died in one could make your kids afraid of doctors.

♦ **Talk about the cause of death, in age-appropriate terms.** If you need some help figuring out how to do this, Helen Fitzgerald's book is a great place to start. In addition, hospitals often have grief counselors who are specially trained in broaching these subjects with children.

♦ **Hug the kids while you're talking to them.** It will help them feel more secure and less out of control.

A Special Note about Suicide

Explaining suicide to a child is especially difficult, but it needs to be done as soon as possible—before he has a chance to hear about it from anyone else. Here are a few other things to keep in mind:

♦ **Explain.** If your child does not know what the word *suicide* means, explain that people die in many ways and that sometimes they kill themselves.

♦ **If the child asks how it happened, be honest but skip most of the details.** Saying that his mother hung herself on a rope is okay; anything more is unnecessary.

♦ **Help the child work through it himself.** Instead of directly answering questions like, "What did she look like when she was dead," Helen Fitzgerald suggests turning the question around and asking something like, "What do you think she looked like?"

♦ **Again, get some guidance.** Because this is such a tough topic to address, it's a good idea to get professional help from a child psychologist, specially trained grief counselor, or even a support group for kids.

Books Dealing with Death

UNDER AGE 7

After Charlotte's Mom Died, Cornelia Spelman, Judith Friedman
After the Funeral, Jane Loretta Winsch, Pamela T. Keating
Badger's Parting Gifts, Susan Varley
Lifetimes: The Beautiful Way to Explain Death to Children, Bryan Mellonie, Robert R. Ingpen
The New King: A Madagascan Legend, Doreen Rappaport
Pulling the Lion's Tail, Jane Kurtz
When Dinosaurs Die, Laurine Krasny Brown, Marc Tolon Brown

AGES 8-12

The Carousel, Liz Rosenberg
Don't Despair on Thursdays!: The Children's Grief-Management Book,
    Adolph Moser, David Melton
Everything You Need to Know When a Parent Dies, Fred Bratman
The Fall of Freddie the Leaf, Leo Buscaglia
I Heard Your Mommy Died, Mark Scrivani
Nothing Grows Here, Jean Thesman
Pleasing the Ghost, Sharon Creech
Something Very Sorry, Arno Bohlmeijer

OVER AGE 12

Coping When a Parent Dies, Janet Grosshandler, Janet Grosshandler-Smith
The Grieving Child: A Parent's Guide, Helen Fitzgerald
*Part of Me Died, Too: Stories of Creative Survival Among Bereaved Children
    and Teenagers,* Virginia Lynn Fry, Katherine Paterson
Personal Problems, Oliver Oldman
*Straight Talk About Death for Teenagers: How to Cope With Losing Someone
    You Love,* Earl A. Grollman

Telling Your Kids You're Gay

Coming out to your kids isn't easy. In fact it can be plenty scary, especially if you're not completely comfortable with your own homosexuality. You might, for example, be concerned about the teasing they'll have to take from their peers. Yes, there's a good possibility that that will happen. But it's better to get it out in the open now. You can't lie to your kids about your sexuality forever.

You also might be worried about whether your kids will reject you or stop loving you. The answer to this one is simpler: if you've always had a solid relationship with your children, they probably won't care whether you're gay or not. The most important thing to them is that you're their father and that although other things have changed in your life, your love and your desire to be with them remains constant.

If you've already told your kids that you're gay, great. But if you haven't, you'd better start thinking about how you're going to do it. Here are some ground rules—a few of which are suggested by Bryan Robinson and Robert Barret in their book *Gay Fathers*—that should help:

♦ **Get comfortable with yourself first.** "The father who feels negatively about his homosexuality or is ashamed of it is much more likely to have children who also react negatively," write Robinson and Barret.

♦ **Tell them if you think they suspect and before they hear it from some-one else.** That way you can control what they hear and answer their questions if they have any.

♦ **Don't rush things.** They're probably going to be somewhat confused by what you're telling them, so allow plenty of time for questions.

♦ **Don't worry that they're too young—there's no such thing.** Describe things in a way you think your child will understand and don't give them any more details than they ask for.

How Your Kids Might React and How You Can Help Them Cope

One can never be sure how kids are going to react to anything, let alone something as major as telling them you're gay. Their response to your disclosure may range from anger and confusion to "So what?"—especially if they knew or suspected before you told them. "Children are perceptive," writes researcher Frederick Bozett. "And it seems as though the walls of closets gay fathers may hide in are sometimes made of glass." Generally, though, your kids, especially if you have girls, will be happy you're being honest with them and their reaction will be positive and accepting.

Still, your coming out will have an impact on their lives and there are a few things you can (and should) do to make sure this impact is as positive as possible:

♦ **Don't demand acceptance from them.** Although acceptance and respect would be ideal, you may have to be satisfied with tolerance. Loving you is very different from loving everything that you do—a message they should learn too. By being tolerant of things that bother you, you'll help them come to terms with you.

♦ **Make sure that your children—especially daughters—have plenty of positive female role models in their lives.** Some girls may interpret your being gay as a rejection of all women, themselves included; having female friends will help take the edge off this fear. Monitor your kids' reaction to your women friends closely, though. If you got divorced because you're gay, your kids may think that if you spend time with close women friends you really do like women and that the whole thing was nothing more than a ruse to get away from their mother.

♦ **Be patient.** Give them some time to let the news—and everything that comes with it—sink in.

♦ **Be understanding.** Kids whose parents differ in any way from the norm are likely to be teased by their peers. This is especially true in the early adolescent years, when kids are dealing with their own sexual identity issues, and when even the slightest abnormality could make your child feel like an outcast among his friends. So even if your child is fine with the fact that you're gay, he may still be very worried about how his friends at school will react.

- **Don't make a big deal of your lifestyle, especially in front of your kids' friends.** Your kids may not have told their friends and will resent the hell out of you for betraying them.
- **Encourage them to talk about how they feel about what you're telling them.** But don't push. Your kids may not have anything to say now, but that will probably change in time. If they do have questions, answer them—without being defensive or getting angry. And if they do have comments, listen carefully and try not to take their criticism too much to heart. If you shut them out now, they won't feel comfortable talking with you later.
- **Be prepared.** Here are some questions your kids may ask you, along with some excellent answers, all of which were suggested by researchers Jerry Bigner and Frederick Bozett in a 1989 article they wrote in *Marriage and Family Review*. Adjust the language level to the age of your child:

QUESTION	SUGGESTED ANSWER
Why are you telling me this?	Because my personal life is important and I want to share it with you. I am not ashamed of being homosexual, and you shouldn't be ashamed of me either.
What does being gay mean?	It means being attracted to other men so that you might fall in love with a man and express your love physically and sexually.
What makes a person gay?	No one knows, although there are a lot of theories. (This question may be a child's way of asking if he or she will also be gay.)
Will I be gay, too?	You won't be gay just because I am. It's not contagious, and it doesn't appear to be hereditary. You will be whatever you are going to be.
Don't you like women?	I do like women but I'm not physically (or sexually) and romantically attracted to them as I am to men. (If your daughter is asking, she might really be wondering whether you like her or not. And children of either gender might really be asking whether you like, or hate, their mother.)

QUESTION	SUGGESTED ANSWER
What should I tell my friends about it?	A lot of people just don't understand, so it might be best to keep it in the family. But I hope you'll discuss it with me anytime you want. If you want to tell a close friend, go ahead and try it out. But you should be prepared that your friend might not be accepting, and might tell others. If you do tell somebody, let me know how it turns out.

Notes:

Helping Your Kids Cope with Their Feelings

One of the major concerns newly single fathers have is how their children will react to the dramatic changes going on in their lives. On the following pages you'll find a discussion of what your children may be going through and how you can best help them cope. (If you're a widower, please disregard the items that are clearly aimed at men whose exes are still alive.) You'll find the most valuable information in the section that covers your child(ren)'s age(s). But because children develop differently and react to stresses in their lives in very different ways, I'd suggest that you also read the sections covering the next oldest and next youngest groups as well.

Infants: 0–12 Months

What They May Be Going Through
- Although they don't understand much language, they're extremely perceptive about what's going on around them and know that something's not right. For example, babies whose fathers are under a lot of stress are less likely to look to them for help. In addition, children this age react to the smell of their parents as well as to the sound of their voices. And if someone's missing, they know who.
- And although they can't express much verbally, they get their feelings out about the stress they're under in many ways: they're often clingy, irritable, and cry more than usual. They may also have sudden changes in sleeping or toilet patterns and will probably show some increased difficulty separating from both you and your ex.
- Overall, kids this age whose parents split up have a distinct advantage over older

kids: in a few years they probably won't really remember the fights you and your ex had and they won't have many idealized memories of the way things used to be. Kids this age whose mother dies have a similar advantage in that they'll avoid most of the emotional trauma of dealing with her death. On the downside, though, they'll never have any real memories of her.

Helping Them Cope

♦ What they're craving most now is consistency in their lives, in their caregivers, and in their routines. So try to avoid making changes in any of these areas. Try not to switch baby-sitters or start a new day-care arrangement right now. If you can't avoid it, at least try to phase it in over a few days with the baby spending time with you and the new caregiver. This will reassure the child that you'll be back.

♦ Build and strengthen your emotional bond with the baby. Spend some extra time together, playing, cuddling, talking, or reading to her. And be affectionate. All this will help reassure her that maybe the world really isn't coming to an end.

♦ Because she's so perceptive and sensitive to emotions, it's especially important that you and your ex avoid any kind of anger or fighting in front of the baby.

♦ Try to smile around the baby as much as you can. Infants and babies get a lot of their cues on how to react in various situations from you and your expressions.

♦ If you're a widower, you can strengthen your baby's connection to his mother by showing him her picture—but only if you can do it without crying. You don't want the baby to associate his mother's image with your sadness.

Toddlers: 1–3 Years

What They May Be Going Through

♦ Kids this age understand a lot more than infants do, but most still can't express themselves—verbally, at least—all that well. They have remarkable emotional radar and can sense trouble around them a mile off. They tend to think the world revolves around them. But the recent events in their lives may have convinced them that the world is completely out of control.

♦ As a result, they're afraid that the parent they're with less has disappeared and they're worried sick about who's going to take care of them.

♦ Separation anxiety can be a real problem at this age (it may either start, return, or get worse). Also quite common are increased tearfulness, clinginess to familiar adults or familiar objects (security blankets, pacifiers, favorite toys), sleep problems, fearfulness, and especially regression in toilet training, behavior, and/or language skills.

♦ A lot of kids this age also have more tantrums and may exhibit extremely (and uncharacteristically) aggressive, dangerous, or even self-destructive behavior toward their friends, family, and even strangers.

Helping Them Cope

♦ As with infants, toddlers need consistency in their lives. They need to know you'll be there for them on a regular basis; they need predictable routines. If at all possible, work with your ex to come up with consistent routines for bedtime, stories, playtime, and anything else you can agree on. And make sure both you and your ex have frequent and regular visits with your toddler. See pages 77–78 for more on this.

♦ Avoid fighting or expressions of anger in front of your child.

♦ Treat your toddler with respect. Explain what's going on in the simplest, yet most honest terms possible.

♦ Encourage him to express his feelings any way he can—in words, physical activity, and pictures. Psychologists Julien Gross and Harlene Hayne recently found that children who drew as they spoke revealed twice as much information as children who were asked only to talk about their experience.

♦ Spend a lot of time one on one with your child, playing, talking, and just being together. Be physically and verbally affectionate and tell your child as often as possible that you love him, that he's important to you, and that you're not going anywhere.

♦ Don't spoil him. Clear boundaries are especially important right now. Not getting them can make your toddler feel even more out of control than before.

♦ Don't worry about regressions. Typically, in times of stress the most recent skill learned is the first to be forgotten. But the more love and attention kids get from their family members, the shorter the time between regression and the return to normalcy.

♦ Be patient. In the short run, toddlers have a very difficult time coping with their parents' separation, but because they're so young, they do better in the long run than kids of any other age except perhaps infants.

♦ Don't blame all their problems on the divorce or the death of their mother. Trying to do so may mean paying less attention to other important factors and can interfere with your ability to respond appropriately to their needs.

Preschoolers: 3–5 Years

What They May Be Going Through

♦ They may have some trouble playing with and getting along with their peers, says researcher E. Mavis Heatherington. This can have a long-term negative effect on children's later relationships and their social and emotional development.

According to Heatherington, kids under six at the time of their parents' divorce have more adjustment problems than any other kids. And there is some speculation that the same could be true of children who lose a parent at this age.

♦ They may play less—especially games involving imagination. Researcher Ross Parke has found that after their parents split, children not only do less imaginative play but do less playing in general and more watching than kids living in two-parent homes.

♦ They may not understand exactly what ending a relationship means, but they definitely know that their regular routines have changed. They may suffer some behavioral regression and may even return to bed-wetting and/or thumb-sucking, clinginess, and aggressive behavior. You're also likely to see an increase in temper tantrums, especially when they're moving from one parent to the other.

♦ They may become uncharacteristically obedient. In many cases this is because they're deathly afraid of being abandoned (the theory being that if either you or your wife left the other, they're next). As a result, they may try to do everything you ask them to, hoping you won't leave. This extra obedience may also come up because they sense your emotional turmoil and feel they have to be especially mature in order to help you out.

♦ Kids this age also still think they're the center of the universe and may hold themselves responsible for the breakup, especially if they had been having any of those I-wish-you'd-just-disappear kinds of thoughts mentioned above. They may also feel guilty about something they did or didn't do, and believe that your breakup is their punishment.

♦ Often, when one parent dies or leaves and the remaining parent seems distracted or emotionally distant, the children end up feeling as though they've lost both their parents. And that's more than any child should have to go through.

Helping Them Cope

All of the advice for helping toddlers applies here, plus:

♦ Don't be too nosy about what's going on with your ex. And don't say anything critical about her. Your children need to know that it's okay to love and be loved by both parents.

♦ Be especially reassuring that you love them and need them and that their place in your life is secure. Also remind them that what's happened between you and their mother had nothing to do with them.

♦ Make sure they understand what's going on. If they don't seem like they do, ask them, for example, if they know why you and their mother aren't living together anymore.

♦ Give them lots of opportunities to express their feelings. Talking, drawing, telling stories, and play acting are all excellent.

♦ Play lots of games that encourage them to use their imaginations. "Imaginative play can be viewed as a major resource by which children can cope immediately with the cognitive, affective and social demands of growing up," says fantasy expert Jerome Singer.

♦ Be absolutely sure to establish and enforce limits. Too many parents feel guilty about what their divorce or breakup is doing to their children and end up spoiling them. The same is often true for widowed dads who feel guilty that their kids have to grow up without their mothers. Clear limits are extremely important at this—and every—age.

♦ Take some time before you introduce your dates or girlfriends to them. (See pages 246 and 252–53 for more on this.)

School-age Kids: 6–9 Years

What They May Be Going Through

♦ Kids' reactions range from nothing (or at least nothing obvious) to near paralysis from depression and poor self-esteem. Regardless of their outward reaction, most children this age have an intense desire for their parents to get back together and can come up with elaborate reconciliation fantasies.

♦ They still feel tremendous guilt. "They're too old to use fantasy to deny the situation," writes Vicki Lansky, "And too young to have the maturity or the independence to remove themselves from all the implications or realize that they are not responsible."

♦ They may take on uncharacteristically mature behavior, trying to take care of your needs and those of their younger siblings. Children often use these "parenting" behaviors as a way to distract themselves from their own problems, one of which is feeling emotionally abandoned by their distracted parent(s).

♦ Feelings of abandonment will be particularly intense if you or your ex has moved in with a new lover or spouse, especially if the new family includes other children. In addition, according to Boston attorney Edward Amaral, a lot of kids this age become suddenly worried that they'll be deprived of such basic necessities as food, clothing, or toys.

♦ They may be furious at you and/or your ex for what they believe you've done to them. They tend to see things in black and white and sometimes take sides, either with the same-sex parent or with the parent they feel was "wronged" most (a definition that will change frequently). Although they may express their anger at the "offending" parent, many kids instead lash out at their teachers and friends.

♦ Distracted by everything else, they may inadvertently let their academic performance start to slip. This is the stage that pioneering psychologist Eric Erickson calls "industry versus inferiority," meaning that children in this general age group are able to focus on other tasks (such as schoolwork or chores) if they aren't overly worried about their relationships with their parents. But if they're denied access to one of their parents through separation, death, or divorce, they may feel inferior and lose the personal inner drive to achieve.

♦ They may come down with new and interesting physical ailments. Some may be real, but many will be little more than attention-getting devices. In some cases, illnesses are an attempt to get you and your ex back together. If your wife has recently died, your child's ailments may be an attempt to get from you the nurturing and love and attention that he used to get from her. "Sometimes," says psychoanalyst Mary Lamia, "these types of illnesses are the child's way of holding on to the lost parent."

♦ Your child may develop something of an obsession with the parent he sees less often. If that's you, your child might wear articles of your clothing all the time, adopt some of your mannerisms, or talk about you constantly to your ex—something she'll probably find incredibly annoying. Kids can also become obsessed with deceased parents.

♦ Children this age crave acceptance by their peers, and acceptance often means blending in. As common as divorces and relationship breakups are, children this age may still be embarrassed by them and are often at a loss for what to say to their friends.

Helping Them Cope

All of the above advice applies, plus:

♦ Make sure the other important people in your child's life—teachers, baby-sitters, coaches—know about what's happening. Ask them to keep you up to date on your child's behavior.

♦ Monitor your children's relationships with their friends. If a gregarious child becomes a loner for a long period of time or if any child stops taking pleasure in activities that used to be fun for him, think strongly about getting some counseling (see page 121 for more).

♦ Ensure that your child has frequent access to both you and your ex. Give him your phone number and let him know he can call anytime. And allow him to call his mother from your house as well. (But don't let this get out of hand; you don't want him calling his mother to complain every time you make him clean up his room.)

♦ Encourage lots of contact with grandparents and other relatives.

♦ Don't talk to your kids about your financial situation, especially if it isn't particularly good. They're already feeling guilty enough as it is.

♦ Ask your child if she needs help talking to her friends or wants any suggestions.

♦ Establish long-lasting relationships with your children. "Parents sometimes become overly involved with their children when they've experienced a loss," says Mary Lamia. "But as soon as they begin dating, the children feel abandoned or second best."

◆ Never pressure your child to take sides and, if she takes yours anyway, say some nice things about your ex.

Preteens: 10–12 Years

What They May Be Going Through

◆ For the most part, preteens go through many of the same things as school-aged children, but much more intensely.

◆ Their thinking is still fairly black and white; they may try to side with the "good guy" against the "bad guy" (both of whose identities may change from time to time).

◆ They may spend a lot time worrying about your emotions and trying to parent you; as a result, they may end up ignoring their own emotional needs.

◆ In front of their friends, they often feel ashamed and embarrassed about your breakup.

◆ Their schoolwork may suffer and so may their relationships with their friends.

◆ They may feel depressed, rejected, and abandoned (boys more so if you've left, girls more so if their mother left). Both boys and girls may announce that they're never going to have children because they would never want to do "this" to them.

◆ They feel utterly powerless to do anything to change their situation. But that probably won't stop them from trying—angry behavior is common at this age and so are rather embarrassing attempts to interfere with your dating life.

Helping Them Cope
All of the above advice applies, plus:

◆ Preteens are especially vulnerable to being put in the middle and to the resulting loyalty conflicts, so be especially careful not to criticize their mother in any way or to do anything that's even close to asking them to choose sides, such as relay messages to your ex or hit them up for information about her and what's going on in her new life.

◆ Support communication and contact with your ex and with other relatives.

◆ Monitor your child's behavior and adjustment with teachers, coaches, and other adults. And watch out for sudden drops in grades, changes in habits or hobbies, or a big shift in the people your child hangs out with. Feeling abandoned and unloved can sometimes drive your child to the "wrong" crowd.

◆ Assure them and then reassure them that although they may feel embarrassed about your divorce or breakup there's really no shame in it. First of all, it's not as uncommon as they might think. And second, although their parents live in different places, they still have two adults in their lives to care for them.

"Why don't you ask your mother? Call her 1-800 number."

- Encourage extracurricular activities: sports, hobbies, and so on. These activities help them build independence, so don't get upset (even though it will hurt a lot) when your child says he'd rather be playing soccer than be with you.
- Remember to set reasonable limits (including curfews) and enforce them. It's tempting to either spoil your child (because you feel guilty) or become too much of a disciplinarian (because you're afraid that your child will try to take advantage of you).
- Continue to provide as much clear, honest information as your children ask for.
- Don't suddenly shift your adult responsibilities onto your children. It's certainly reasonable to ask them to do a little more at home, such as helping to keep the house straight, some basic meal preparation and clean-up, and maybe even some occasional short baby-sitting stints with a younger sibling. But remember, your preteen is still a child and you're the adult.
- Don't rely on your child to be your friend. Don't cry on his shoulder, talk about finances, or complain about how tough it is to get a date, even if your child seems to be enjoying the discussion. All these kinds of things can make your child feel responsible for you and your feelings and can make him suppress his own.

Teens: 13–18 Years

What They May Be Going Through

- Your breakup with his mother has come at a particularly inconvenient moment for your teenager—a period when he wants to be independent and spend more of his time with his friends than with you. He will probably resent the additional responsibilities you may expect him to assume in your newly structured family. He may also resent any limits that your tighter budget may impose on him.
- Because they are older and have a greater understanding of divorce, adolescents seem to adjust to it fairly well—at least in the short run. "If the home situation is particularly painful adolescents, more than younger children, have the option to disengage and seek gratification elsewhere such as in the neighborhood, peer group, or school," writes E. Mavis Heatherington. According to Heatherington, about a third of children and adolescents disengage in this way, and this can be a mixed blessing. Many teens become more mature, develop deeper friendships, and explore extracurricular activities and other interests. But others, trying to be too independent too fast, run away from home altogether, slip into drug or alcohol abuse, have sex too early, or behave in other less-than-positive ways.
- Depression is a major problem for teens and you need to watch out for its symptoms from the start of your breakup. Your teen may become emotionally distant, have problems in school, or lose interest in friends and other activities.

"If you can hear me, give me a sign."

Divorce researcher Judith Wallerstein found that a third of children and teens of divorce were still moderately to severely depressed five to ten years after their parents' divorce.

♦ "Adolescents tend to be egocentric," write Laurence Steinberg and Ann Levine, authors of *You and Your Adolescent.* "They see divorce as something you are doing to them. Getting angry at the parent who is moving out is dangerous, because that parent might not want to see them anymore. Getting angry at the parent with whom they will be living is also dangerous, because that parent might abandon them, too." So they express anger in other ways, usually by suppressing their feelings and pretending that nothing out of the ordinary is happening in their lives. As Edward Amaral puts it, "Their anger stems from their grief, but it is also directed at their parents' 'selfishness' in breaking up the family at the very time they relied so heavily on it."

Helping Them Cope

All of the above advice applies, plus:

♦ Allow and encourage their independence and their relationships with their friends.

♦ At the same time, reasonable, firm limits are especially important. Although your teen is battling for independence, she may be quite worried that you won't be able to take care of her. Maintaining limits shows her that you're still in charge and that she has a solid foundation on which to rely.

♦ Give them more input into scheduling. Teenage girls sometimes prefer to live with their mothers, while boys may prefer their fathers. If your kids want to spend more time with their mother, let them, but don't let yourself be cut out altogether.

♦ Try to schedule some one-on-one time with your kids to talk or just to hang out.

♦ Don't rely on your teenagers to be your emotional support. At this stage in their lives they need to be establishing their own independence and that's hard to do if your emotional neediness makes them feel obligated to take care of you and guilty for not wanting to.

♦ Be very, very patient. Judith Wallerstein found that two-thirds of kids who were teenagers when their parents split up were still having emotional, social, or educational problems five years later. Half were still having problems ten to fifteen years after their parents' breakup.

♦ Maintain as close a relationship with your teenager as you can. Your teenager's relationship with you—his father—is going to be a major predictor of his or her long-term adjustment to your breakup.

♦ Don't be afraid to get them into therapy. Teens (as well as younger kids) whose parents divorce or split often have difficulties establishing and maintaining relationships with lovers and spouses later in life and can even have trouble keeping a job (another kind of commitment). Teens whose mothers die have fewer of these problems, but therapy can help them greatly with their grief and loss.

General Coping Strategies

Here are some additional strategies you can use to help your children cope—regardless of their ages:

+ **Try to get along with your ex as well as you can.** The three most signifi-cant factors in post-divorce adjustment for children are the degree of parental conflict, the degree of legal conflict, and the mother's hostility toward the father, says attorney Michael Oddenino.

+ **Put your personal feelings about your ex aside.** "Parents must add to the already great burdens of their own distress an awareness of and sensitivity to the effects of divorce on their children, as well as an ability to separate their own feelings about their spouse as spouse from a view of the other spouse as parent," writes Edward Amaral.

+ **If possible, you and your ex should try to come up with a consistent approach to discipline and limit-setting.** The more consistency your chil-dren have, the better. A word of caution: consistency is good, but don't feel obli-gated to adopt *all* of your ex's way of doing things. You're a parent, too, and you have an equal say in how you're going to raise your children.

+ **Try not to blame your child's problems or adjustment difficulties on your ex.** "It is fairly common for the parent initiating the divorce to perceive the children as doing just fine, whereas the abandoned parent perceives the children as troubled or damaged," says Vicki Lansky. This was exactly the case with me: every time my children had any kind of emotional or physical ailment I immediately looked around for some way to blame it on my ex. While this kind of thinking may make you feel better, it's completely unproductive and probably not very accurate either. And even if you're right, how does that help your children?

+ **Avoid (or put off) any more major changes.** Their parents' breakup is enough of a shock. Moving to a new house, switching schools, and having to find new friends can be too much.

+ **Keep up their routines.** Children who adjust best are the ones with the few-est disruptions to their school, homework, meal, extracurricular activity, chore, and bedtime routines.

+ **Don't dismiss your children's desires (and occasional plots) to get you and your ex back together.** Let them have their fantasies, but make sure they understand that it's not going to happen.

+ **Keep your emotions under control.** Your kids will model their own coping behavior on yours. If you fall apart or get depressed and withdrawn, they prob-ably will too; if you run around blaming everyone else and acting like a victim, so will they. But if you can keep it together—at least in front of them—they will too. Of course, this does *not* mean that you should stifle your feelings and plaster a fake smile on your face. It just means don't wallow in your grief.

Trying to Avoid Conflict

Before your divorce or breakup, you and your partner undoubtedly had your share of fights and stress. When you were together, you had a variety of reasons for trying to work things out. You may have thought the relationship was worth saving, for example, or you may have tried to stay together for the children. Now that the relationship is over, though, you may think that there's no real incentive to staying on civil terms. But you're wrong. In fact, it's never been more important to treat her well.

Quite simply, the most important influence on children's long-term adjustment to a divorce or breakup is the level of conflict between the parents. "Conflict and divorce can put children on a trajectory that leads to serious problems later on," writes psychologist and researcher John Gottman. Gottman has found that children whose parents' relationships are filled with criticism, defensiveness, and contempt "are much more likely to show antisocial behavior and aggression toward their playmates. They have more difficulty regulating their emotions, focusing their attention, and soothing themselves when they become upset. In addition . . . the kids had an increased number of health problems such as coughs and colds. These children also seemed to be under more chronic stress."

Of course, it's going to be impossible to completely eliminate conflict from your relationship with your ex—if you could have, you'd probably still be together. But what you can do is make a real effort to keep your animosity and fighting away from your children—especially when you're arguing about the children themselves.

Seeing their parents fight harms kids in two ways, says Shirley Thomas: it can frighten them, bringing up feelings of fear, panic, and even abandonment; it also teaches them that yelling and screaming (or worse) are effective ways of dealing with problems.

There's no way to shield your kids from every disagreement you have with your ex. And that may actually be a good thing. Our children instinctively model their behavior after ours, and if they see you and your ex disagreeing—provided you can do it with respect—they'll learn some helpful ways of dealing with conflict. Kids who never see their parents disagree and then work together on a compromise or a resolution will have a very tough time doing so with their friends, peers, coworkers, and future lovers.

What If You Slip

No matter how much you try, the time will come when you lose it and you bite your ex's head off—right in front of the kids. When (not if) this happens, apologize to your child as soon as possible. Tell him that you understand how scary it must be to see his parents fighting and explain that his mother and you are really trying to work things out but that sometimes even adults say things that aren't particularly nice. You should also take the opportunity to remind the child that no matter what he

When It's Time to Call in the Professionals

Sometimes, despite all your efforts, your children will need more help than you're capable of providing. This doesn't mean that you're a bad parent, just that you know your limitations. Here's what you should be looking for:

- Any kind of regression—a return to bed-wetting after being dry, thumb-sucking, becoming clingy after being having been independent, and so on—that doesn't disappear within just a few weeks.
- Withdrawal—from friends, family, or once pleasurable activities.
- Alienation from old, long-term friends or a sudden change in the crowd your child hangs out with.
- Problems at school that last more than a semester.
- Wild or prolonged mood swings.
- Profound grieving for the other parent that doesn't improve after a few months.
- Any other behavioral problem in which the symptoms stay the same for months at a time without any improvement
- For young kids: uncharacteristic fighting, aggressive behavior, or drastic change in school performance.
- If you feel that you simply can't cope with your child's reactions on your own.

If you have sons, pay particular attention to them. By the time they're only four or five, boys in our society know perfectly well that "big boys don't cry." As a result, boys are far more stoic than they ought to be. But stoic behavior could be a sign that your son isn't dealing with his emotions the way he should. In addition, be aware of your own reactions to his behavior. You may subtly treat his clinginess and tears as signs of weakness and get angry at him when you really should be comforting him instead.

When looking for a therapist for your children, talk to several candidates before making your decision. Be sure to select someone who has a lot of experience dealing with children of divorce or children whose mothers have died. It's also very important to find someone who appreciates your desire and need to play an important role in your child's life. Not every therapist does.

Finally, consider getting your child into therapy *before* you notice any of the symptoms listed above. By doing so, a sharp therapist may be able to help your child start dealing with his emotions in a productive, healthy way. And that might keep a lot of those symptoms from developing in the first place.

thinks or what he heard, he's not responsible for either the disagreement or your breakup with his mother.

Because this kind of slip is likely to happen again, here are a few things you can do on a daily basis to minimize the potential damage to your child. Some of these were suggested by John Gottman.

♦ Never, never use your children as weapons in your battles with their mother. This includes limiting her access to them, having them deliver nasty messages, putting pressure on them to choose sides, or trying to alienate them from her. (See pages 181–87 for more on this.)

♦ Don't allow your kids to put themselves in the middle. According to Gottman, because children are often frightened by what's happening with their parents, they try to step in to help mediate or resolve the conflict—a job that's way to big for any child. Make sure your children know that although you appreciate the thought, you and their mother will have to resolve your problems on your own.

♦ Encourage the kids to keep talking to you about their feelings.

♦ Say some nice things about their mother once in a while. And let them know that it's perfectly fine for them to do the same thing. Giving them the opposite message is essentially asking them to choose sides.

♦ Be honest when talking about their mother—but not too honest. If she drinks too much, don't say she's a filthy drunk. Instead, tell them she has a sickness that's called alcoholism and that she's getting help to make her better.

♦ Do everything you can to reassure your child that despite the fighting, you and his mother love and need him very much.

Gender Concerns

The breakup of their parents' relationship is hard on all children, but it's especially hard on boys. One major explanation for this is that while parents allow and encourage their daughters to express their emotions and deal with them, they too often "forget" about their sons' emotional needs and subtly (or not so subtly) encourage them to be tough and to suppress their feelings rather than express them. But boys' fears, worries, anxieties, and other emotions don't go away; they just get expressed in other ways.

It's really not that much of a surprise, then, that boys from broken families have more interpersonal problems with their friends. According to Ross Parke's research, boys growing up in single-parent homes were ignored more and isolated more often by their peers than boys in two-parent homes. And very few boys from single-parent families were selected by their peers as best friends. They're particularly vulnerable in the preschool years. They generally watch more than they participate, and when they do participate, they're less imaginative, less cooperative, seem to be less happy and more anxious, and seem to enjoy playing less than their two-parent peers. Boys from single-parent homes also have more problems with their teachers, perform worse in school, and are more likely to act out their anger physically than boys from two-parent homes.

Some experts believe that women may be responsible for at least some of boys' increased problems coping. "A woman angered by divorce may transfer her resent-

"Hey, Ben! We're in Maine now. We don't have to perform."

ment from her ex-husband to her son, especially if he resembles his father," writes Mary Mattis, author of *Sex and the Single Parent*. Overall, women tend to pay less attention to their sons than to their daughters; it's a pattern that starts very early on: boys aren't breastfed as often or for as long as girls, and mothers typically don't respond to their cries as quickly as they do to girls'. Be careful, though—men bear some responsibility here as well, having a tendency to pay more attention to their sons than to their daughters.

Girls have their difficulties too. According to divorce researchers Judith Wallerstein and Joan Kelley, "Girls tend to recover significantly faster than boys from the initial unhappy reaction to the parental separation." But girls are prone to experience what some researchers have called a "sleeper effect," meaning that many of girls' separation-related problems often don't show up until adolescence or adulthood. And a number of these problems have to do with their relationships with men. E. Mavis Heatherington's research indicates that women whose parents split up years before get married younger, are more likely to be pregnant when they marry, and are more likely to marry men who are less educated and less economically secure than women who grew up in two-parent families. And researcher Sandra McLanahan and her colleagues have found that women who grew up in broken homes are more likely to get divorced themselves.

There's one thing that may be able to mitigate almost all of divorce's negative effects on children: you. John Guidubaldi and a number of other researchers have found that the more contact children—especially boys—have with their fathers, the better off they are. Keep this in mind when you're thinking about the kind of custody arrangement you're going to ask for.

For Widowers

Although children whose mothers die deal with their loss in a way that's very similar to children whose parents divorce or split up, there are some interesting differences you should be aware of. Some of these were suggested by widowhood expert Jane Burgess (see page 125).

Helping Your Children Cope with Their Mother's Death

For the first few months after your wife's death, you may find it very difficult to cope with your children's emotional reaction to losing their mother. That's completely natural and doesn't mean that you're insensitive to their needs. It's hard to comfort someone else when you're grieving yourself. But hard as it is, you don't really have a lot of choice.

Like adults, children go through several phases of grief, including denial, anger, guilt, and depression. And like adults, they express these feelings in many different ways. This makes perfect sense, of course. But problems can arise if your children don't grieve the way you think they should. Some children react angrily; others are in denial. Some react immediately; others, not for months or even years after the death (this is especially common for boys who, even at very young ages, have taken to heart the cultural message that big boys don't cry). Some mourn, some play, and others do both at the same time. Sometimes they want to talk about the death all the time, sometimes not at all (again, the more common reaction for boys). Some may focus completely on schoolwork and extracurricular activities; others may lose whatever interest they had in school.

Whatever their reaction, the most important thing you can do is to let them grieve the way they want to. The love you have for your wife is very different from the love your kids have for their mother, and the bottom line is that you can't force them to feel exactly what you do exactly when you do. Trying to do so will only make them believe that there's something wrong with their feelings and with them. This is especially true if your child is under three. Kids that age can't possibly grasp what's happened, and they need to laugh and play.

One of the most important things you can do to help a child of any age grieve is to encourage her to express what she's feeling. Sometimes talking is the best way to do this, but don't get frustrated if she asks you the same question a hundred times a day. Sometimes drawing a picture is a more effective way for a child to deal with her powerful emotions. Sometimes it's reading or having you read a story about how

CHILDREN WHO LOSE THEIR MOTHER	CHILDREN WHOSE PARENTS DIVORCE OR SPLIT
◆ May have a hard time accepting the loss, may be overwhelmed by grief, and will undoubtedly want their mothers to come back. But most kids understand that Mom won't be back. This helps the child better cope with the grieving process.	◆ Hope and fantasize that their parents will get back together. This hope often delays the children's acceptance of the divorce and their ability to move on.
◆ Feel secure knowing they'll always be with their father.	◆ Feel very insecure about where they're going to be living and with whom.
◆ Rarely blame themselves for the death of their mother. They can understand that usually no one is responsible for death.	◆ Often feel that the breakup was their fault.
◆ Have a lot of support for keeping the memory of their deceased mother alive. You'll probably talk very glowingly about your wife and you'll keep pictures of her on the walls.	◆ Don't get as much support in this area as they should. Parents don't often talk about each other very favorably and it's rare to find a picture of one divorced parent prominently displayed in the home of the other.
◆ Will see the surviving members of the family come together to support each other in their time of stress.	◆ Will see families take sides, divide property, and argue. Relationships among family members are often strained.
◆ Are comforted and supported by their fathers and feel confident in their love.	◆ Are sometimes used as weapons by their parents and often feel confused about whether their parents love them or not.

other children have handled similar situations. There's a list of age-appropriate titles on pages 104–5. And sometimes all it takes is just being together, curled up on the couch, holding each other silently. Whichever way you choose, don't push: your child may simply not want—or be ready—to deal with her grief right now. Trying to force her to do so will only drive her away.

Here are a few other things you can do to help your kids cope in these difficult times:

♦ **Keep up as many of their normal routines as possible.** Although they've been badly shaken, going to school, doing their homework and chores, having regular meal times, visiting friends, and doing their extracurricular activities will reassure them that the world hasn't really come to an end.

♦ **Don't keep your own grief a secret.** Although grief is a natural process, your children will look to you as a model for what's okay and what's not. Your crying may help them cry as well, but being stoic will make them think that tears are inappropriate.

♦ **But manage your emotions.** They've already lost one parent and seeing you fall apart emotionally will make them afraid that they might be losing the other.

♦ **Help them remember.** When they do something nice, tell them how proud their mother would be of them. Making scrapbooks, photo albums, and arrangements of special gifts and other mementos from their mother will help them keep her memory alive and come to terms with her loss at the same time. But if the children aren't interested in doing this now, don't force the issue.

♦ **Reassure them their mother's death doesn't mean that you'll be next.** Again, they need to feel that their world is still secure and that you'll be there to take care of them.

♦ **Reassure them that they're not to blame.** Children sometimes say that they wish their parents were dead or that something terrible would happen to them. In most cases, of course, nothing does happen. But if it does, the child may hold himself responsible. Kids need to know that no matter what the Blue Fairy told Pinocchio, wishes—especially bad ones—don't come true.

♦ **Spend some extra time with your boys.** Boys are less likely to express their grief and, as a consequence, sometimes have a tougher time dealing with this type of loss.

♦ **If your child can't or won't talk with you, encourage her to seek out someone else.** It's best to find another adult or older friend since other children may not understand what's happened, may not know how to react appropriately, or may even get scared.

♦ **Watch for their physical reactions.** For some reason, children's grief often comes out as a stomachache, headache, or other physical complaint. And if your wife died of an illness, your child may become obsessed by it and develop similar "symptoms" himself. If your child has any kind of physical reaction, be sympathetic; don't accuse him of faking or tell him to cut it out. But if it lasts more than a few days, if a fever develops, or if the pain or discomfort seems truly extreme, call your doctor.

♦ **Let your child be a child.** Don't ever tell your kids that they're going to have to be "the lady of the house" or "the man of the house" now. This puts way too much pressure on them.

Staying Involved With Your Kids

"When society relegates you to the status of second-class citizen vis-à-vis your children, it is easy to doubt your worth as a father," writes psychologist Richard Warshak, author of *The Custody Revolution.* "The doubts are reinforced when you see your relationship with your children deteriorate or become more superficial— as often occurs under the constraints of the typical visiting schedule."

But doubts aren't the only feelings that most noncustodial fathers experience. There's also:

- Depression and sadness at the constant good-byes.
- Fear of being cut off from your children completely or that they don't need you or love you anymore.
- Anger at the system and your ex.
- Shame at not being able to protect your children from the hurt they're feeling.
- Frustration at not being able to be a real father because you're not part of an intact family.
- Helplessness for being unable to teach your children your values and philosophy of life or to make sure they're equipped to meet the world.
- A sense of futility at not being able to change anything.
- Worries about not having the skills or training necessary to actually take care of your children.
- Disappointment that your visits are too short or that your interactions with the kids aren't "normal" like they were before your breakup.

Those feelings, combined with the limited contact noncustodial fathers are allowed to have with their children, lead some of them to gradually fade out of their children's lives.

In a particularly dark moment you might suddenly decide that dropping out of your kids' lives altogether would be the best solution for everyone. But it's really the worst. Being a presence in your children's lives—even on a limited basis—has great benefits for your kids and for you. And not being there has some devastating effects.

What you're going to read in the section below may make you angrier, more depressed, and more scared than you were before. But that's not why it's here. I've included it simply to drive home three important points:

1. Don't let yourself fade away. You are extremely important to your children—in a lot of ways you might not even have thought about.
2. Children who don't have a lot of contact with their fathers can pay a heavy price.
3. By being as actively involved with your children as possible, you'll be doing a tremendous amount to make sure they turn out okay.

When Fathers Aren't Involved

Crime
Children growing up without active father involvement in their lives are more likely to be jailed for juvenile offenses than kids whose fathers are involved. More than 70 percent of adolescent murderers and 60 percent of rapists in this country grew up without a father. If you look at the one factor that most closely correlates with crime, it's not poverty, it's not unemployment, it's not education, said former U.S. Attorney General William Barr. "It's the absence of the father in the family."

Education
Children growing up in homes without a father are twice as likely to repeat a grade than children in two-parent families. As adolescents, they have lower test scores, lower grade-point averages, poorer school attendance, and more than double the risk of dropping out of high school altogether. They're less likely to enroll in college and less likely to graduate. And later in life they are more likely to be unemployed or out of work.

Psychological or Behavioral Problems
Children whose parents separate are about three times as likely to have emotional or behavioral problems. They're more anxious, more hostile, more withdrawn, and less popular with their peers. They're significantly more likely to engage in early— and unsafe—sexual activity, get pregnant, abuse drugs, and experience conduct and mood disorders. "This effect is especially strong for children whose parents

"Daddy can't help you son. Daddy's a product of the 'me' generation."

separated when they were five years old or younger," says psychiatrist David Fergusson and his colleagues. And other researchers have found that children raised by divorced or never married mothers are less cooperative and score lower on intelligence tests than kids from intact families. Interestingly, these effects tend to show up earlier in life for boys than for girls.

General Health
"Children living apart from their biological fathers experience more accidental injury, asthma, frequent headaches, and speech defects," says researcher Debra Dawson. They're 4.3 times more likely to smoke cigarettes as teenagers, according to sociologist Warren Stanton and his colleagues. And they're significantly more likely to live in poverty.

Now that I've got your attention and you've seen the damage that dropping out of your kids' lives can do, let's take a look at something much more positive: the many ways being involved can help your children—and you.

When Fathers *Are* Involved:
What You Can Do and Why It Matters

We all know that babies are better off when they have two parents to love them, cuddle them, and contribute to their college fund. And even though mothers are the ones who breastfeed, get up in the middle of the night, and undoubtedly change more than their fair share of newborn diapers, you play a unique and very important role in your child's life—right from the start. The fact is that your children will benefit greatly in all kinds of ways from the different interests, hormones, and ways of being that you bring to them.

So what, exactly, do fathers do? Well, to start with, they tend to allow their infants more freedom to explore, while mothers are usually more cautious. Fathers also encourage their children's independence by promoting exploration, and they even speak to them differently than mothers do (fathers generally prefer *doing* practical, educational things to *talking* about them).

But the area in which your unique parenting style is probably going to be most obvious—and most important—is play. Anyone who has ever watched parents in action can attest that women tend to play quieter, more visual, and more verbal games with their children, while men are far more physical and cause more excite-

MANKOFF

"Pass 'em, Pop."

ment—even with tiny infants. Both my daughters, for example, spent most of their first year on an extended roller coaster ride on my back and could stand up on my shoulders—without using their hands—before they were eighteen months old.

Not surprisingly, babies are among the first to notice that their parents have very different styles, and they react accordingly. "Babies know that men and women behave differently and they seek out their mothers and fathers for different reasons," says Gary Levy, director of the Infant Development Center at the University of Wyoming. "Even as young as just a few months old, when babies want to be comforted, they look for their mothers. But when they want to play, they look for dad." Researcher Alison Clarke-Stewart has found that when given a choice of play partners, more than two-thirds of 2½-year-olds choose their fathers over their mothers.

While the differences between fathers' and mothers' parenting styles certainly make for fascinating conversation, the big question still remains: So what? Do all these differences really make a difference to anyone? In a word, absolutely.

Playing Nerf basketball with your kids in the living room or doing somersaults with them on the bed is always fun, of course, but this rough-and-tumble play style offers a lot more than just a good time. On the most basic level, when wrestling and rolling around on the floor, you're teaching your children some valuable lessons in self-control. "While they're roughhousing with their fathers, infants are already learning some valuable lessons in self-control," says fatherhood researcher John Snarey. "They're also learning how to express and appropriately manage their emotions and to recognize others' emotional clues, and that biting, kicking, and other forms of physical violence are simply not acceptable."

You can influence your children's emotional lives in other ways as well. "The kids who did best in terms of peer relationships . . . were those whose dads validated their feelings and praised their accomplishments," writes psychology professor John Gottman. "These fathers were Emotion Coaches, who neither dismissed nor disapproved of their kids' negative emotions, but showed empathy and provided guidance to help their kids deal with negative feelings." Specifically, Gottman found that fathers' acceptance of and assistance with their children's sadness and anger at five years of age was related to children's social competence when they were eight. Kids with supporting, emotionally accepting fathers were less aggressive, had better relationships with friends, and had less trouble in school.

Having a good, active relationship with your children may also make them smarter! "The evidence is quite robust that kids who have contact with a father have an advantage over kids without that kind of contact," says Norma Radin, a professor emeritus at the University of Michigan who has conducted research on fathers for more than twenty years. And these benefits are evident very early in life. In one study, Radin found that children who were raised by actively involved fathers scored higher on verbal ability than children raised by less involved fathers. In another study, toddlers whose fathers took a special interest in child care were consistently rated two to six months ahead of schedule on tests of development, problem-solving skills, and even social skills. In addition, Radin believes that "there's a strong connection between kids' math skills and the amount of contact they have with their fathers."

Interestingly, the kind of playmate you are may also have an influence on your children's cognitive development. Fathers who are good at peek-a-boo or ball tossing and bouncing, for example, have more cognitively advanced children than those who can't keep their children interested in their games. And even if you aren't all that into play, you can contribute to your kids' intellectual capacity by encouraging them to be

Boys and Girls

While it seems somehow intuitive that you would have an influence on your son's development (after all, you both share that pesky Y chromosome), too many fathers fear that they can't possibly have much of an impact of their daughters. Wrong.

POSITIVE WAYS YOU CAN IMPACT YOUR SONS

♦ The more socially and emotionally nurturing a father is to his young son, says Snarey, the better the boy's academic skills, success in school (and later, in college), and scores on IQ and other standardized tests. Norma Radin says that, generally speaking, the more involved a boy's father, the more empathetic the boy will be—and the better behaved.

♦ You provide a role model for your son that his mother can't provide—and neither can her new husband or boyfriend.

♦ You can help him avoid gender stereotypes. Getting hugged and kissed by you and seeing you clean and cook will help him understand that men can and do nurture, and that being a nurturing father is something to aspire to.

♦ Boys who don't have contact with their fathers run the risk of becoming too dependent on their mothers, says researcher Neil Kalter. That can make them grow up doubting their masculinity. The results of this self-doubt are often devastating. A large percentage of boys in prison or involved in gang activity, for example, grew up without a father in the home. And they settle on crime and violence as a way to prove that they're "real men."

POSITIVE WAYS YOU CAN IMPACT YOUR DAUGHTERS

♦ Ross Parke found that girls whose fathers play with them a lot tend to be more popular with their peers and more assertive in their interpersonal relationships. Other research has found that extremely competent and successful women frequently recall their fathers as active and encouraging, playful and exciting.

independent. In one study, researcher Alison Clarke-Stewart found that the earlier (within reason) the father expected his child to be able to handle a pair of scissors or take a bath alone, the more advanced his child's intellectual development.

Best of all, these benefits of involved fatherhood seem to last a lifetime. Researchers Carol Franz, David C. McClelland, and Joel Weinberger contacted people in their early forties whose parents had been interviewed thirty-six years earlier about their child-rearing practices. They found that the people who had

♦ You provide an example for your daughter of how she can expect to be treated by the men in her life.
♦ You help break down gender stereotypes. Getting hugged and kissed by you and seeing you clean and cook will help her understand that women aren't the only ones who do those things.
♦ If your ex is saying mean and hateful things about you, your daughter may assume that all men are that way. Being there and behaving well will enable you to undo the damage.
♦ You can show her that you'll support her in her future work endeavors by taking her with you to work and letting her see what you do there.

"No man is going to tell me what to do, even if he is my mom!"

experienced the warmest relationships with their fathers when they were five exhibited the highest levels of sympathy and compassion for others, had longer, happy marriages, and developed generally better social relationships.

So does all this mean that just being around will magically make your kids smarter, more confident, and better adjusted? Not a chance. While the amount of time you spend with your kids is extremely important, what you do when you're with them is more important. Incompetent fathering—just like incompetent mothering—can have a variety of negative effects.

Gottman found that kids whose fathers were cold and authoritarian, derogatory and intrusive had the hardest time with grades and social relationships. They are, says Gottman, even worse off than kids who live in homes with no father at all. "Kids with humiliating, nonsupportive dads were the ones most likely to be headed for trouble," he says. "They were the ones displaying aggressive behavior toward their friends, they were the ones who were having the most trouble in school, they were the ones with problems often linked to delinquency and youth violence."

In contrast, dads who are nurturing, responsive to their children's needs, and respectful of their feelings and desires have kids who are better adjusted.

Being There for Your Kids Is Good for You Too

Kids aren't the only ones who benefit from spending time with their fathers. More than twenty years ago Maureen Green, author of *Fathering,* wrote, "One of the first things a father learns from his children is that his needs can match theirs. They look to him for instruction; he can enjoy giving instruction. The children look to him as a model and being a model adds an extra dimension to his decisions. His ambitions and achievements look different to him if he can look at them through their eyes as well as his own. Fathering, in short, may be good for men as well as for children."

Being a presence in your children's lives may also be good for your health. Conventional wisdom tells us that men's health is more affected by their work than by their family relationships. But according to researcher Rosalind Barnett and journalism professor Caryl Rivers, "Problems in a man's relationship with his child had a significant impact on his physical health, while his problems at his job did not. . . . The men who had the fewest worries about their relationships with their children also had the fewest health problems. Those who had the most troubled relationships with their children had the most health problems."

Taking an active role in your child's life can help you in other ways as well. According to Snarey, involved fathers tend to have more successful careers. They may also have a greater ability to understand themselves as adults and to take care of others. Men who take an active role at home are—by the time their children are grown—better managers, community leaders, and mentors. Overall, they're more concerned with the generation coming up than with themselves.

Involvement over the Years

The bottom line of all this is that you can have a major impact on your children's physical, intellectual, and emotional/social development. You can do these things whether you're a custodial parent and have your children every day or you're a non-custodial parent and see them only a few days a month. Here's how:

Birth–6 Months

Over the course of the first few months of life, your infant will gradually gain control of her muscles, evolving from a little creature who can hardly lift her head to some-one who can actually get her body to perform on demand. She'll also go from pas-sively observing everything around her to actively interacting with the people and things that make up her world. If you have a child this age, and you haven't already read my book *The New Father: A Dad's Guide to the First Year,* I'd strongly suggest you get a copy now. It will take you through the first year of your baby's life—and of your fatherhood—in great detail. Following are some great ways you can stay involved with your baby and help her grow.

PHYSICALLY

♦ Play lots of games that stimulate your baby's senses. Let her smell everything in your kitchen (even the moldy stuff in the back of the refrigerator) and taste a few drops of things other than milk. Make sure she has a wide variety of things to look at—photos, mirrors, toys, people. Expose her to lots of textures—smooth, soft, rough, bumpy. And be sure she has lots of different things to listen to—bells, whistles, your whole CD collection, and, most important—plenty of conversation.

♦ Stimulate muscle development with reaching games. Hold a favorite toy just out of reach above her head, below her, to the sides. But don't tease or torture her.

♦ Pay attention to her signals. If she keeps turning her head away from you or looks like she'd rather be sleeping, don't force her to play.

♦ Play tracking games. Hold a ball about a foot in front of your baby's nose and slowly move it from side to side. Watch her follow it and smile as she sees how delighted you are.

INTELLECTUALLY

♦ Read. At this age, you can read just about anything to your baby, from the *Iliad* to the installation guide for your dishwasher. What's important, says Jim Trelease, author of *The New Read Aloud Handbook,* "is that the child becomes accustomed to the rhythmic sounds of your reading voice and associates it with a peaceful, secure time of the day." So set up a regular reading time and place. Again, monitor the baby to make sure she's happy and interested; if she's not, stop.

♦ Play if-then games. Any kind of game that teaches cause and effect (if Daddy blows up his cheeks and you poke them, it makes a funny noise) is great.

♦ Play a lot of music. Whether you leave the radio on or carefully select a program, make sure there's plenty of variety in style, key, and tempo. Some recent evidence indicates that listening to classical music at this age helps babies' brains develop and may even make them smarter.

EMOTIONALLY/SOCIALLY

♦ At this age, what your baby needs from you is security and love. The best way to provide this is to spend a lot of time together getting to know each other and getting used to each other. It doesn't really matter what you're doing (although the stimulating activities described above are much better than watching television), or whether you're inside or outside. If you do go outside, strollers are nice, but if your back can handle it, a front pack is nicer because it gives you and the baby more body-to-body contact.

♦ Pay attention to your baby's signals—smiles, babbling, and looks—and respond to them by touching, talking, and looking. Babies learn the important lesson that their actions can actually affect the people around them.

6–12 Months

In the second half of the first year, your baby is going to go learn to crawl, sit up, and maybe even take a step or two (probably holding on to something). He's learning huge amounts about his environment. In the early part of this time frame your baby thinks that any object or person he can't see simply doesn't exist. But within just a few months, he'll know that if you leave the room you'll be back and that that toy he dropped over the rail of his crib is down there somewhere. He can now tell the difference between adults and children and especially between family members and strangers. By twelve months he'll have a vocabulary of six to eight words and a bunch of animal noises, and he'll be able to understand quite a bit more.

PHYSICALLY

♦ Play, play, play. See pages 130–34 for more on the advantages of play for your kids. For small-motor (coordination) development, play lots of games that involve picking up, organizing, stacking, nesting, pouring, tearing, crinkling, and crushing objects. Puzzles are especially good starting at about a year, but get only the kind that have separate holes for each piece (each piece should also have a peg for easy lifting). For bigger muscle development, try pushing balls back and forth, playing hide-and-seek, and chasing each other around the house on your knees. And (starting when your baby is eight months old) for building hand-eye coordination, try spilling a bunch of Cheerios on your baby's highchair tray and letting him pick them up. Whether he eats them or puts them back in the bowl is up to him.

♦ Don't spend a lot of money on fancy toys. Babies this age are more likely to be interested in labels and packing material than the toys themselves. When you do get toys, make sure they're safe: no mechanical parts, no wires or strings, nothing small enough to fit all the way into the baby's mouth, and no parts that can be chewed off. Most toy manufacturers now produce a wide variety of safe, fun toys that come with labels telling you the age the toy is most appropriate for.

INTELLECTUALLY

♦ Play hiding and finding games, such as looking for a favorite toy that you've hidden under a napkin, to reinforce the important notion that things exist even when you can't see them.

♦ Play imitating and pretending games. They're excellent for developing imagination and for teaching babies about emotions.

♦ Play with blocks. "Taken from a psychological view-point," wrote Albert Einstein, "this combinatory play [creative arts, blocks, puzzles] seems to be the essential feature in productive thought—before there is any connection with logical construction in words or other kinds of signs which can be communicated to others."

♦ Keep reading. By ten months your baby will want to sit and turn the pages (two or three at a time); at eleven months, she may follow characters from one page to the next; at twelve months, she'll be able not only to turn one page at a time, but to answer questions like, "What does the duckie say?" The best reading position for your baby is seated on your lap with her back to your chest. Hold the book with your arms around her and read from over her shoulder.

♦ Keep playing music. The more—and the greater the variety—the better. And don't forget about singing. Your baby doesn't care whether you sound like Placido Domingo or a bull on its way to the slaughter.

EMOTIONALLY/SOCIALLY

♦ As with younger babies, your six- to twelve-month-old most needs to know you love her and that you'll always be there for her. Doing any and all of the above activities—especially those that involve physical contact—will help you and your child build a strong relationship.

♦ Start establishing regular routines right now. Getting your child used to eating, reading, going out, and sleeping at pretty much the same time every day will help build her sense of confidence and security.

♦ Spend some time holding, hugging, and cuddling your baby, and be sure to tell her often that you love her. Even if you think she doesn't understand what you're saying, your smiles and your voice tell her a lot more than you think.

1–2 Years

Your new toddler is developing at an alarming rate. Over the course of this year he'll go from barely being able to stand on his own to being able to run (although he may have some trouble making fast turns). He'll progress from using one word at a time to putting together two- (and maybe three-) word combinations. He's consumed by a primal urge to discover how the world works and he'll pick up, crawl over, and put into his mouth just about anything. By his second birthday he will have discovered that a more effective way of learning how things work is to imitate daddy, which he'll try to do whether you're sweeping, washing the car, brushing your teeth, or sitting on the toilet. He's also developed a pretty healthy ego, believing that the world revolves around him.

If you have a child this age, and you haven't already read my book *The New Father: A Dad's Guide to the Toddler Years,* I'd strongly suggest you get a copy now. It will give you a detailed look at how your child is going to be developing from now through his third birthday, and it is filled with lots of tips on the best ways to stay involved. In the meantime, here are some things to keep in mind:

PHYSICALLY
♦ Kids this age generally love vigorous physical activity that helps them build their larger muscles: chasing each other, running through the weeds, jumping up and down on the bed, climbing a jungle gym, swinging on a swing, and so on. Make sure your child has some time every day to run around. But as usual, take your direction from your child about when he needs a break—and make sure he gets one. Parks with fences that kids can't open are ideal: your child can't run away and you might actually get a few minutes to relax with a book. And in case you were wondering, it's a little too early for tricycles.
♦ To help promote manual dexterity and coordination, encourage your child to build towers from Duplo (the large-size Lego), stack blocks, twist keys in locks, pour sand from one bucket to another, build mud pies, dial the (disconnected) phone, squeeze the juice out of a lemon, and anything else that makes him use his fingers and hands. Use real objects, such as keyboards and phones, whenever you can. And avoid overly complicated toys. Manufacturers love to sell "busy boxes"—toys that have dozens of little buttons to push and levers to turn and things to squeeze—but most kids this age don't have much use for them.
♦ Be particularly careful about safety—where your child is playing and what he's playing with.

INTELLECTUALLY
♦ Games that promote an understanding of consequences. Have your child turn the lights on and off or push the play and stop buttons on your VCR. Does he understand what happens?
♦ Computers. If your child has a good grasp of consequences, he may be ready for

a basic introduction to computers. But you'll have to find a special child key-board—no letters, no numbers, just buttons with pictures, colors, shapes, and maybe a telephone receiver. As with most things, pay attention to what your child wants. He's going to want to spend a lot of his time practicing all the neat things he can do with his body and may not enjoy sitting on your lap looking at a computer screen for very long.

♦ Reading is getting more and more important. Start (or keep up) a nightly read-ing routine. Let your child select the reading matter—even if it's the same story for the 419th time in a row. If you get bored, spice things up by changing a few key words once in a while and waiting to see whether your child will catch your mistake. You can also make your reading experience more interactive by includ-ing flap books and letting your child open and close the flaps.

♦ Start creating art: it builds a great awareness of color. Nontoxic paints and markers are essential. Stay away from crayons, though, as they can get ground into your carpets or eaten. Another necessary medium is Oobleck, a moldable dough kids love to play with. Here's the recipe: Pour 1 pound of cornstarch into 1½ cups cold water and add a few drops of your child's favorite food coloring. Mix together until smooth and start having fun. Make sure you're in a good mood before you start any art project: it's going to be messy. You can do it either outside, where clean-ing up will be easier, or inside, but before you start, spend a few minutes cover-ing every surface in your house with newspaper.

♦ Preparing food can teach your child many valuable lessons about textures, measur-ing, and how things change shape when they're mixed, heated, or cooled. Jello is particularly well suited because it even requires cooking. As with art, be patient; making food with a child can be a tremendous mess—but an even more tremen-dous amount of fun.

EMOTIONALLY/SOCIALLY

♦ Let your child ask for help before you jump in. Learning to do things on his own is an important part of building self-esteem and self-confidence.

♦ Do things together. Kids this age love to do exactly what you do, so let them "help" you by vacuuming the rugs, cleaning up spills, and even shaving you (with an electric razor or a bladeless safety razor) or smearing themselves with your shav-ing cream.

♦ Encourage them to start playing with peers. You'll be amazed at how quickly they make friends at the park or playground.

♦ Don't treat boys and girls differently (see pages 122–24 and 132–33).

♦ Routines for meals, bedtimes, and so on are increasingly important to children at this age.

♦ Play imagination games. "Pretend play actually fosters cognitive and social development," wrote famed child psychologist Bruno Bettelheim. Children who have well-developed pretending skills tend to be well liked by their peers and

"See? Easy."

to be viewed as peer leaders. It also helps them take the point of view of others and improves their ability to reason about social situations.

2–3 Years

Your two-year-old's control over her body is growing by the minute—she hardly falls down anymore, can build impressively tall towers out of blocks, and can draw a pretty round circle. She can probably dress herself, although buttons and zippers are still going to give her some trouble. The biggest developments this year, though, are verbal—on her second birthday she can probably understand 200 to 500 words and use 20 to 100. But by the time she's three, she'll understand the majority of the conversational language she'll use for the rest of her life. Attention spans vary greatly, with some kids able to sit patiently through a double feature and others not able to make it through a preview. She's increasing her understanding about the consequences of her behavior and she's pretty much able to play cooperatively with another child. She's also getting more independent and won't mind being left alone for a while as long as you're nearby.

PHYSICALLY

♦ Most of the information your child gets about the world comes from play, so do as much as you can. If you have girl, don't hold back—she's just as hardy as any boy. But no matter what flavor your child is, don't push. Just like adults, kids need down time.

♦ For large motor skills, running, jumping, chasing, kicking things, spinning till you drop, dancing, gymnastics, pillow fights, and, finally, bike (actually tricycle) riding are excellent.

♦ For small-motor skills, try puzzles (a maximum of ten pieces), painting, stringing large beads, pouring, and measuring.

INTELLECTUALLY

♦ Reading. Your child will want to do a lot of "reading" on her own now, so set up a bookshelf so she can get her own books whenever she wants to. Despite her independence, be sure to read to her every day.

♦ Computers. She's got those pesky if-then problems down pretty well by now and should be ready for computers. She'll probably be able to handle a mouse by her third birthday. Be sure to have rules: no food or drink anywhere near the computer (but get a plastic keyboard protector anyway), no fighting near the computer, and, if you kick the machine, you're done for the day.

♦ Talk, talk, talk. "The amount of live language directed to a child was perhaps the strongest single indicator of later intelligence and linguistic and social achievement," say Ohio State University researchers Barbara and Philip Newman. Talk about everything you're doing and why you're doing it and identify everything she points to. Expand on what your child says. If she says, "Truck drive," for example, you reply, "Yes, the truck is driving by." Finally, don't correct grammatical or pronunciation mistakes. Just put the word or idea into a correct sentence and move on. If she says, for example, "Me want baba," you can ask, "Do you want your bottle?"

♦ Play matching games (you can do this with an ordinary deck of cards), alphabet games, and number games. The idea is to get your child familiar with these basic concepts.

♦ Get a basic book about constellations and find some of the easy ones in the sky. Have your child try first.

♦ Keep television to a minimum and let your child watch only when you're there so you can explain what she's seeing. Shows like *Sesame Street* can help your child learn more about numbers, shapes, sizes, and letters, and Mr. Rogers and Barney can help them with their feelings and emotions. Videos can also be good at this age because you can control the content that your children watch and stop the tapes anytime to explain important points.

EMOTIONALLY/SOCIALLY

♦ Encourage independence. At this age you can let your child (but don't force the issue) play by himself for a while in his room or in a fenced, childproofed yard as long as you're nearby.

♦ Take an active role in toilet training, especially if you have a son. On average, boys aren't toilet trained until sixteen months after girls are. Part of the reason is that boys don't want to imitate what their mothers do and mothers really can't demonstrate how—or how much fun it is—to pee standing up. And be sure to let him watch you!

◆ Your child needs confidence and encouragement, so compliment her often, tell her you love her, and make sure she knows what a great job you think she's doing.

◆ Spend time just being together. Go on a picnic in the woods, take a trip to the zoo, or go to a lake and feed the ducks.

◆ Roughhouse.

3–5 Years

The preschool years are a time of continued physical, verbal, emotional, and social growth. Kids this age generally have excellent control over their bodies; they can catch, throw, and kick a ball; and long before they're five most will be able to write the letters of their names and some will be able to recognize the rest of the alphabet as well as numbers from 1 to 10. They're also just beginning to form their gender identity, with girls and boys suddenly expressing a desire to spend more of their time with same-sex kids. Here's how you can stay involved:

PHYSICALLY

◆ Your child should have some time for vigorous physical activity every day. Some of it can be structured, such as the games discussed above, and some should be unstructured—just plain running around making noise.

◆ Play ball! Start with a large ball (8 to 10 inches in diameter); stand a foot or two away from him and drop the ball into his outstretched hands (you may have to show him how to hold his hands the first few times). As your child gets more comfortable catching and throwing, increase the distance between you. Don't expect too much too soon; your child won't be ready to catch a high fly or a long bomb for at least a few years.

◆ Biking (tricycling) is fun to do together, but watch out. If you're walking while your child is on wheels, get a bike with a handle on the back seat; otherwise you'll throw your back out leaning over to push.

INTELLECTUALLY

◆ Read. Your preschooler is going to be an active participant now. Let her fill in the last words of sentences, and use the book as a launching point for other discussions: ask her to tell you what's going on in the illustrations or to explain what a particular character is doing or what he's feeling. If you need a break, most local libraries have kids' story readings.

◆ Play vocabulary-building games. Pants are pants but what about trousers and slacks? Kids also love to use homonyms (words that have different meanings but sound the same) and will giggle endlessly at sentences like, "We should meet at the store to buy some meat."

♦ Art. Do portraits of each other, draw still lifes together. Other projects, such as collages, making sculptures out of Oobleck (see page 139 for recipe), cutting pictures out of magazines, finger painting, and stringing beads, build coordination as well as an appreciation of color, line, and art in general.

♦ Make sock puppets. All you need are some old socks, yarn, thread, pieces of felt, and squiggly eyes (which you can get fairly cheap at a variety store). Besides being fun to make, they offer kids a great opportunity to engage in imaginative play.

♦ Expose them to music. Not only should they be listening to music all the time, but now's the perfect age for them to start playing the piano and/or the recorder. Both are relatively simple instruments and allow them to make reasonable-sounding music almost immediately. Even if you don't want to start them on lessons, they can toot around on a kazoo or imitate you when you tap out various rhythms on the front porch.

♦ Expand their world by taking them on field trips. Malls, parks, and even local businesses are wonderful places for learning all sorts of things. Many cities, of course, have wonderful children's museums (if yours doesn't, a grown-up museum is just fine to start), and aquariums are always a splash.

♦ Now's just the right time to get your child interested in science. You can do simple experiments, such as shaking a clear plastic bottle of soda to see how bubbles form, or activities that promote an awareness of size differences. For example, fill a measuring cup with rice and then pour it into a large bowl. Then refill the cup. Ask your child which container has more rice in it.

♦ Give your child an allowance. See pages 234–35 for more.

EMOTIONALLY/SOCIALLY

♦ Make your kids part of your life. Take them along when you go food shopping, apartment hunting, or to the bank. They don't know that such chores are boring; they just want to be with you. You should probably draw the line at activities that would require them to be silent or immobile for long periods of time, such as ice fishing or deer hunting.

♦ Spend time getting to know your child. Watch him carefully to figure out what he likes to do and what he doesn't. Get down on the floor and play with him on his level, and play the games he wants to play.

♦ Talk to your child. Ask a lot of questions about what he's thinking and feeling. It's especially important to do this with boys because they're somewhat less likely to volunteer information than girls. And make sure to talk to him about your day. Doing this lets him know that you value his company and, by extension, him.

♦ Encourage his friendship with other kids. Invite his friends over to play or let

*"It's a poor craftsman, son,
who blames his tools."*

him go to someone else's house. Having friends helps kids build social skills
and encourages them to be independent.
* Praise him. Parents spend way so much time criticizing and saying no and stop
that they forget to remark on the good things their kids are doing. So give your
child a hug and a compliment (at least one) every day. Displaying his artwork in
a prominent place is also a great self-esteem booster.
* Keep a record. Shoot videos, take pictures, keep a journal, or do tape-recorded
interviews with the kids. And let them help; they can sort photos or come up with
a few questions to ask you.

5–10 Years

From the time your child starts kindergarten at about age five, school will become
the focus of her life. And over the next few years she'll go from being able to read her
name to plowing through two-hundred-page novels. But "If you talk to children about
why they like going to school—or what they enjoy about school even if they aren't
having a good time overall—their answers are likely to describe the social experience more than the academic," writes psychologist Lawrence Kutner. "Friendships,
sports teams, cliques, and other social groups become an increasingly important
part of children's lives." The ongoing process of separating from you and joining the
outside world is getting more obvious by the day. Your school-aged child has her own

social life—one that often doesn't include you—and she's perfectly capable (or at least she thinks she is) of scheduling her own engagements and other activities. Here's how you can stay involved:

PHYSICALLY

♦ Kids this age need a lot of exercise—half an hour daily should be considered a minimum. Some they'll get at school, some they'll have to get at home.

♦ If your very young school-aged child can handle her trike pretty well—negotiating tough turns, weaving through a crowd of people without doing any major damage, and pedaling backwards—she's ready for a two-wheeler (although she'll need training wheels for a little while). When buying a first bike, try to get one with foot brakes. Hand brakes are too complicated to master at the same time as balance.

♦ Encourage her to get involved in team sports, but make sure not to push her into something she doesn't want to do. Take direction from her. Your child may very well be a good enough athlete to compete in future Olympics, but is that what she wants or is it what you want? If you push too hard, her resentment may drive her away from sports altogether.

♦ If they prefer to get their exercise alone, roughhousing is still a welcome activity for most kids this age, as are shooting baskets and jogging.

♦ Be sure your kids have the right safety equipment for whatever sport they're doing: helmets for bike riding and mountain climbing, life jackets for river rafting, knee pads and wrist pads for skateboarding or In-line skating, protective cups (for boys) for baseball, and so on.

♦ Encourage them to build things—model airplanes, simple radio receivers, or simple furniture. These activities not only help with coordination but with such skills as measuring and following directions (including cleaning up when they're done). Supervise them at all times and make sure they wear goggles and carefully observe your basic safety rules.

INTELLECTUALLY

♦ Reading is still tremendously important and you should read to your children every day until they ask you to stop, which they probably won't do until they're at the very end of this age group. With new readers play word games, such as finding smaller, familiar words hidden in larger words ("parking," for example, contains "park," "ark," and "king"). And ask them to read you a paragraph or two —or maybe even a whole book—once in a while; it's a great way for them to develop pride and confidence in their reading abilities. Once they begin to read fluently on their own, make sure they spend at least some time on their own with a book or newspaper. More advanced word games are fun at this stage too, such as seeing how many words can be made from the letters on a particular license plate ("ALD," for example, is in "bALD," "wALDo," and "sALteD").

♦ Encourage them to work on their writing skills by keeping a diary or journal.

♦ Talk to your child. Talk about her day (and yours) while you're driving home from school. Talk to her about current events.

♦ Keep up her allowance, and find other ways to talk with her about math concepts. At the grocery store, for example, have her do comparison shopping. Ask her to figure out whether one big box is really cheaper than two smaller ones, or to weigh produce and estimate how much it will cost.

♦ Teach her how to read a map and let her navigate—even if you get "lost."

♦ Plant a garden. Fertilizing, tilling, and planting are great opportunities to learn about nature. Use a journal to keep track of what was planted and, when the first buds came up, how much water they received, what they looked like, how tall they were at one day, three days, a week, two weeks, and so on. It's a fun way to introduce kids to the scientific process. Radishes, carrots, corn, beans, tomatoes, lettuce, pumpkins, and strawberries grow almost anywhere and don't require all that much care.

♦ Get your child interested in conflict resolution and creative thinking. Encourage her to explore a range of options before acting and talk about the consequences of each choice.

♦ Encourage participation in art, music, and anything else (from raising roses to breeding iguanas) she's interested in exploring on her own.

EMOTIONALLY/SOCIALLY

♦ Find a common interest, whether it's tinkering on your car, playing basketball, or going to the opera, and develop it together.

♦ Give your child the opportunity to take on more responsibility. This can mean getting a job watering the neighbor's garden, doing some meal planning (or even cooking), and scheduling the activities for a whole weekend.

♦ Help her develop her moral or spiritual side (which does not necessarily mean anything religious). Whether you take your child to a church or synagogue or mosque, or just talk about things at home, what's truly important is that she learn how to treat other people—especially those less fortunate—in a kind and ethical way.

♦ Take an interest in your child's friendships. You can do this by helping her schedule play dates and sleepovers and by offering to invite a friend or two along on one of your outings. And make sure she sees you interact with your friends as well.

♦ Give your child lots of opportunities to develop her own skills and interests. And support her in this any way you can.

♦ Take an interest in your child's schoolwork. Go to PTA meetings, attend parent-teacher conferences, help out with homework, and/or volunteer in your child's classroom. All these things help your child understand that you're interested in her all the time.

♦ Teach your child what to do in scary or difficult situations, such as getting lost in an amusement park, dealing with a stranger's offer of candy or invitation to get into a car, having a run-in with the school bully, being offered drugs or alcohol, and so on. Don't scare her. The object here is to get her to start thinking on her own about the best ways to handle these kinds of situations and to reinforce the all-important message that she's important to you.

11–18 Years
This is going to be a time of great conflict for your child. Kids in this general age group are yearning for independence while still being controlled by their parents, teachers, and other adults, say Charlene Giannetti and Margaret Sagarese, authors of *The Roller Coaster Years.* They worry about their appearance while nature is wreaking havoc with their bodies; they are on the brink of adulthood, yet have trouble controlling their childlike impulses; they're fascinated by the world and want to explore it; they're learning to formulate their arguments; they're developing their individual skills; and they're putting together their own values and moral framework. And it's up to you to help them do it.

PHYSICALLY
♦ As big as your kids are, roughhousing with them isn't going to be as easy as it used to be. And your kids probably aren't going to be as interested anyway. But that doesn't mean that they shouldn't be active. They need at least half an hour of physical excercise a day, but as they get older, they're going to be responsible for selecting their own activities themselves.
♦ Encourage them to stay—or get involved—in team sports. And set a good example by being physically active yourself. If they're interested, invite them to join your softball team, swim or run with you, play racquetball together, or even tag along to your yoga class. Another way to keep them (and yourself) interested is to coach a team they're on.

INTELLECTUALLY
♦ As with physical activity, the older your children get, the less direct a role you can play in their intellectual development. But this doesn't mean you should step out of the way. You can still have a major impact by encouraging them to think clearly and creatively and helping them further develop the intellectual skills they learned when they were younger. But a lot of your impact will come more from setting a good example and supporting what they want to do and less from directing them. If they don't already know more about the Internet than you do, you might be able to show them how to use the computer to help them research their term papers or a particular subject that interests them.
♦ Reading is an essential skill and you should do everything you can to promote it. Encourage them to spend time reading every day and make sure they see you reading. Take them to book readings at your local bookstore and spend time

*"Just what exactly is your generation going to do
about my generation's social security?"*

telling each other about what you're reading—including critical discussions of
what you've found on the front page of the newspaper.
♦ Support their interest in art and music. Make sure they have the right equipment
(including good-quality instruments) and the right teachers. Take them to concerts and gallery openings, and if they're interested but don't want to go with you,
get them tickets and send them with a friend.
♦ Continue their allowance so they have money of their own, but ask them to participate by helping you put together a family budget.
♦ Encourage them to think creatively, especially with other people. When dealing
with any kind of problem, focus on these four steps: identify the problem; brainstorm about all the possible solutions—even the ones that sound silly; identify
the best and the worst options; and implement the best one.

EMOTIONALLY/SOCIALLY
♦ Give them more responsibility and encourage their independence. This can mean
everything from letting them baby-sit for younger siblings or neighborhood kids and
letting them drive your car, to helping them investigate and plan overseas trips.
♦ Have clear, reasonable expectations and limits—some kinds of activities (drugs,

alcohol, R-rated movies) may not be acceptable in your home. Impose curfews and rules and enforce them.

♦ Support their friendships (unless they're hanging out with a truly bad crowd) and their interest in popular culture. Kids this age are consumed with the notion of belonging and being accepted by their peers; sometimes seeing the right movies, going to the right concerts, wearing the right clothes, and even an occasional ear piercing (even for boys) is what it takes to do that. Keep up to date on what's cool, but don't get too involved: the last thing your child wants is to have a dad who acts like a teenager.

♦ Encourage them to get involved in their community. Volunteering at a recycling center or serving meals at a homeless shelter on Thanksgiving are important ways of reinforcing a sense that they're citizens of a larger world. It's crucial that you set a good example by doing some of the same activities. I still remember as a ten-year-old sitting down with my father and going through the dozens of solicitations he received from charitable groups and watching him write check after check to the ones we both decided were most worthy.

♦ Stay involved in your children's lives. Be a scout leader or a coach for their soccer team, give a lecture in their classroom, drive the kids on a field trip. If you stay involved with them, they'll stay involved with you.

♦ Respect their feelings. A few years ago, when your kids were younger, they probably thought you were the coolest thing going. But now you're more of an embarrassment. If your daughter (or son) has four or five friends over for a slumber party, don't even think about trying to hang out with them. If you're driving the car pool and they want you to pick them up or drop them off around the corner, do it (as long as it's safe). You might also want to cut back on kissing them in public. And don't get your feelings hurt if they stop wanting to go the movies with you. No self-respecting teen wants to risk being seen with a chaperone.

♦ Make sure they know they can always talk to you about anything and everything. Talking—and listening—is what relationships are based on. Hopefully, they know this already.

♦ Try to find some common interests to share: hiking, biking, board games, art, movies, music, sports, camping, going to museums. And take an interest in their activities, but don't fake it.

♦ Be careful with jokes and teasing. Fathers tend to joke around with their teens more than mothers do and this isn't always a good thing. "If fathers make everything into a joke, their adolescents may start to suspect them of not taking their feelings seriously," writes researcher Reed Larson.

♦ Respect their privacy.

♦ Keep an eye out for unusual behavior: depression, a dramatic drop in school performance, a sudden loss of interest in friends or activities, and so on (see page 121 for more).

A Dad's (Brief) Guide to Puberty

"At no other time, except during infancy, does the human body change so dramatically as it does during puberty," says Chrystal De Freitas, author of *Keys to Your Child's Healthy Sexuality.* You remember what all those changes are about, right? Hormones raging through your child's body, preparing it to reproduce (isn't that an absolutely horrifying thought?). Puberty is going to be tough on your child, and it may not be all that easy on you either. So read on:

What Your Child May Be Going Through

BOYS

♦ His penis and scrotum will get bigger, pubic hair starts appearing, his voice will change, he may start getting acne, and he'll grow hair under his arms.
♦ He may become obsessed with comparing his progress to that of his friends.
♦ He'll have his first wet dreams, which he may find anything from confusing to scary as hell. He may think he's wet the bed or that something is drastically wrong.
♦ The process usually starts at age 11 or 12 (although the range is roughly from 9 to 14) and can take 4 to 8 years to complete. If puberty hasn't started by the time your son is 15, make sure you tell his pediatrician.

"Come along, son. We are at but the beginning of a
long and arduous journey."

An Extra Note If You Have a Girl

If you're a noncustodial father and have your children only part-time, it's fairly safe to assume that your daughter will have the necessary discussions on puberty and menstruation with your ex. But if you're a widower, a primary custodial father, (or even a noncustodial father who wants to know how to handle these things), follow these three steps:

1. Get yourself a few books on adolescent child development and carefully read the sections on girls' puberty. Chrystal De Freitas's *Keys to Your Child's Healthy Sexuality* and *You and Your Adolescent* by Laurence Steinberg and Ann Levine are excellent resources.

2. Ask your daughter if she has any questions about the ways her body is changing and let her know that you'll always be there for her if she wants to talk about anything. Chances are, though, that she'll be far too self-conscious to discuss those intimate details with you—a man. But making the offer in a loving, supportive way will let her know that you care, and that's what's really important.

3. Offer to put your daughter in touch with an adult female friend or relative with whom she may feel more comfortable talking about these things.

"Sorry, sweetie. All I know is guy-stuff."

How It Might Affect You

♦ You may have fond—or horrible—memories of going through puberty yourself. When I was 11 or 12, I remember comparing pubic hair counts and penis measurements with my friends in the bathroom.

♦ You may be proud that your son is becoming a man.

♦ You may suddenly find yourself feeling competitive with him.

What Your Child May Be Going Through

GIRLS

♦ Her breasts will start to develop, she'll start growing hair on her genitals and under her arms, her skin may start breaking out, and she'll begin menstruating.

♦ She'll probably be quite concerned about how she's developing compared to her friends.

♦ The process can start as early as 9 or 10 (the range is typically 8 to 14) and usually takes 18 months to 7 or 8 years to complete. If puberty hasn't started by the time your daughter is 15, make sure you tell her pediatrician.

♦ Girls may feel fat, embarrassed, and ill-at-ease in their new bodies. Girls who

---

Some Advantages to Being a Single Dad

Being a single father—whether you're a custodial or a noncustodial one—has some definite drawbacks. But not all the news is bad. Here are a few of the advantages, some of which were suggested by Jane Nelsen, author of *Positive Discipline for Single Parents,* to doing your parenting on your own:

♦ You may begin feeling better about life in general. Finding out that you really can handle the demands of fatherhood will do wonders for your confidence level and your self-esteem.

♦ You'll have the chance to develop your own style as a parent. In most homes, women are the ones who establish the parenting style. But now that you're flying solo, you can do things the way you want to.

♦ If your ex used to handle all the cooking, cleaning, and child care, being on your own and having to do everything for yourself may force you to become more self-sufficient and responsible. It may also broaden your cooking repertoire—eating tuna out of the can every meal may be fine for you (it certainly is for me), but it isn't for your children.

♦ You may be able to improve or strengthen your relationship with your kids. "Children develop into capable people when they experience the pride and joy of making a contribution," writes Nelson. "Participating in shared responsibility—being part of a team—is one way they can gain this experience."

start developing early usually attract boys' attention and they're often stereotyped as loose or easy.

How It Might Affect You

♦ Your daughter's puberty can be a very difficult time in your relationship. "Girls may become flirty with their fathers in much the same way they were when they were three," write Don and Jeanie Elium, authors of *Raising a Daughter*. "But now the fathers notice their daughter's developing hips and breasts and may get 'turned on.' Thinking that these feelings are abnormal and shameful, they push their daughters away to avoid their feelings and to protect their daughters from them."

♦ Besides being confused by your daughter's physical changes, it's not uncommon to feel embarrassed or slightly put off by the whole menstruation thing.

A Final Word

When considering the activities discussed above, remember that your kids need down time, so don't feel that you have to cram a hundred things into a single weekend. Take a look at the Visitation Dos and Don'ts chart on pages 93–96, and, if you need more suggestions, check out some of the listings in the Resources section.

Staying Involved for Long-distance Dads

Some wise person once said that you can measure distance in miles or in tears. And when it comes to being a long-distance dad, truer words were never spoken. You might, for example, be one of the nearly 40 percent of single fathers who, according to the U.S. Census Bureau, have no court-ordered access to their kids at all. Or you might have a court order but still can't see your children because your ex kidnapped them or is interfering with your access in some other way. Or you might have joint custody and things might be fine between you and your ex, but your child lives so far away that you're able to see her for only a few weeks in the summer and an occasional school holiday during the year.

Wherever you live, whether it's an entire continent away from your child or only a few blocks, not being able to see her is going to be hard for both of you and will have an impact on your relationship. But don't confuse physical distance with emotional distance. Too many long-distance fathers think that since they can't see their children the kids don't love them or need them anymore, or that they can't still play an important role in their kids' lives or have any kind of impact on the kind of people they grow up to be, and they let communication fade or even die out. But nothing could be further from the truth; your kids will always love and need you— no matter how far away you are. It's also very important for them to know the stories and legends that make up the history of your side of their gene pool, and that's something they can't get anywhere else.

Maintaining an emotional bond between you and your children won't be easy. But it's nothing you can't do and it's everything you must. Here are a few things you need to do:

+ If your child can't come to you, go to her. Fly or drive to her mother's house, check into a hotel, and spend a weekend doing things with your child there. If you and your ex are getting along and you live within driving range of each other (and that could be more than a thousand miles), you might be able to convince her to meet somewhere in the middle. Denny's restaurants all over the country are being used for exactly this purpose. You might even be able to check into a nearby hotel and spend a weekend with your child. It's a lot of driving, but I've met several single fathers who drive five or six hours every weekend just to see their kids.

+ Stay up to date on your child's life. If your ex won't help you, write your child's teacher and school principal. Ask them to send you copies of report cards, notices of school events, vacation schedules, and so on. You probably won't be able to attend any of these events, but at least you'll know what your child is up to. Be aware, though, that teachers and principals are under no real obligation to comply with your request if you don't have at least some kind of joint legal custody. So if you do, be sure to enclose a copy of your custody order. If you don't, be sure to ask them in the nicest, least threatening way possible.

+ Call and write. See below.

Phone Call Guidelines

For some long-distance dads, phone calls are great. They give you and your children a chance to hear each other's voices, tell stories, or even to sing songs with each other. But for others, the phone isn't the best option. If your ex is still feeling hostile toward you, she might not allow you to talk to the kids. And even if she does, there's no guarantee that they'll be there when you call. And even if they are home, there can still be problems.

Trying to talk on the phone to a child under six is going to be hard: they don't have a long enough attention span to make conversations particularly fulfilling. And trying to talk to a teen or preteen may be even harder. You'll have to compete with boyfriends or girlfriends, sports, shopping malls, whatever's on the television or the radio, call waiting, and dozens of other things that seem more important to them than you for the moment. It's not hard to end up feeling shortchanged and, if you let yourself, angry and frustrated.

None of this, of course, is to say that you shouldn't talk to your children on the phone. Actually, I believe you should talk to them as often as possible; but know what to expect. Here are a few guidelines that can make your phone interactions more fulfilling and more successful:

♦ Try to call at the same time every week (or every day or every month). As we've said before, kids love routines. The more regular the calls, the more they'll look forward to them and the better your chances that they'll actually be home when you call.

♦ Work out a schedule with your ex so you don't get the kids in the middle of dinner, homework, or soccer practice.

♦ If you're dealing with a teenager, start off asking whether it's a good time to talk. Be prepared for—and try not to take offense at—a "No." If that's the response, though, reschedule the call for a time that works for both of you.

♦ If your ex answers the phone, *always* be civil. Thank her for helping you keep in contact with your kids. (Yes, this may make you want to vomit, but do it anyway.) Do *not* get drawn into a fight. You're calling to talk to your children. If she has something the two of you need to discuss, schedule another time to do so.

♦ Try to make your calls more than just conversations. Watch a favorite television show together. You can mutter comments to each other during the show, talk over the commercials. This can be even more fun if you're both chomping on popcorn at the same time.

♦ Make sure the children always have your phone numbers and let them know it's okay for them to call you anytime. You can make this a lot easier by getting yourself a toll-free number; they're cheap and in many cases can be hooked up to your existing home phone.

Letter Writing

Whether you're unable to communicate with your children by phone or you're looking for a great way to augment your communication, writing is the perfect solution. You don't need your ex's permission and you don't need to schedule a time, and, except in the rarest of circumstances, there's no limit to the number of written contacts you can make (it's still possible, though, for your ex not to deliver your letters to the children).

"Writing letters to children not only helps the child, it also gives the father a way to feel he has a say or impact in his child's life," says researcher Sandra Petronio. "The act of writing often is an opportunity to reveal feelings through a 'safe' vehicle of communication. There is time to think through the content of the message." In fact, Petronio has found that fathers and children are more trustful of each other and more apt to disclose their feelings in letters. This type of trust and open communication is what all good father-child relationships are about. Best of all, unlike a phone call, your child will have a chance to read and reread your letters as often as she wants, giving her the chance to reexperience your love over and over.

For many men, writing a letter—especially one to a child—is a frightening task. Worries about what to say, how to say it, whether you're a good writer, whether you'll be funny or cool enough are bound to surface. If any of these thoughts are keeping

QUESTION STYLE	SAMPLE QUESTIONS
Basic	What's your favorite TV show?
Silly	What is your dog's favorite TV show?
True/False	You should never eat anything bigger than your head. True __ False __
Multiple choice	What does your room look like? A. Neat and clean B. Not too bad C. Disaster area
Yes/No	Do you help your mom around the house? Did you get the present I sent for your birthday?
Yes/No/Other Options	Do you like school? Yes___ No ___ A little ___ A lot ___
Lists	What are the names of all your pets?
Activities	Ask your child to draw a picture of something (an alien from Mars, a cucumber with glasses). Ask your child to write a short story about something.

you from starting to write, remember this: your child probably isn't going to be checking your spelling and punctuation, and she won't really care whether you're funny or nerdy. You're her father and she just wants to know you love her, that you're interested in her, and that despite the distance between you, you're committed to being in her life. Taking the time to write a letter is a great way to show her that you do.

Before you get started, here are a few dos and don'ts to keep in mind:

♦ Do be honest and open. The more clearly you reveal how you feel in your letters, the more likely your child is to react positively to those private feelings, thoughts, and experiences, says Petronio. Exchanging messages this way leads to closer father-child relationships.

♦ Don't write too much at a time. Most kids will be so intimidated by a twenty-five-page letter that they may be afraid even to start reading it.

♦ Don't use your correspondence with your child to criticize his mother, to finagle a way to get back together with your ex, or to criticize the ex's new boyfriend or husband. The purpose of writing is to communicate with your child, so stick to that.

If You Have to Take an Extended Trip

No matter how close you live to your children, the time may come when you'll be away from them for a while—on business, perhaps, or an extended vacation. And while a few weeks or months away might be easy for you to handle, it's going to be a lot harder for your kids, particularly if your absence happens sometime in the early months or even years after you become a single father, and especially if your kids are young. Here are some ways to stay involved while you're gone and to minimize the hurt:

♦ Tell them where you're going and how long you'll be gone. And if you know your itinerary, let them know how to reach you by phone, fax, letter, or e-mail.

♦ Send them regular letters or postcards—the more colorful the better.

♦ Send them small care packages that let them know you're always thinking of them: a pine cone you picked up on a hike up a mountain, the soaps and shampoos from your hotel rooms, whatever.

♦ If you can't avoid missing a special event (birthdays, school plays, piano recitals, and so on) call *before* the actual event and then send a gift. My older daughter was crushed when an unavoidable trip made me miss her first school play, but the flowers I had delivered that night were a huge hit.

♦ When you come back, schedule a special time to show them the pictures you took and tell them the story of your trip.

♦ Do be creative. Send along an occasional video or audio tape, write a story (or put it on tape), paint a picture, send along mementos (even the smallest things, like a few pebbles or a piece of snake skin to go along with your description of your weekend camping trip, can help your child feel a part of your life), family pictures, magazine or newspaper clippings about things your child is interested in, books you remember from when you were young or that you think your child would love, and so on.

♦ Do include a self-addressed, stamped envelope so they can reply. You'll get answers a lot faster that way.

♦ Don't set your expectations too high. Most of the time your children aren't going to be able (or maybe even want) to answer in the same detail that you write to them.

♦ Do try other ways of writing. If the kids have e-mail or a fax machine at their other residence, try communicating that way. If they don't (and you can afford it), consider buying them whatever kind of hardware they need to stay in touch.

Creative Writing

Figuring out what to write about isn't always easy. If you need some assistance, The Write Connection Company (listed in the Resources section) sells a complete kit, including sample topics, activities, and even stickers and stationery.

You might also be able to gain some creative letter-writing inspiration in a hard-to-find book, *Questions from Dad* by singer-songwriter Dwight Twilley. A frustrated long-distance dad himself, Twilley came up with a way to establish an "unprece-dented line of communication" with his daughter, Dion, that has "shattered the distance barrier—forever."

Twilley's simple approach involves little more than sending your child a never-ending series of what he calls "tests" that your child can fill in and return directly to you. (They really aren't tests, though, just a fun way of asking questions.) To get you going, a few of the question styles Twilley suggests as well as a few of his sample questions are listed on page 156.

The purpose of this approach is to make communication with your child—and his communication with you—easy and fun. Of course the questions you ask and the activities you select will vary. All you have to do is use your imagination. Ask about everything you can think of, from the politics of pizza and what to do with a rusty nail to the humiliation of chores and the hazards of shopping. Almost nothing is off-limits (except questions about your ex and any new men in her life). Start off easy, though, maybe twenty questions the first time. And be sure to send a self-addressed, stamped envelope.

Notes:

Discipline: Getting Your Kids to Cooperate

At one time or another, all parents struggle with discipline, establishing and enforcing limits, and getting their kids to speak to them respectfully and do what they're supposed to do. Single parents, though, often have more trouble with these issues because they're so exhausted, depressed, and overwhelmed by life in general that anything other than putting food on the table and clothes in the closet seems like too much to handle.

The results shouldn't surprise you. "Divorced parents tended to show less affection and to have less control over their children's behavior," writes E. Mavis Heatherington. "Children were somewhat more disruptive and disobedient than children of intact families."

Interestingly, if you're a widower, you probably won't experience quite as many of these problems. Unlike divorced fathers, widowers are more secure in their fatherhood role and aren't worried that they'll lose custody of their children to someone else, says widower expert Jane Burgess. In addition, children who lose a parent generally grow up a little faster than their peers after their loss. They seem to understand instinctively how important it is to pull together and support each other and they'll usually take on more responsibilities at home—often without having to be asked.

But whether you're divorced, unmarried, or widowed, you may find yourself slipping into one of these common discipline patterns:

♦ **You might become more lenient.** You may feel guilty about having hurt your children and may believe that by being lax you'll be cutting them some slack. You might also be more lenient because you're feeling competitive with your ex, thinking that by not establishing rules to follow or even giving the kids chores to do they won't stop loving you. Even sole or primary custodial fathers fall into this trap because they're often worried that their exes will regain custody and they hope that their children won't want to leave the rule-free and chore-free environment they've been living in.

♦ **You might become stricter.** You might be feeling so out of control and so unable to handle things that you institute tons of arbitrary rules that even you would have a tough time following. And the consequences you come up with are often far in excess of the infraction (no television for a month for not finishing a homework assignment).

♦ **You might become inconsistent.** This is probably the most common pattern of all. You might, for example, be lax about getting the kids to clean up their room for a month or two and then, out of the blue, demand that they get it spotless in the next fifteen minutes or lose their dessert for a week. Children have a "tendency to treat the parent as they are being treated," writes Stuart Kahan. "If they see craziness and inconsistency going on about them, they will also be crazy and inconsistent. It will not help you in your attempt at disciplining them."

Obviously, all three of these patterns are remarkably ineffective. Here's how you can keep yourself out of them:

♦ **Be consistent.** Not only on a day-to-day basis right now, but consistent with the way you and your partner used to do things before you became a single father. In addition, try to work with your ex to come up with a discipline plan that's consistent between homes and agree to back each other up on how you'll enforce limits. If you can't, you'll have to be firm in telling your kids, "In your mom's house you follow her rules, but in this house you'll have to follow mine."

♦ **Establish and enforce reasonable limits.** No child will ever admit it, but the truth is that they need to know who's boss and they need that person to be you. "With all the changes suddenly happening around him or her, a child could imagine the world falling apart," writes Helen Fitzgerald. "In order to feel secure and to know that life has not been totally disrupted, your child needs the usual rules and daily routines to continue as well as they can." Setting your expectations too high, though, can also be a problem, frustrating your kids and making them feel bad or inadequate when they can't comply.

♦ **Link consequences directly to the behavior.** "I'm taking away your hammer because you hit me with it," or "Since you didn't get home by your curfew, you can't go out with your friends tonight."

♦ **Don't worry.** Unless the limits you set are completely insane, your child will not stop loving you for enforcing them.

♦ **Choose your battles.** Some issues—those that involve health and safety, for example—are non-negotiable. Others don't really matter. Does it really make a difference if your child wants to wear a red sock and an argyle one instead of a matched pair?

"When I was your age I didn't have a corner to stand in."

♦ **Give limited choices.** "Either you stop talking to me that way right now or go to your room."

♦ **Encourage your kids to be independent.** "When parents do too much for children, to 'make up' for the fact that they have only one parent, the children don't have a chance to develop responsibility, initiative, and new skills," writes Jane Nelsen in *Positive Discipline for Single Parents*. But don't go too far here. Your kids still need a structure (see above).

♦ **Understand your child's behavior.** "Misbehaving children are using a code to tell us what they're feeling and experiencing," writes Nelsen. So how do we decipher the code? According to Nelsen, kids misbehave for one or more of the following reasons:

◊ They want attention.

◊ They want to be in control.

◊ They want to get back at you for something you did.

◊ They're frustrated and they just want to give up and be left alone.

From my own experience, I can tell you that trying to punish a child without understanding why she's doing what she's doing is a little like taking cough syrup for emphysema: the thing that's bugging you goes away for a while but the underly-

"Soon you will be entering a phase, son, in which you will no longer pay attention to anything I have to say. Please let me know when that changeover occurs."

ing problem remains—and keeps getting worse with time. The most direct way to do this is to ask your child; in many cases she'll tell you. If she won't tell you or doesn't have the vocabulary to do so, make an educated guess ("Are you writing on the walls because you want me to spend more time with you?").

Understanding your child's motives is only part of the battle. To be a more effective disciplinarian, you'll also need to pay close attention to how your child's misbehavior makes you feel, how you respond to it, and how the kids respond to your response. The chart on pages 164–65, which is based on Jane Nelsen's work, will help you put all the pieces of this puzzle together and come up with some solutions that might work better than what you're doing now.

Family Meetings

Although my parents and I have had our share of disagreements about whether they did a good job raising my sisters and me, one thing we all agree that they did absolutely right was to have regular family meetings. These meetings, which we had once a month or so, gave all of us a chance to air our concerns and work together to solve problems. As my sisters and I got older, it also gave all of us a chance to simply slow down and catch up on what the others were up to. By getting us involved in everything from assigning chores to resolving huge fights, my parents gave us the feeling that we were important members of the family and that our opinions—while they might not always be implemented—would at least be listened to with respect.

My sisters and I have some pretty clear memories of how our family meetings ran and I've augmented these with some suggestions from Kathryn Kvols's book *Redirecting Children's Behavior,* and from author Cheryl Erwin.

♦ **Schedule them regularly.** The schedule should be proportionate to the amount of time you have with your children. If you're a custodial father, once every week or two is fine. But if you see them only every other weekend, once every other or every third visit is fine. Schedule them for a time and place where you won't be interrupted by the phone, the television, or anything else.

♦ **Keep them to a reasonable length.** Tailor the length to your children's ages and attention spans. Fifteen minutes is about right for kids under six, forty-five minutes is a good max for any age (unless the kids want to go longer). You want your kids to love these meetings, not dread them.

Corporal Punishment

Spanking is far and away one of the most divisive parenting issues, and one that seems to lead to all sorts of heated debates every time I write or talk about it. If you don't spank (or hit) your children, you can skip this section altogether. If you do, consider this: most parents who hit their children do so because they're angry, not as a way of solving problems. Not surprisingly, researchers have found that hitting kids does a great job of attracting their attention but a lousy job of promoting any long-term change. In fact, hitting children does little more than teach them to resort to violence and aggression to solve their problems—not exactly the kind of message you want to convey to your children.

Author Doug Spangler suggests that fathers who hit their children are sending some very specific messages:

♦ It's okay to hit another person.
♦ It's okay to hit another person who's smaller than you.
♦ It's okay to hit someone you love.
♦ It's okay to hit someone when you feel angry and frustrated.
♦ Physical aggression is normal and acceptable under any circumstances.
♦ Fathers are to be feared.

Children who are hit by their parents are more likely to suffer from poor self-esteem and depression, and have a greater chance of ending up in abusive relationships and of accepting lower-paying jobs as adults.

Understanding Your Child's Misbehavior

IF YOUR CHILD'S GOAL IS . . .	HE OR SHE MIGHT BE THINKING . . .	THIS MIGHT MAKE YOU FEEL . . .	AND YOU MIGHT REACT BY . . .	
To get attention (to keep others busy or to get special services)	♦ "I'm important only when I'm being noticed or getting special treatment." ♦ "I'm important only when I'm keeping you busy with me."	♦ annoyed ♦ irritated ♦ worried ♦ guilty	♦ reminding ♦ coaxing ♦ doing things for the child that he could really do for himself	
To be in control	♦ "I belong only when I'm the boss or when I'm proving no one can boss me." ♦ "You can't make me."	♦ angry ♦ provoked ♦ challenged ♦ threatened ♦ defeated	♦ fighting ♦ giving in ♦ thinking, "You can't get away with this" or "I'll make you."	
To get even	♦ "I don't think I'm important so I'll hurt someone else." ♦ "I can't be liked or loved."	♦ hurt ♦ disappointed ♦ disbelieving ♦ disgusted	♦ retaliating ♦ getting even ♦ thinking, "How could you do this to me?"	
To give up and be left alone	♦ "I'm not important because I'm not perfect, so I'll convince others not to expect anything from me." ♦ "I am helpless and unable. It's no use trying, because I won't do it right."	♦ despair ♦ hopeless ♦ helpless	♦ giving up ♦ doing things for the child that he should be doing for himself	

YOUR CHILD MIGHT THEN RESPOND BY . . .	YOU MIGHT WANT TO TRY ONE OR MORE OF THESE OPTIONS INSTEAD
♦ stopping temporarily but starting the same behavior again later or doing something else equally annoying	♦ Pay more attention to your child. ♦ Avoid giving special treatment. ♦ Tell your child only once what you want her to do and then impose a "natural" consequence. ("Because you cut my favorite tie in half you're going to have to buy me another one using money from your allowance.") ♦ Tell her you love her. ♦ Hug her or give other nonverbal signs that you care. ♦ Redirect her behavior. ♦ Have family meetings and encourage her participation.
♦ intensifying his behavior ♦ giving in, but very reluctantly ♦ feeling she's wrong when you're upset ♦ being passive-aggressive	♦ Ask your child to help you solve the problem. ♦ Withdraw from the conflict—resist the urge either to fight or give in. ♦ Make sure your child knows the routines, the rules (limits), and the consequences. Then, if he misbehaves, don't talk, follow through immediately. ♦ Be firm, kind, and encouraging. ♦ Give limited choices. ♦ Use family meetings.
♦ retaliating ♦ intensifying or escalating the same behavior or choosing some other weapon	♦ Avoid punishment and retaliation. ♦ Let your child know how you feel. ♦ Encourage your child to tell you what's wrong. ♦ When dealing with her feelings, use reflective listening (restate or rephrase what she's said to make sure she knows you're hearing exactly what she's saying). ♦ Apologize when it's appropriate. ♦ Encourage her to air her complaints at family meetings.
♦ retreating further ♦ becoming passive ♦ ignoring you ♦ showing no improvement	♦ Show your child you have faith in him. ♦ Work on gradual rather than instant solutions. ♦ Stop criticizing your child immediately. ♦ Praise your child and be especially encouraging of every positive thing he does. The average child receives 400 negative comments a day compared to only 32 positive ones, according to Kathryn Kvols. ♦ Don't feel sorry for your child. ♦ Put your child in situations where he can succeed, concentrating especially on areas he's interested in. ♦ Teach new skills in areas where he may feel deficient. ♦ Focus on the child in your family meetings.

- **Be flexible.** Not every meeting has to be devoted to family business. Once in a while take advantage of the time together to do something fun.
- **Start each meeting with something nice.** Everyone at the meeting should say something complimentary to at least one other person and be the recipient of at least one nice comment from someone else. And each person who receives a compliment needs to accept it graciously and say thank you. If you're like me, this part of the meeting might be enough to make you want to gag. But it's important because it keeps the meeting from turning into a gripe session that everyone will hate.
- **Keep a sheet of paper on your refrigerator or bulletin board so people can write down topics to discuss at the next meeting.**
- **Elect a secretary and a leader for each meeting.** The secretary writes down the final decisions and the leader keeps things on track. Make sure everyone gets a chance to do each. The kids will take the whole process more seriously if they get to run the show once in a while.
- **Listen to everyone's proposed solutions, no matter how ridiculous.**
- **Make decisions by consensus, not majority rule.** In other words, everyone has to agree on a solution or the topic will have to be tabled until the next meeting. If you go with majority rule, the person in the minority will feel left out or hurt.
- **End each meeting with a special treat.** A special snack, a game, a song, a video. But be careful not to turn these treats into bribes for attending the meetings.

Notes:

Keeping Things Nice

Imagine that your child is graduating from high school next week. Will you and your ex throw a joint party? Will the two of you sit next to each other at the ceremony or on opposite sides of the room? Or will you be so angry at each other that one of you will refuse to be there at all if the other one's going to show up?

In the late 1970s Rutgers researcher Kenneth Kressel found that therapists, clergy, and lawyers all believed that couples who stayed friends after splitting up were basically crazy. The prevailing wisdom went something like, "If they get along so well, why did they split up?" More than two decades later, not much has changed. Professionals still raise their eyebrows at divorced and separated couples who aren't at each other's throats and even the former lovers themselves imagine that they'll spend their time arguing and fighting over the kids or that they'll never speak to one another again. But despite what you might think (and what you might see in the media), this is true only half the time.

In the first few years after couples split up they tend to fit into one of the following four categories, says University of Southern California researcher Constance Ahrons:

PERFECT PALS (12 PERCENT OF THE TOTAL)
- Were probably great friends before getting involved romantically and still consider each other great friends now.
- Often make a joint decision to end their relationship.
- Support each other's parenting, help each other out with child care, and make all their decisions keeping in mind the best interests of the children. They'll

have no problem planning a joint birthday or graduation party and inviting everyone on both sides of the family.

♦ May still be angry, but respect each other as individuals and maintain an interest in each other that goes beyond the children. They might spend time together as friends and call just to chat. They also usually maintain close relationships with their former in-laws.

COOPERATIVE COLLEAGUES (38 PERCENT OF THE TOTAL)

♦ Accept that they wouldn't have much to do with each other if it weren't for the children.

♦ Still harbor some anger toward each other and have their disagreements, but manage to work them out cooperatively, recognizing that compromise is important for the sake of the children.

♦ Probably won't call each other up to talk about things that have nothing to do with the kids and probably won't have joint parties, but they'll both attend important events and might even sit together.

ANGRY ASSOCIATES (25 PERCENT OF THE TOTAL)

♦ May still be very angry and bitter with each other about the circumstances that led to the breakup.

♦ Are rarely able to have any kind of discussion without it turning into an argument.

♦ Will attend an important event but won't sit anywhere near each other.

♦ Are not very supportive of each other's parenting and sometimes (inadvertently) put their kids in the middle.

♦ Wish there would be less antagonism and more communication about the kids.

FIERY FOES (25 PERCENT OF THE TOTAL)

♦ Regard each other as the enemy. If asked, they can't remember anything good about their relationship at all.

♦ Almost never see each other or have any kind of communication at all.

♦ Spend a lot of time in court or threatening to go there.

♦ May deliberately undermine each other's parenting by interfering with visitation, or alienating or even kidnapping the children.

♦ Often ask the kids to side with one parent against the other.

♦ Wouldn't be caught dead in the same room at the same time.

♦ Are as angry five years after the breakup as when it first happened.

♦ Wish there would be less antagonism and more communication about the kids.

♦ Fathers often fade out of their children's lives within a few years.

Whether you and your ex end up as "perfect pals" or "fiery foes" depends to a great extent on how well the two of you can cooperate with each other—right from the beginning. The kind of relationship you and your ex establish over the

*"It's a very sad story, honey. I'm a single parent because
I devoured your father."*

first year or so after your breakup will set the tone for your relationship for the rest of your lives.

Here are two more important reasons why keeping things pleasant between you and your ex is so important.

1. Unless you have primary or full custody, your ex controls your access and regulates your contact with your children. If she doesn't enjoy, or at least tolerate, the contact she has with you, your relationship with your children could be in trouble.

2. "High levels of conflict and little cooperation tended to hinder father-child contact and especially father's involvement," write Constance Ahrons and her coauthor, Richard Miller, "while low conflict and high support facilitated the continued father involvement in the children's lives."

Meetings

If you're going to be an involved father, there's almost no way to avoid having at least some contact with your ex: you'll bump into each other at parent-teacher conferences or school plays or while transferring the kids between houses; she may answer the phone when you call her house to talk to your children. And whether or not you see

Watch out for These Communication Killers

Dealing with your ex will probably be a little strained even under the very best of circumstances. And to make things worse, there are a number of common factors than can seriously undermine any hope you might have had of achieving good, healthy, open communication with each other. Not all of these will apply to you, of course, but if one (or more) does, be aware of its destructive potential and try to put it aside during your interactions with your ex.

♦ If she was having an affair, you may be trying to get even in a variety of ways; or if you were having an affair, you might be tempted to give in to anything she asks for, no matter how idiotic.

♦ If she left you, you may be falling all over yourself trying to get her to take you back; if you were the one who left, she may be begging you to come back.

♦ If you were like most men in relationships who try to avoid fights by smiling and saying, "Yes, dear," you may be doing the same now. Or you might be doing the opposite, turning every opportunity into a huge fight, thinking that since there's longer any incentive to stay together, you're free to be a jerk.

♦ The stress of dividing up your property and your debts may have raised all sorts of unpleasant issues.

♦ You may be angry that even though you and your ex aren't together anymore she still calls you up all the time asking you to help her do all those things you used to do: take care of her taxes, fix her car, move heavy objects, and so on.

♦ Your lawyers may have whipped the two of you into an antagonistic frenzy and made you both a lot more hostile toward each other than you really need to be.

each other in person a lot, you'll still have to discuss dozens of kid-related things, such as visitation schedules, school, extracurricular activities, health and safety, and insurance. Even if you and she are getting along great right now, each interaction you have is a potential fight.

That's why it's important to have a plan in place that will allow the two of you to discuss the things you have to discuss while minimizing the risk that you'll end up biting each other's heads off. If you and your ex aren't in the perfect pals category, schedule regular meetings to talk about kid-related business. She might take your calling at any old time or pulling her aside after a soccer game as an attempt to control her life (in some cases she'll be right). You can meet quarterly, monthly, or even more frequently if you feel the need. But before you get out your calendar, both of you should agree on the following ground rules:

- Decide in advance what you're going to discuss at the upcoming meeting.
- Keep all of your discussions focused on the children. Anything else is out of bounds (unless you agree to talk about it). All solutions should have the children's best interest—not yours—as their goal.
- Be polite to each other. No swearing, name calling, or insults.
- Give each other the benefit of the doubt.
- No questions or comments about each other's personal life.
- Either of you can request a break at any time, and the other must agree.
- If you can't reach an agreement on a particular issue, table it until the next meeting.
- If you can't work things out after a reasonable number of meetings, get some mediation.

Some Communication Basics

If communication between you and your ex had broken down before the two of you broke up, you may have forgotten how to talk with each other in a civil, productive manner, so here's a little refresher. Even if you and she are getting along wonderfully, pay attention; things have a nasty way of changing, and not always for the best. Here's how it works:

1. Each person says what he or she has to say—uninterrupted. Stay away from phrases like "You always . . ." "You never . . ." or anything else that you know is guaranteed to put a quick end to your conversations.
2. The speaker asks the listener to repeat—in his or her own words—the main points of what the speaker said. "I understand what you're saying" isn't enough here. Saying the words helps promote understanding—not necessarily agreement, just understanding.
3. The speaker confirms whether the listener has heard what was originally said. If there was some kind of misunderstanding, the speaker repeats the original comment and the listener summarizes again. Repeat this step until the speaker is satisfied that the listener has truly heard and understood.
4. Go back to Step 1, but switch roles: the speaker becomes the listener, the listener the speaker.

Some Guidelines for Running a Meeting

- Pick a time and place that suits both of you. If you're worried about tempers flaring, consider meeting in a public place where the fear of embarrassing yourselves will probably keep you from getting in each other's face too much.
- Show up on time.
- Know your position on each of the agenda items in advance. You might want to make a little cheat sheet with all your most convincing arguments.
- Remember your ground rules (above).

Taking the High Road

Communication and cooperation are supposed to be two-way streets, but things don't always turn out the way they're supposed to. No matter how much of a jerk your ex is and no matter how horribly she treats you, it's critical that you learn to be a *mensch* (that's Yiddish for "a decent human being" or "someone who does the right thing"). Hopefully, if she sees you taking the high road for long enough, she'll eventually decide to join you there. Here are some things that can help make you the mensch you and your kids need you to be:

- ◆ Remember that everything you do has to be done with the best interests of the kids in mind.
- ◆ Unless your ex is doing something truly dangerous, let her parent the way she wants to. She may have been a rotten partner, but that doesn't mean she's a rotten mother.
- ◆ Don't use the kids to relay messages to your ex.
- ◆ Honor your commitments. This means not being late, keeping your promises, following the terms of your parenting agreement to the letter, and making your child-support payments on time.
- ◆ Share information. Send your ex a copy of any information you get about your kids that you think she doesn't have or would be interested in. This includes report cards, notices of parent-teacher meetings, school photographs, and even copies of the kids' art projects.
- ◆ Remember that you can't control her but you can control yourself.
- ◆ Keep your comparisons to a minimum. Yes, she may be living in a mansion while you're sleeping in your old bunk bed in your parents' garage. But that's just the way things are.
- ◆ Be flexible. Kids get sick, and plans change. But don't be so flexible that you let your ex take advantage of you. Stand up for your rights when it's appropriate to do so.
- ◆ Don't deliberately do things that you know will annoy her.

- ◆ Start your meeting with points you're most likely to agree on. Don't move to the next point until you've either settled it or agree to table it.
- ◆ Keep focused on the issue at hand. If things seem to be falling apart or if you feel that you're heading down that old familiar path toward a fight, take a break immediately.
- ◆ Brainstorm about solutions. This means that you both come up with as many solutions as you possibly can to a given problem and go over each of them— even the idiotic ones—eliminating those that are clearly unworkable.
- ◆ Don't make it personal. If you don't like a proposal your ex has made, tell her you

- Listen to what she says to you. Try to find the truth in it. Who knows, she may actually come up with something that can help you.
- Give her the benefit of the doubt, at least for a while. Don't assume that she's deliberately doing things to hurt you.
- Get some help. If your anger at your ex is so consuming that it gets in the way of your parenting, you really need help dealing with it.
- Apologize to her if you've done something wrong. It might hurt do to this, especially if she never apologizes to you, but it's the right thing to do.
- Don't assume you know what she'll say or how she'll react in a given situation. Yes, you may have been together for years, and yes, she may have reacted that way every other time this situation has come up, but people can and do change. Give her a chance. And if she does react the way you thought she would, at least you won't be surprised.
- Force yourself to make reasonable compromises. Granted, now that you're a single father, you've lost one of the biggest natural incentives to cooperate with your ex: the desire to keep your relationship together. But knowing when to compromise may be more important now than it was then.
- Try to keep from getting defensive. One of the most painful things your ex can do to you is question whether you have what it takes to care for your children. If your ex makes this kind of accusation, before blowing up take a second and honestly ask yourself whether there's even a glimmer of truth to what she's saying. If there are areas in which you really need help, you might want to sign yourself up for a parenting class at your local community college.
- Stop relying on her for approval. You're a big boy now and it's up to you to do what *you* think is right.
- Learn to work around her anger. Do not get dragged into a shouting match, no matter how tempting. There's absolutely nothing good that can come from it. Instead of responding to her unreasonable demands, ignore them. And remember, you can always take a walk. You do not have to stick around and be abused—verbally or otherwise.

don't like the proposal and why. Don't tell her that it (or she) is stupid. That's the quickest and surest way to end your meeting early—and antagonistically.

- Take notes. Keep track of everything you decide on. Make sure to give your ex a copy.
- Keep it short. Any longer than an hour is risky. End it on time and try to schedule the next one before you leave.

Changing Relationships with Other People

There's no question that your new status as single father has had a dramatic effect on you relationships with your children and, if you're divorced or unmarried, with your ex. But be prepared: it will also impact a variety of other relationships.

Your Ex's Side of the Family

It seems natural that your ex's side of the family would side with her—and against you. But things are not always quite so clearcut. Even if you and your in-laws were the best of friends, your breakup with your ex will be tough on everyone. You may regret not being able to spend as much time with them as before, and they may find themselves caught between wanting to have a relationship with you and needing to support their daughter.

If you and they didn't get along before, your breakup certainly won't do much for your relationship. For you, this may be a good thing: no more of those annoying family get-togethers, while for them it provides the perfect excuse for taking their hate for you to an all-new level.

If your former in-laws haven't taken sides and things between you are still warm (or at least civil), reassure them that your breakup with their daughter won't affect their relationship with your kids in any way. (I've gone out of my way to emphasize that idea by letting my kids go to their maternal grandparents' for special occasions on "my" days. That may be why to this day I still get a holiday box of peanut brittle from my former mother-in-law.)

Even if your relationship with your former in-laws is hostile, it's still important that you support their relationship with your children (unless there are serious health or safety issues). Never, never, never say anything to your children about how you feel. Those people may not be your family anymore, but they're still your kids'.

Your Children's Changing Relationships with Your Ex's Side of the Family

Knowing that you support their relationships with your former in-laws teaches your children a wonderful lesson: ending a relationship with one person doesn't mean ending a relationship with everyone. It will also keep the children from feeling that they're being disloyal to you by loving people who aren't part of your family anymore. So never, never threaten to cut the kids off from the relatives or vice versa.

If you're a noncustodial parent you won't have to worry too much about encouraging your kids' relationships with their other family. But if you're a custodial parent you might have to, since your former in-laws probably won't feel comfortable approaching you about spending time with the kids. This means that even if your relationship is somewhat tense, you'll need to take the initiative—by staying in touch with them to make sure they're able to see the kids often enough, by offering to include them in family activities, or by suggesting times that they and the kids can get together.

Widowers: In-law Problems

Although you might think that your wife's death would bring both sides of the family together, this isn't always the case, especially if you didn't get along very well with her parents before she died. They may, for example, resent (somewhat irrationally) that you're alive while their daughter is dead, or suspect that you're in some way responsible for her death. If they're fairly traditional, they may wonder whether you'll be able to do a good enough job raising your children without a mother around and tell you as often as they can what a horrid job you're doing.

If your in-laws are behaving this way there's not really much you can do about it except to ignore them or tell them that they have no say in the way you parent. If necessary, remind them that no matter how they feel, they absolutely may not criticize you or anything you do in front of your children, and that doing so may result in their not being able to see their grandchildren as often as they'd like. But try not to let things get this far. You may be showing your in-laws who's boss, but you'll be punishing your kids in the process.

Your Side of the Family

Your parents will probably react in much the same way as your ex's do. And part of their reaction will have to do with the kind of relationship they had with your ex. If they didn't like her, they'll probably take your side completely and may want to celebrate your getting out of something they think you never should have been in. But if they were close to her, it will be a little more complicated. If she left you, they may feel rejected and hurt. If you left her or were having an affair, they may be furious at you for having destroyed a perfectly good marriage.

Whether they approve of your new situation or not, most relatives, unless they're seriously screwed up, come around eventually, showing their support in a variety of ways: baby-sitting, offering you a shoulder to cry on, or helping you out financially. My parents, for example, offered to pay for my therapy, which I needed a lot of after my divorce. Sometimes, though, getting help from relatives—especially parents— can be very difficult and can bring up all sorts of issues you'd rather not deal with. Taking (or borrowing) money from them, perhaps for the first time in years, for example, or having to move back into their house (see page 178) can strain even the best of relationships. This raises an interesting problem: your relatives may not want to offer to help you because they don't want to offend you. And you may not want to ask because you're too embarrassed. But if it turns out that you need the kind of help relatives can provide, ask for it. You'll be doing everyone a favor.

Your Children's Changing Relationships with Your Side of the Family

If you're a custodial parent, your relatives' relationship with your children won't change much. But if you don't have custody of your children, your breakup will probably alter their relationship quite a bit, because your ex, having primary custody of the children, can essentially control how much time your children can spend with your side of the family. The emotional attachment your children and your relatives have with one another can suffer greatly from a lack of contact. Here are some things you can do to reduce the chance that this will happen:

+ **Don't hog the kids.** Since their time with you is limited, you may not want to share them with anyone else. But you need to allow them some time to be with their grandparents and other relatives—sometimes together as a family, sometimes without you.
+ **Never let your parents say anything bad about your ex in front of the children.**
+ **Check your relatives' motives.** They may shower the children with gifts, take them shopping, or invite them to the theater and other special places. Sometimes this is just for fun and that's okay. But sometimes it's a subtle attempt to buy the children's affections by making the time your kids spend with your side of the

A Special Note about Grandparents

"Inter-generational relationships are important to all children's development," says Patrick McKenry, a professor family relations and human development at Ohio State University. "However, following a divorce, these relationships can be even more important. They can foster additional social support—and different types of support—not received from the parents." Grandparents also give children a sense of community, of belonging to an ongoing family, one with a past as well as a future.

Unfortunately, children often have a lot less contact with what McKenry calls "non-custodial grandparents"—your parents if you don't have custody, your ex's if she doesn't. Try not to let this happen. Many kids are quite close to their grandparents and "losing" them in a divorce or separation can be quite a blow, often leading to depression.

"Your father was just about your age when he began to swear."

What If You've Moved Back Home

If you're a widower, chances are you won't have to move out of your current home. But if you're divorced or were never married, chances are you will. And if you're like a lot of newly single fathers and don't have the resources to get a new place right away, you may find yourself living at your parents' house for a while. In my case, it took me about two months after selling my house to find an apartment that was cheap enough and big enough for me, the kids, and my office. As mentioned above, moving back into your parents' house—even if it's only temporary—can be difficult. Here are a few of the issues that might come up:

- **Privacy.** How much control are your parents going to have over how you run your life while you're living under their roof? Can they set a curfew? Can they restrict your dating or at least your bringing women home? (It might be a little hard to have dates over anyway if you're sleeping in a bunk bed in your old room.)

- **Strings.** Can you live there for free or are they expecting you to pay rent, do yard work, or make your bed? At the very least you should chip in for groceries, do some laundry once in a while, and try to keep the place clean.

- **Space.** I slept in my parents' guest room (they'd turned my old room into an office!), which was okay when I didn't have the kids. But when the kids were there, it got kind of cramped.

- **Identity.** While moving home can make you feel loved and secure, it can also make you feel like a child again—a feeling you might find somewhat uncomfortable.

- **Resentment.** Your parents might be glad (or at least tolerant) that you're there, but they might feel that they're being taken advantage of if you use them as baby-sitters every night.

- **Relationships.** Being back at home might put you and your parents into more regular contact than either of you would like.

family more fun than the time they spend with their mother's side. This may seem like a good idea but it almost always backfires, making the kids expect gifts and treats every time they see someone from your side.

- **Make sure your parents mail or deliver birthday and holiday gifts to your house.** No matter who has the kids on those days, the presents—even if they get delivered a little late—should clearly be coming from your side of the family. If they're delivered to your ex's house, the kids may never know that gifts are coming from your side of the family, and they may take that as a sign that they aren't loved anymore.

"Big date tonight, Dad. Can I borrow the cardigan?"

Relationships with Your Children's Teachers and Schools

Because so many fathers leave anything having to do with school up to their wives or girlfriends, they often never have a chance to develop any kind of relationships with their children's teachers or school administrators. This is big mistake. Your kids spend a big chunk of their day at school, and if you aren't on top of what's happening there you're going to miss a lot of what's going on with your child.

If you have joint legal custody (which you probably do), you have the right to know everything that could possibly affect your child at school, such as psychological or academic testing, and you have a right to a copy of every single piece of paper your child brings home from school—report cards, notifications of book and bake sales, and invitations to try out for the soccer team.

Unfortunately, just because you're a man, teachers and administrators may assume that you either don't have any rights or aren't really interested. If so, straighten them out, gently but firmly. When it comes to your rights, all you should have to do is show them a copy of your joint-custody decree. When it comes to demonstrating your level of interest, the best way is to do some volunteer work at the school. Personally, I always find it incredibly annoying that people assume that mothers are interested in their children and that fathers have to prove they are, but there's not much you can do to change that right now. The bottom line is that the more time you spend at the school, the better the people there will get to know you and the more they'll respect you. The best part of all is that since they probably aren't expecting very much from you anyway, they're likely to regard even the slightest effort on your part as an act of heroism. And while you're at the school, spend a few minutes getting to know the school secretary. She's the one who probably does the actual mailings.

No matter what you do, though, you'll still have to keep pushing to be kept informed. It took more than a year for the folks at my older daughter's school to do what I asked them to, despite the fact that I volunteer in the classroom an hour a week (and my ex doesn't), that I coordinate (and help cook) three school-wide spaghetti lunches a year (and my ex doesn't), and that my ex and I share custody and expenses, including tuition, equally.

Keeping current on what's happening at your kids' schools is only part of the job. You also need to make sure your kids are doing their homework, are showing up for band rehearsals, and are properly dressed for field trips. This can be especially hard when the kids are going back and forth between houses—an assignment that your child starts at your ex's house may be due on a day she's at yours. You may feel that keeping track of homework and other school-related things is your child's responsibility, and if they're older than about ten, you're right. But because you're the grown-up, you need to help them any way you can. Not turning in assignments or constantly forgetting them can really hurt your kids. Their teachers may criticize them, their grades may suffer, and maybe worst of all, their friends might make fun of them.

The best way to handle this type of problem is to work with your ex to make sure that both of you are fully up to date on everything having to do with your children's school life and that you establish consistent rules for homework at both houses. If you can't do that, you may have to ask your children's teachers to send you duplicates of all relevant assignments.

Notes:

When Things Go Wrong

Access Interference

The goal of the family law system is supposed to be to protect the child's relationship with both parents. But if you were thinking about relying on the courts to protect your relationship with your children, you'd better think again. As we've talked about earlier, the courts and the legal system place plenty of barriers between fathers and their kids—the most notable being giving primary custody to mothers about 85 percent of the time. But judges and legislators aren't the only ones who don't fully appreciate father-child relationships.

"Many times, mothers will disrupt visitation by getting the kids involved in something really fun just before the father gets there," says Dr. Richard Warshak, author of *The Custody Revolution*. "That way, if the father tries to enforce his visitation, the kids will see him as the bad guy—the guy who made them stop having fun."

In their landmark book, *Surviving the Breakup*, researchers Judith Wallerstein and Joan Kelly found that 20 to 50 percent of custodial mothers "actively tried to sabotage the meetings by sending the children away just before the father's arrival, by insisting that the child was ill or had pressing homework to do, by making a scene . . ." or by simply refusing to let the father have his court-ordered time with his children. Translated into plain numbers, this means that each year, more than six million children are denied access to their fathers.

Mothers' interference with fathers' access comes out in other, more subtle, ways as well, say Wallerstein and Kelly. Your ex might resist accommodating your necessary schedule changes, "forget" that you were coming, insist that you follow a rigid schedule on each visit, refuse to allow your child to go with you if you bring along a friend—male or female—"in a thousand mischievous, mostly petty, devices designed to humiliate the visiting parent," they write, "and to deprecate him in the eyes of his children."

Getting Your Access Enforced: Good Luck

Theoretically, at least, judges have the power to fine your ex, cite her for contempt of court, or even jail her. But don't hold your breath. The first obstacle, of course, is money. It will cost you an average of about $4,000 to file a single court action to enforce your visitation. And even if you've got the money and even if you win, there's no guarantee that anything will change. While family court judges are quite willing to lock up men who get behind on their child support, they are extremely reluctant to do anything to punish mothers who refuse to comply with visitation orders. In 1989, for example, Cyndy Garvey, the ex-wife of former Dodgers star Steve Garvey, was found guilty of forty-two counts of willfully violating a court order that permitted her ex-husband to visit his daughters. She received a suspended sentence.

A recent survey in Indiana turned up 272 fathers who had gone to court to try to enforce their court-ordered visitation. Only 62 percent were actually granted a hearing and absolutely zero mothers were jailed for having violated a court order. And 77 percent of the men who had hearings reported that the access-denial problem actually got worse after going to court. The message from all this is pretty clear: there are no consequences—for women, anyway—for violating court orders.

So what can you do if your ex interferes with your court-ordered access to your children? Well, to start with, try reasoning with her. Gently remind her that you have a court order and that by keeping you from the kids or the kids from you she's violating the law and, worst of all, hurting the children. You might also follow up with a firmly worded but nonantagonistic letter. If the situation doesn't change for the better, have your lawyer talk to her lawyer or have him write a sternly worded letter directly to her.

If after all that she continues to block your visitation, you need to do the following:

♦ Remain calm. No swearing, breaking things, or other outbursts, especially in front of the children.
♦ Get someone to witness the ways your ex interferes with your access.
♦ Take detailed notes, including everything she says, your responses, the kids' responses (if you know), and anything else that seems relevant.
♦ If it's legal in your state (check with your lawyer), consider tape recording a typical scene—from the moment you approach her house to collect the kids until the moment you leave without them. Speak slowly, bring a copy of your visitation order with you, and make sure the recorder catches what she says.

The Subtlest Interference

Even if your ex doesn't obstruct your access to your children, she might still interfere with your time together. How? By insisting that you follow certain parenting rules when the kids are with you. She may have simply bought into the "motherhood mystique" (page 48) and believe that she instinctively knows how to take care of children better than you do. Or she may believe that when you have the kids you're just lending her a hand, like some kind of hired help. Either way, you're likely to find her attitude frustrating and perhaps even humiliating.

If you can, talk to her—without making accusations—about how you're feeling, and remind her that she can be any kind of mother she wants to be, but unless you're doing something negligent or dangerous she has no say in the way you father.

♦ Make a police report. Bring a copy of your visitation order and schedule to the station house and ask for an officer or sheriff to accompany you back to her house to enforce your rights.

♦ Go to court. Even though it's expensive and your chances for success are limited, caving in without a fuss will give her the idea that you don't care and that she can continue to abuse you any way she likes.

♦ Show up for your visitation—even if you know your ex is going to interfere with it. Somehow your kids will get the message that you're not giving up.

♦ Get to know your children's teachers, soccer coaches, swimming instructors, and anyone else you can think of who can keep you informed of events that your ex might not bother to tell you about. You also might want to volunteer for the PTA and do other things that make you a known—and respected— commodity.

♦ Don't do anything stupid. Don't, for example, even think about kidnapping your child (see page 194). And don't stop paying your child support. Yes, this seems like the best way to force your ex to comply, but it will probably land you in jail. As far as judges are concerned, child support and access are two completely separate issues and you'll get into trouble if you try to link them. Besides that, you'll be giving your ex yet another excuse to keep the kids away from you, and you could force her (in her mind, anyway) to take more drastic steps, such as parental alienation (pages 184–87) or kidnapping (pages 191–94).

♦ Get involved in a local or national fathers' rights group. You'll meet a lot of other men in the same situation and learn from their experience. In addition, even if there's nothing you can do to make your own situation any better, you might be able to help someone else.

For Gay Dads Only

When it comes to having problems with exes, gay fathers are no exception. So if your ex is hostile toward you or your lifestyle (which is especially likely if your homosexuality was a major factor in your breakup), be sure to read pages 60–62. And if you think her anger is severe enough, you should be prepared for her to turn the children against you. If you think this is a real possibility, read about parental alienation on pages 184–87.

In many cases, your ex's fury may be dissipated with some joint counseling and/or mediation. But whether that works or not, remember this: your children need you just as much as any straight father's kids need him. So do not give in to anyone's pressure to give up custody or settle for less visitation, no matter how guilty you feel, no matter how much you might want to get your ex off your back. Doing so may make one of the grown-ups involved feel better for a while, but it will hurt your kids in the long run.

Whether your breakup with your ex was angry or amicable, you'd do well to keep the following points in mind at all times, say attorney Hayden Curry and his colleagues:

♦ Be sensitive to the feelings and needs of your ex.

♦ Avoid going to court if at all possible.

♦ Even if you're sure that avoiding court is hopeless, try again and keep trying.

Parental Alienation

In most cases, when a relationship breaks up parents are able to place their individual problems and needs behind those of their children. Even when the split-up is extremely angry and filled with conflict, these parents manage to keep their eyes on what's really important. Perhaps the most effective means of doing this is by supporting their children's relationship with the other parent.

Sometimes, though, one parent may put his or her own emotional needs first and may look for ways to manipulate or inflict some kind of pain on the other. And to a parent who's really intent on doing this, children are particularly effective weapons. Most commonly, this means that a parent will ask the children to ally themselves with that parent, often to the exclusion of the other. This type of parent may also begin a subtle campaign to brainwash his or her children against the other parent.

Sound far-fetched? It isn't. In a 1991 study sponsored by the American Bar Association, researchers Clawar and Rivlin found that 80 percent of children of divorce showed evidence of being "brainwashed" to think less of one parent than the other.

Overall, this type of behavior—the brainwashing and asking the children to take sides—is part of what Dr. Richard Gardner, a child psychiatrist at Columbia University, has identified as Parental Alienation Syndrome (PAS). And according to Gardner (and most other researchers in the field), 90 percent of the alienating parents are mothers.

PAS exists on various levels. Here's a brief look at each one, with some identifying factors suggested by Dr. Gardner and Dr. Peggie Ward, who has also done extensive research into PAS. If you recognize *any* of these symptoms, read page 187.

Mild

The mildly alienating mother won't actively try to turn your child against you, but she doesn't really see the need for father-child contact. She's likely to say things like, "If you really want to see your father it's up to you." She also doesn't see a lot of value in father-child communication between visits, and although she won't discourage it, she won't do anything to facilitate or encourage it. She's put off by the idea of being anyplace at the same time you are and will tell your child that if you're there, she won't go. She also is quite willing to consider moving out of the area (with your child), completely disregarding how important you are to your child.

Moderate

The moderately alienating mother is considerably less veiled in her criticism of you, saying things to the kids like, "You can see your father, but you know how I feel about it," or, "If you don't go see your father now, he'll take us to court." She makes a more concerted effort to undermine the image your child has of you by destroying pictures of you, artwork you made, or anything else that might remind your child of you. She'll "accidentally" tell your child negative stories about you ("Your father is a drug addict—oops, I shouldn't have said that," or, "If you only knew the horrible things he's done . . ."). When you come to pick up the kids, she may refuse to allow you into her house and may not even let you ring the doorbell. She argues with you, calls you names, and makes outlandish accusations within earshot of the kids. The message, subtle yet clear, is that there's something wrong with you and that your child is better off without you.

Overt

The overtly alienating mother is convinced that the father is—and always was— a worthless individual who should be kept away from his children. If she sees you, she won't be even close to civil. She tells lies to the kids about you ("He never pays his child support," or "Don't be alone with him—he'll hurt you"); tries to convince the kids you don't love them ("Your dad told me he hates you"); criticizes you openly ("Your father is such a jerk"); makes the children keep secrets ("Don't tell your father what we did this weekend"); may even threaten to withdraw her love from the children if they express a desire to see you or spend time with you; and may tell the kids that you're the one completely responsible for the breakup. She may also neglect to inform you about special events or even emergencies and will then tell the children that you didn't show up because you don't care about them. And she may tell your children that the new man in her life is their "new daddy" and to forget about the "old" one.

Severe
When things get this far the child has become completely brainwashed and believes every bad thing your ex has said about you. The child and the mother are in what psychiatrists call a *folie-à-deux,* a shared psychotic delusion. "At this stage the child is so enmeshed with the alienating parent that he or she agrees totally that the target parent is a villain and the scum of the earth," says Ward. "The child takes on the alienating parent's desires, emotions and hatreds and verbalizes them to all as his own." When alienation is this severe, your children will make up just about any excuse for why they don't want to be with you. And it's quite common for the child's hatred to extend beyond you to your family, friends, or anyone else with whom the child once had good relations.

Don't Do This at Home
I've used the word *mother* to describe the alienating parent, but there's a chance that you'll recognize your own behavior in the descriptions I've given. If you do, stop any alienating behavior immediately and spend some time thinking about why you're doing it. You may think that you're hurting your ex, but in reality you're hurting your child a lot more. First of all, you're teaching your child that it's okay to lie to achieve a goal. Most important, though, "The effect will be to place the child in a severe loyalty bind, a position wherein the child believes she must choose which of her two parents she will 'love' more," writes Peggie Ward. "To have to choose between parents is itself damaging to the child, and, if the end result is the exclusion of a parent from the child's life, the injury is irreparable."

And finally, you may be placing yourself at risk. If your ex accuses you of alienating the kids against her and a judge agrees, you could find yourself with limited, supervised visitation (see page 87 for more on this).

False Allegations of Abuse

Perhaps the most horrific alienation weapon used these days is the accusation of child abuse. If you are accused, you *will* be presumed guilty—unless you can disprove the charges. "And that's not easy," says Peter Firpo, an attorney who specializes in abuse cases. "By the time you even hear that you're accused, your child has probably been seen by a therapist or a child protective services officer who sees his or her role as to 'validate' the accusation." And things move pretty quickly from

What to Do If Your Child Is Being Alienated

Recognizing the symptoms of parental alienation is one thing; doing something about them is yet another. Here are some things you must do if you suspect that your child is being alienated:

- Strengthen your relationship with your child. Even if your ex makes the prospect of picking up your child seem unpleasant, do it anyway. The better your relationship with your child, the less the chance that she'll believe the bad things that your ex is saying about you.
- Respond at the first signs. In the milder stages your ex many not even be aware of what she's doing. Telling her about it gently may be enough to stop it.
- Reassure your ex that you aren't trying to hurt her. Many alienating women do so out of a fear that the child's father is trying to take the child away. If you can get your ex to see that you have no such intention, she may stop what she's doing.
- Ask your ex to talk to you—and listen to what she says. Alienation is often the result of feeling unheard or misunderstood. The more she talks to you about what's bugging her, the less she'll try to use the kids to punish you.
- Notify your attorney immediately. Courts are paying more attention these days to the ways mothers and fathers facilitate each other's relationship with their children. A parent found to be deliberately interfering could end up with less custody instead of more.
- Try not to push her buttons. Annoying your ex, posturing, making loud and obnoxious demands about your rights could push her even further.
- Cooperate with your ex—but not too much. Some fathers are so eager to work things out that they inadvertently let an angry, manipulative ex-wife manipulate them right out of a relationship with their children.
- Learn more about what's happening. Richard Gardner's book *The Parental Alienation Syndrome* is an excellent resource.
- Have your children undergo a psychological evaluation—but only if you're truly suspicious. A well-trained psychologist may be able to tell you whether your child is being alienated.

there. The instant you're accused of having molested your child, all your contact with the child will be cut off until the question gets heard in court, and that could be anywhere from a few days to a few months later.

If you think your ex is the type who might use this kind of weapon, it's important to start trying to protect yourself right now. Here's how:

- Never let yourself get suckered into a fight, particularly on the phone. Your ex and her lawyer are just looking for evidence that you're violent and unstable.

Don't answer questions like, "Why did you touch Sally down there?" Categorically deny her accusations, and end the conversation immediately.

♦ Tape your conversations with her. But before you turn on your recorder, check with your lawyer to make sure doing so is legal in your state. It's a tricky area of the law, so be careful.

♦ Stay squeaky clean during the entire divorce and custody process: don't drink, don't drive too fast, don't even stiff a waitress on her tip. A sharp lawyer (employed by your ex) can make something as innocuous as a speeding ticket into just another example of what an irresponsible brute you are.

The SAID Syndrome

Charges of abuse are, of course, made against men in intact families, but they are far more common in cases of divorce, coming up in as many as 30 percent of custody disputes. A variety of studies have concluded, however, that 75 to 80 percent of these divorce-related abuse allegations are completely false.

In the late 1980s and early 1990s psychologists identified what is now a clinically recognized syndrome, Sexual Allegations in Divorce (SAID), which identifies a set of behaviors that are almost unique to divorce-related false accusations and, if present, should raise a red flag with investigators.

Generally speaking, women who make deliberately false allegations are obsessed with hurting their ex-husbands as much as possible. They'll frequently coach their children into making statements against the father and will shop around until they find a therapist, a doctor, or some other professional who will support their claims. In contrast, parents who are genuinely concerned about their children typically hope that the child was not sexually abused and tend to be relieved when an investigator concludes that abuse is unlikely.

Here are a few other clues that an accusation may be SAID-related. One or more of these may indicate that the accusation is possibly false:

♦ The mother brought the initial accusation, not the child.
♦ The allegations surfaced long after the relationship ended.
♦ The mother had never made any accusations of abuse during the relationship.
♦ The father recently remarried or started a relationship with another woman.
♦ The father recently received a more liberal custody or visitation package.
♦ The child seems to have been coached, uses age-inappropriate words, or looks to the accusing parent for approval while describing the alleged abuse.
♦ Money or custody issues are still unresolved and in hot dispute.

Child Protective Services (CPS): Not Your Friends, Not Your Child's Either

In 97 percent of the cases where the police conduct an actual investigation into

What to Do If You're Falsely Accused

Being falsely accused of having abused your child will probably scar you for life. It also may change forever your relationship with your child and even the way your friends and family look at you. There are some steps you can take, however, to minimize the toll that a false accusation will take on your life and on your child's:

♦ Control your emotions. Assuming you're innocent (if you're not, please close this book immediately and turn yourself in), you'll probably feel like strangling your ex and her lawyer. And while that may make you feel better, it won't help your case. Most attorneys agree that loud, irrational, aggressive behavior will just make the law-enforcement personnel, judges, psychiatrists, and anyone else involved in your case more suspicious and negatively inclined toward you.

♦ Cooperate fully. Not doing so will raise all sorts of suspicions.

♦ Respond quickly and aggressively. You have two vital missions at this point, suggests attorney Jeffery Leving: to protect your child from further trauma (the never-ending psychological and medical examinations that abuse accusations always entail) and to defend your innocence.

♦ Hire a lawyer with a strong track record in handling sex-abuse cases. This may mean that you'll have to replace your current lawyer or bring in an expert to work with him or her. It may be expensive, but "incompetent or inexperienced counsel may cost you your children, your reputation, and your freedom," writes Leving.

♦ Agree to submit to an outside psychologist's examination only if he or she will also examine your ex's mental state.

♦ Give your ex the benefit of the doubt. This one is especially hard— especially after the walls of the system have started closing in on you. But the fact is that she may have seen something she genuinely thought was a symptom of abuse. Try to imagine how you'd behave if you'd seen something suspicious. Your goal should be to get the truth out, not to get revenge.

an abuse charge, they are not able to substantiate the allegations, so no criminal charges are filed. But to the dismay of the thousands of men (and a few women) falsely accused each year, this doesn't mean that the investigation will end, or that they'll be able to see their children anytime soon. Even after the police drop the criminal investigation, CPS can still conduct its own. And to help them do so, the courts have given them extremely broad powers.

For example, CPS workers armed with nothing more than an allegation—and without a court order or a hearing—can force fathers and children into therapy for an unlimited amount of time, can compel fathers to take lie detector tests, and can deny them access to their children—even if they have a court order allowing such access.

In many cases CPS farms out part of its investigations to outside therapists who should be able to weed out obviously false charges. But all too often the therapists CPS uses are "validators" who, like the referring CPS worker, have already made a decision before hearing what all the parties—including the father—have to say. When Dr. Richard Gardner, a noted expert in child-abuse investigation, asked various "validators" why they did not interview the father as part of their evaluation, he was frequently told, "[The father] would deny it anyway so there's no point in my seeing him," or "My job is not to do an investigation; my job is only to interview the child to find out whether the child was sexually abused."

A number of these "validators" also use other incentives to back up allegations of abuse—even when they know they're false. In a recent grand jury investigation of CPS wrongdoing in San Diego, California, a number of therapists testified that they were afraid they'd be dropped from CPS's list of outside therapists (and, of course, suffer the corresponding drop in income) if they didn't confirm CPS's recommendations.

Other Abuse Accusations

An accusation of domestic violence may have nearly the same effect as an accusation of sex abuse: no access to your child until a judge rules on the charge. But keep in mind that, as strange as it sounds, men are the victims of domestic violence at least as often as women. The problem is that men rarely see their wives' shoves, slaps, or thrown dishes as violence.

Now's the time to change your thinking. If your ex has been violent toward you— or the kids—file charges immediately. This does two things: it helps protect the kids from further abuse, and it helps protect you if she attempts to bring charges against you.

Don't Overreact

Although 90 to 95 percent of the accusers in divorce-related abuse allegations are women, men are not immune from the hate and rage that too often result in this type of behavior. As you've seen on these pages, an allegation—even a well-meaning one—can have devastating consequences. So before you even think of publicly accusing your ex of having hurt your children, take a deep breath and consider whether there are any reasonable explanations for whatever it is you're worried about. (Diaper rash? A bruise? A legitimate medical problem? and so forth.) If you're still worried, talk it over with your ex, but don't do it in a way that would make her defensive. Your objective is simple: to find out what's wrong with your child. Treat your ex the way you'd like to be treated in a similar circumstance.

Kidnapping

Every year some 350,000 children are kidnapped—not by strangers, but by one of their parents. Now before you panic, consider this: the vast majority of these "family abductions" are in fact custody-related delays, such as one parent returning a child a few minutes late after a court-ordered visitation. Most last from only a few days to a week (only 10 percent go on a month or more). And only 17 percent of the searching parents really don't know where the missing child is.

Relaxed? Well, don't be. There are still more than 3,000 children a year who are snatched and hidden away during ugly custody battles, according to Tim Riley, an expert in statistical assessment. And many of those children are gone for years or never come back at all.

Fathers and mothers are just about equally likely to abduct their children, but as Canadian criminologist John Kiedrowski points out, the circumstances are quite different:

MOTHERS WHO KIDNAP THEIR CHILDREN . . .	FATHERS WHO KIDNAP THEIR CHILDREN . . .
♦ Take the children after a custody order is issued. They're disappointed when the father gets a more favorable custody arrangement or visitation schedule than they had hoped for.	♦ Take the children before a custody order is made. They expect that the court will give custody to the mother.
♦ Tend to be unemployed.	♦ Tend to be employed.
♦ Generally keep the children over two months.	♦ Generally keep the children a week or less.
♦ Take the child with the express goal of keeping him from the father.	♦ Take the child with the goal of getting to spend more time with him.

About three-quarters of child abductions involve kids ages two to twelve (about 35 percent are under five, 22 percent are six to eight, and 26 percent are nine to eleven). Babies under two years old and teens are rarely kidnapped. Kids are far more likely to be abducted from their home (or at least one of them) than from a school or day care.

Red Flags to Watch Out For

Here are some signs that should make you at least raise your eyebrows:

- Your ex has threatened that "one of these days" she's going to take the kids away from you.
- She's extremely angry at you and is looking for ways to punish you.
- She has been unsuccessful in trying to alienate the children from you.
- She's been unsuccessful in trying to get you to reconcile with her.
- She has accused you or is currently accusing you of having abused your children.
- You recently were awarded custody or fairly liberal visitation against her wishes.

What You Can Do to Reduce the Risk

If your ex is intent on kidnapping your children, there's not much you can do to prevent it from happening entirely. Still, there are some precautionary steps, several of which were suggested by Child Find of America, that you can take to make it less likely:

- Stay on good terms with your ex. The closer and more cooperative the two of you are with each other, the less motivation either of you will have to want to deprive the other of the children.
- Don't play visitation games (interfering with or preventing her visitation, bringing the kids back late when you have them). If she's angry at you already, this will only make it worse.
- Have a legally binding custody agreement that specifies who is to have the children when and restricts either parent from taking the children away without the agreement of the other. You'll have a very difficult time getting anyone to pay attention to you if you can't prove that you have at least some custody of your child.
- Talk with your children. Teach them what to do in case of an abduction. Tell them often that you will always want them; that unless they've attended your funeral and have seen that you have died—and this is not likely to happen—that you are alive and searching for them.
- Apply for a passport for your child, then tell the State Department not to issue another one in the child's name to anyone else. This will make it a lot harder for your ex to take the children out of the country.
- Keep an up-to-date file with important information on your ex: her social security number, driver's license number, license plate number, credit card information, and employer (including phone number and address), as well as contacts for as many of her relatives and friends as you can keep track of.
- If she's threatening to take the kids, find someone to witness her threats or make a tape recording of them.
- Let the police know. Give them a copy of your custody decree and tell them why you're worried.
- Give copies of your custody decree to your child's day-care center, school, or

baby-sitters. Also give them a list of the people who are authorized—and those who are not authorized under any circumstances—to take your child.

♦ Make sure your child knows his name, your name, your address, your phone number, and how to make collect phone calls. He needs to know that he has the right to find a way to contact you no matter who forbids it. If he's old enough, you also might want to have him memorize the phone number of the National Center for Missing or Exploited Children (NCMEC) at 1-800-THE LOST (843-5678) or Child Find America at 1-800-I-AM LOST (426-5678). Both organizations help parents seek out their lost or missing children.

What to Do If Your Child Has Been Abducted

1. Immediately file a missing person report with your local police department— and be sure to bring a copy of your custody order. Under the Federal Uniform Child Custody Jurisdiction Act you should be able to get your custody and visitation orders enforced in all fifty states. But you'll have to push hard. Law enforcement is notoriously reluctant to get involved in these issues. If you think your ex and child have left the country, say so; the police may be able to notify their counterparts in the country or region you suspect.

2. Contact the NCMEC or Child Find.

3. Contact your lawyer. Even if your ex had primary custody, kidnapping is a clear violation of your custody decree, and your judge needs to know about this right away. It's also especially important to get your attorney involved early because you're not likely to get a lot of help from anyone else. Police departments and even the NCMEC and Child Find are extremely reluctant to help men, even if they're the custodial parents.

4. If you're sure your ex and child have left the country, send a fax to the US Department of State, Department of Children's Issues, at (202) 647-2835. Be sure to include the following:

   ◊ Child's full name (and any aliases)
   ◊ Child's date and place of birth
   ◊ Child's passport number, date, and place of issuance
   ◊ Copies of any court orders or police reports
   ◊ Your ex's full name (and any aliases)
   ◊ Her date and place of birth
   ◊ Her passport number, date, and place of issuance
   ◊ Her occupation
   ◊ Probable date of departure
   ◊ Flight information
   ◊ Details of ties to a foreign country, such as the names, addresses, and telephone numbers of friends, relatives, place of employment, or business connections there

Don't Even Think about It

+ If you're worried that your ex is abusive or dangerous, try—and keep trying—all legal means to get the situation addressed.
+ Kidnapping is a horrible thing to do to your children. They'll miss their mother, just like they'd miss you if the situation were reversed. If you're worried that your ex will keep you from seeing your child, the solution is not to keep your child from your ex.
+ It's against the law. When you get caught—and you undoubtedly will—you'll be going to jail for a while. Do you really want your kids to see you that way?
+ It always backfires. The kids will act out, blame you (rightfully) for keeping them from their mother, and probably end up hating you in the long run.

Notes:

Striking a Balance between Work and Family

Most fathers, single or otherwise, are "torn between the need to provide economically for the family and the desire to be a nurturing father," writes author David Giveans. Finding the right balance between these two seemingly mutually exclusive options is difficult enough when you're doing your parenting with a partner. But it's especially challenging when you're a single father, and all the more so if you're the primary custodian.

The simple fact is that you can't maintain much of a relationship with your children if you don't spend time with them. Fortunately, although you may never be able to resolve your work/family conflicts completely, there are a few ways you can maximize your time with your family, minimize your stress, and avoid trashing your career.

Making Some Changes

Flexible Scheduling

"One of the conditions for men to become and stay highly involved in childrearing is for their work hours to be and continue to be flexible," writes John Snarey. If you don't have primary custody of your kids, you might want to consider running one of the following flexible scheduling options past your employer:

- On days when you don't have your kids you'll work ten-hour days so you can take your kid-days off.
- If that doesn't work, suggest that on days when the kids will be with you that

*"Sorry to get you out of school this early, son,
but I need your help with this computer."*

you'll work a different schedule, perhaps 6:00 A.M. to 2:00 P.M. instead of the usual 9:00 to 5:00.

♦ Consider telecommuting a day or two a week (see pages 197–98 for more on this). It probably won't reduce the number of hours you work, but it will give you time with your kids that you might have spent stuck in traffic or sitting on the subway.

If you're the primary custodian, the flexible scheduling options discussed above may help solve some of your work/family conflicts. If not, you might want to consider some of these slightly more bold possibilities (assuming, of course, that you can afford them):

♦ Job sharing. You and another person—perhaps another single parent—divide up the responsibilities of the job. You would probably use the same office and desk. A typical job-share schedule might have you working two days one week and three days the next, while your workplace partner does the opposite. One warning: be very careful to negotiate a continuation of your health benefits. Many employers drop them for less-than-full-time employees.

♦ Switch to part-time, which is more or less the same as job sharing, except you probably won't have to share a desk with someone else.

♦ Become a consultant to your current employer. This can be a great way for you to get a lot of flexibility over your workday. There are also tax advantages, particularly if you set up a home office (see more on this in the next section). At the very least, you'll be able to deduct auto mileage and a percentage of your phone and utility bills and maybe even part of your rent or mortgage. But be sure to check with an accountant first; the IRS uses certain "tests" to determine whether someone is an employee or a consultant. If, for example, your client provides you with an office, a secretary, business cards, and a company car, you're an employee, no matter what your consulting contract says. Also, remember that if you become a consultant, you'll lose your benefit package. So be sure to build the cost of that package (or the amount you'll have to pay to replace it) into the daily or hourly rate you negotiate with your soon-to-be-former employer.

Working at Home (Telecommuting)

Far too many managers believe in the importance of daily "face time" (actually being seen at the office). The truth is that face time is highly overrated and often unnecessary. In all the years I've been writing, I've worked for dozens of magazines and newspapers, most of which are several thousand miles from my home. And in most cases I've never even met my editors. One of the disk jockeys at the San Francisco radio station where I host a parenting show lives in Washington, D.C. She records her music introductions on high-quality tapes and overnights them to us. I'm the first to admit that being a writer (or a DJ) isn't a typical job. But millions of Americans do work that doesn't require their physical presence in any particular place at any particular time (engineers, computer programmers, and just about anybody else who sits at a desk). If you're not a construction worker or a retail salesman, you might be a prime candidate for telecommuting.

Now don't get too excited; it's not as if you and your boss will never see each other again. Most telecommuters are out of the office only a day or two a week. And if it's going to be a workable option at all, telecommuting is something you'll have to ease yourself (and your employer) into. Like the other flexible work options discussed in this chapter, telecommuting is designed to give you more time with your family. But if you think you'll be able to save money on child care or have your baby sit on your lap while you crunch numbers, you're sorely mistaken.

If you want to give telecommuting a try, here's what you'll probably need:
- A computer (compatible with your employer's system)
- An additional phone line or two
- A modem
- A fax machine (or a send/receive fax/modem)
- A quiet place to set things up

For me, one of the major advantages of telecommuting is that I don't have to shave every day and I can work in my underwear (and yes, it's nice to be able to work out or take an occasional nap in the middle of the day). But there are a few disadvantages.

If You're an Employee

Although the number of family-friendly companies is growing every year, most employers remain somewhat skeptical. The first thing to do when proposing any kind of schedule change is to make sure that you're in the office during your employer's "core" time (for most that's 11 A.M. to 2 P.M.). Knowing that you'll be around for meetings and lunches with clients may make your employer more receptive to your request.

If your company is still resistant, you might want to let them know that a significant amount of research on workplace flexibility has found that the more satisfied working parents are with their work/family balance, the more satisfied they are with their jobs. Companies that support their employees in striking this balance experience less turnover and absenteeism and have employees who are happier and more productive. But companies that are rigid in their thinking about work and family often end up with quite the opposite situation: greater turnover and economic losses, say personnel experts Fran Sussner Rodgers and Charles Rodgers. "Employees who perceived their supervisors as unsupportive on family issues reported higher levels of stress, greater absenteeism, and lower job satisfaction."

Primary among them is the lack of human contact; you may hate that train ride into the city or the annoying guy in your car pool, but after a few months alone in your house, you might actually miss them. You might also miss going out to lunch with your coworkers or even just bumping into them in the halls. And if you have a tendency to be obsessive about your work (as I do), you'll have to train yourself to take frequent breaks. I can't tell you how many times I've realized—at ten o'clock at night—that I haven't eaten all day and that the only time I went outside was to take the newspaper in from the porch.

What If You Can't Find a Good Work/Family Balance?

Unfortunately, not every father is going to be able to come up with a workable, flexible schedule that allows him to be with his kids as much as he'd like to be. You might have an employer who refuses to compromise. Or you might be working a job that simply doesn't allow for any flexibility. Or you might just want more time with your children than any schedule can reasonably allow. Whatever your situation, it's important to avoid falling into either one of these common work/family traps.

♦ **Trying too hard to make up for lost time.** There's nothing like a long day at the office to make you realize just how much you miss your children. And when

STRIKING A BALANCE BETWEEN WORK AND FAMILY

If You're an Employer (or a Supervisor)

"Companies compete to woo skilled women," says *Wall Street Journal* columnist Sue Shellenbarger. "But many still assume that men will continue to work regardless of how they are treated as fathers." Now that you're aware of how hard it is for single parents, you're in a unique situation to change this Neanderthal attitude and help men (and women) get more involved with their families.

♦ Change your own schedule. Many of your male employees will be reluctant to approach you with proposed schedule changes. So if you know someone has just become a single father, raise the issue with him first. Chances are he'll be grateful.

♦ Make your workplace more family-friendly. If you have enough employees, organize classes and support groups for new parents and especially for single parents. Even if you don't have many employees, you can still offer free (or subsidized) on-site or near-site child care. You can also encourage your employees to take advantage of part-time, job-sharing, or flexible scheduling options. Overall, your company's policies should recognize that all parents (as opposed to just mothers) are responsible for their children's care and development.

♦ Don't worry about the cost. As mentioned above, companies with family-friendly policies find that the costs of implementing such programs are more than compensated for by increased morale and productivity, reduced absenteeism, and lower turnover. They're also a great recruiting tool.

you get home, you might be tempted to try to make up for lost time by cramming as much active, physical father/child contact as you can into the few hours before bedtime (yours or your kids'). That's a pretty tall order, and just about the only way you'll be able to fill it is to be "overly controlling, intrusive, and hyper-stimulating," writes psychiatrist Stanley Greenspan. So before you start tickling and wrestling and throwing your kids around, spend a few minutes reading or cuddling or talking about your respective days, quietly getting to know each other again.

♦ **Guilt.** Besides making you miss your kids, a long day at the office can also make you feel guilty about the amount of time you're away from them. Now a little guilt is probably a good thing, but it's awfully easy for parents to let their guilt get out of hand. And the results are not good at all. "In order to make the emotional burden easier," writes Greenspan, "some parents distance themselves from their children." It's critical, then, that you find some middle ground between being overly controlling and distancing yourself from your kids. The best way to do that is to make sure that whenever you're with your children, you're there 100 percent. Forget the phone, forget the newspapers or the television, forget washing the dishes, and forget eating if you can. You can do all those things after your kids go to sleep or before they wake up in the morning.

Who Takes Care of the Kid While You're at Work?

School-age Kids

If your kids are over five, they're most likely in school and you won't have to worry about who's taking care of them during the day—regardless of whether they're with you full-time or part-time. But what about the hours between the time school lets out and the time you get home from work? There are, of course, all sorts of alternatives: setting up regular play dates with their friends; enrolling them in after-school sports, arts, or science programs; letting them spend the time at grandma and grandpa's house; hiring a sitter (for more on sitters, see below).

Kids under Five

If your kids aren't in school yet, you've got a completely different—and much more complicated—situation to deal with. If you're a widower or have primary custody of your kids, the responsibility for finding good-quality child care is all yours. But if your ex is the one with primary custody, the decision is mostly hers. This does *not* mean, however, that you shouldn't participate (or at least try to) in the decision. The people who care for your children—even when they're with your ex—can have a major impact on their health and development. So read the following sections carefully and get involved in the child-care selection process as early as you can.

When it comes to finding someone to take care of your small children, there are two basic options:

♦ In-home care, provided by a sitter (who doesn't live there), an au pair (who probably does), or a nanny (who might or might not).
♦ Out-of-home care, either in a caregiver's home (called family day care) or at some kind of organized facility (child-care center, preschool, or nursery school).

In-Home Care

If you're a widower or the primary custodian, in-home care is probably the most convenient option. You won't have to worry about day-care schedules, and your young children will be able to stay in the environment to which they have become accustomed. In addition, they'll receive plenty of one-on-one attention, and, if you stay on top of the situation, the caregiver will keep you up to date on their development. Finally, by remaining at home, your children will be less exposed to germs and illness.

In-home care can also work well even if you have your kids only part-time, especially if they're with you for a week or two at a stretch. But if you and your ex live close to each other and your kids are in an out-of-home situation when they're with your ex, it's probably best to utilize the same arrangement when they're with you.

Leaving your children alone with a stranger can be daunting and traumatic, especially the first time. On the one hand, you might be worried about whether you really know (and can trust) the caregiver. You might also be worried—as I was—that no one will be able to love or care for your kids as well as you do. On the other hand, you might experience what psychologist and parenting guru Dr. Lawrence Kutner calls the "natural rivalry" between parents and caregivers. "As parents, we want our children to feel close (but not too close) to the other adults in their lives. We worry that, if those attachments are too strong, they will replace us in our child's eyes." Fortunately, no one will ever be able to replace you—or your love. But there are many wonderful caregivers out there who can give your baby the next best thing. You just need to know how to find them.

HOW TO FIND IN-HOME CAREGIVERS
The best ways to find in-home caregivers are:
♦ Agencies
♦ Referrals from trusted friends or acquaintances
♦ Bulletin boards (either caregivers respond to your ad, or you respond to theirs)

The first thing to do is to conduct thorough interviews over the phone. This will enable you to screen out the obviously unacceptable candidates (for example, the ones who are only looking for a month-long job, or those who don't drive if you need a driver). Then invite the "finalists" over to meet with you and your children in person. Make sure the kids and the prospective caregiver spend a few minutes together, and pay close attention to how they interact. Someone who approaches your children cautiously and speaks to them reassuringly before picking them up is someone who understands and cares about your kids' feelings. And someone who strokes your children's hair, strikes up a conversation, or offers to do a magic trick is a far better choice than a person who sits rigidly staring at your children from across the room.

Another good "test" for potential caregivers is to have them spend a few minutes playing with your kids. Does the applicant suggest a game or song or ask your children to bring a favorite book, or does she seem at a loss for ideas?

When you've finally put together your list of finalists, get references—and check at least two (it's awkward, but absolutely essential). Ask each of the references why the baby-sitter left his or her previous jobs, and what the best and worst things about him or her were. Also, make sure to ask the prospective caregiver the questions listed below.

When you make your final choice, try to take off from work for the person's first few days so you can all get to know each other, and, of course, so you can spy.

Practical Matters

WHAT TO ASK THEM

Here are some important questions to ask prospective in-home caregivers. You may want to add a few more from the sections on out-of-home options.

- What previous child-care experience have you had (including caring for younger relatives)?
- What age(s) of children have you cared for?
- Tell me a little about your own childhood.
- What would you do if . . . ? (Give several examples of things a child might do that would require different degrees of discipline.)
- When would you hit or spank a child? (If the answer is anything other than "Never," find yourself another candidate.)
- How would you handle . . . ? (Name a couple of emergency situations, such as a gushing head wound or a broken arm.)
- Do you know baby CPR? (If not, you might want to consider paying for the caregiver to take a class.)
- What are your favorite things to do with kids?
- Do you have a driver's license?
- What days/hours are you available/not available? How flexible can you be if an emergency arises while I'm at work?
- Are you a native speaker of any foreign language?

OTHER IMPORTANT ISSUES TO DISCUSS

- Compensation (find out the going rate by checking with other people who have caregivers) and vacation.
- Telephone privileges.
- Complete responsibilities of the job: feeding, bathing, diapering, changing clothes, reading to the kids, and so on, as well as what light housekeeping chores, if any, will be expected while the children are sleeping.
- English-language skills—particularly important in case of emergency (you want someone who can accurately describe to a doctor or 911 operator what's going on).
- Immigration/green card status (for more on this and other legal complications, see pages 203–4).

You might want to draw up an informal contract listing all of the caregiver's responsibilities—just so there won't be any misunderstandings.

A NOTE ON BACKGROUND CHECKS

Even if your candidates have answered all your questions satisfactorily, how do you *really* know who she is? The best way to find out is to do a thorough background check. No, this doesn't mean hiring some kind of tough private investigator to rough up the candidate's neighbors, nor does it entail lifting a set of fingerprints off the glass of lemonade she drank from. All you need to get started is her social security number and her signature on a release that will allow you to take a look at her driving record and criminal and civil background reports. Your local police or sheriff's department will be able to tell you what you need and how to obtain the information you're looking for.

Live-in Help

Hiring a live-in caregiver is like adding a new member to the family. The process for selecting one is similar to that for finding a non-live-in caregiver, so you can use most of the questions listed above for conducting interviews. After you've made your choice, try out your new relationship on a non-live-in basis for a few weeks, just to make sure everything's going to work out to everyone's satisfaction.

AU PAIRS

Au pairs are usually young women who come to the States on year-long cultural exchange programs administered by the United States Information Agency (USIA). Legally, au pairs are nonresident aliens and are exempt from social security, Medicare, and unemployment taxes (see below for more on taxes and payroll).

What an au pair provides is up to forty-five hours per week of live-in child care. In exchange, you pay a weekly stipend (currently about $150) as well as airfare, insurance, an educational stipend, program support, and full room and board. On average, having an au pair will set you back about $12,000 for the full year.

You can hire an au pair through one of only about eight USIA-approved placement agencies. You could hire one through a non-USIA agency, but the au pair would be subject to immediate deportation and you could get slapped with a $10,000 fine.

Having an au pair can be a wonderful opportunity for you and your children to learn about another culture. One drawback, however, is that they can stay only a year, then it's *au revoir* to one, *bonjour* to another. In addition, it's important to remember that from the young woman's perspective, being an au pair is a cultural thing. In theory she's supposed to do a lot of child care and other work, but in reality she may be far more interested in going to the mall with her new American friends or hanging out with your neighbor's teenage son.

Taxes and Government Regulations

If you hire an in-home caregiver or family day-care provider, here are some of the steps you may have to take to meet IRS, INS, and Department of Labor requirements:
- ◆ Get a federal ID number (you may be able to use your social security number).
- ◆ Register with your state tax department.
- ◆ Register with the Department of Labor.
- ◆ Calculate payroll deductions (and, of course, deduct them).

- File quarterly reports to your state tax board.
- Calculate unemployment tax.
- Get a worker's compensation policy and compute the premium (usually a percentage of payroll rather than a flat fee for the year).
- Prepare W-2 and W-4 forms.
- Demonstrate compliance with Immigration and Naturalization Service guidelines.

If the prospect of doing all this doesn't make you want to quit your job to stay home with the kids, nothing will. Your accountant may be able to take care of some or all of these pesky details for you.

Out-of-Home Care

FAMILY DAY CARE

If you can't (or don't want to, or can't afford to) have someone care for your child in your home, the next best alternative is to have your child cared for in someone else's home. Since the caregiver is usually looking after only two or three children (including yours), your child will get the individual attention he needs as well as the opportunity to socialize with other children. And since the caregiver lives in his or her own house, personnel changes are unlikely; this gives your child a greater sense of stability.

Be sure to ask potential family day-care providers what kind of backup system they have to deal with vacations and illness (the provider's). Will you suddenly find yourself without child care or will your child be cared for by another adult whom both you and your baby know?

PRESCHOOLS, NURSERY SCHOOLS, AND OTHER GROUP SITUATIONS

Many people—even those who can afford in-home child care—would rather use an out-of-home center. For one, a good day-care center is, as a rule, much better equipped than your home, or anyone else's for that matter, and will undoubtedly offer your child a wider range of stimulating activities. But remember, "There is absolutely no relationship between the amount of money a child-care center charges and the quality of care your baby will receive," writes Lawrence Kutner. "The best child-care centers invest in hiring and retaining the best people, not buying the most toys."

Many parents also prefer group day care because it usually offers kids more opportunities to play with one another. In the long run, most parenting experts agree that being able to play with a variety of other kids helps children become better socialized and more independent. The downside, of course, is that your child won't get as much individual attention from the adult caregivers. In addition, interacting with other kids usually means interacting with their germs; children in

> ## To Grandmother's (or Grandfather's) House We Go
>
> If your parents, in-laws, or other relatives live in the neighborhood, they may provide you with a convenient, loving, and low-cost child-care alternative. According to a recent survey by the U.S. Census Bureau, about 16 percent of children under five years old are being cared for by their grandparents while their parents are working—half of them in their grandparents' homes. Other relatives account for an additional 8 percent of all child-care arrangements for preschoolers.

group day care tend to get sick a lot more often than those cared for at home (whether yours or someone else's).

WHERE TO FIND OUT-OF-HOME CAREGIVERS

You're most likely to find out-of-home child-care facilities through word of mouth or by running an ad in a local parenting newspaper. Perhaps the easiest (and safest) alternative is through Child Care Aware, a nationwide campaign created to help parents identify quality child care in their communities. Contact them at (800) 424-2246. But don't base your final child-care decision on *anyone's* recommendation. Spend some time at each potential site and ask a lot of questions. Here are some excellent ones, a number of which were suggested by Child Care Aware, the National Association for the Education of Young Children (NAEYC), and the American Academy of Pediatrics. The answers should all be Yes, except where indicated.

ABOUT THE CAREGIVERS

- Do they seem to really like children? Do the kids seem to like them?
- Do they get down on each child's level to speak to the child?
- Are the children greeted when they arrive?
- Are the children's needs quickly met even when things get busy?
- Are the caregivers trained in CPR, first aid, and early childhood development? (At least one should be.)
- Are they involved in continuing education programs? (As many as possible should be.)
- Does the program keep up with children's changing interests?
- Will the caregivers always be ready to answer your questions?
- Will they tell you what your child is doing every day?
- Are parents' ideas welcomed? Are there ways for you to get involved if you want to?
- Are there enough caregivers for the number of kids? (The NAEYC recommends that a minimum of two adults should care for a maximum of 8 infants, 14 two- and three-year-olds, or 20 four- and five-year-olds. If your children are older and in an after-school program, the National School-Age Care Alliance

recommends that ratios should vary according to the ages and abilities of children, with at least one qualified adult in charge of a maximum of 10 to 15 children over six.)

ABOUT THE FACILITY

- Is the atmosphere bright and pleasant?
- Is smoking prohibited on the premises?
- Is there a fenced-in outdoor play area with a variety of equipment that meets current safety standards?
- Can the caregivers see the entire playground at all times?
- Do the children have daily opportunities to participate in a variety of active and quiet activities, including free play, art, music, and group and individual play? Is there a wide variety of age-appropriate toys, books, and materials available? Is there more than one of each toy so that the kids don't have to wait in long lines to play?
- Are there different areas for resting, quiet play, and active play?
- What precautions are taken to ensure that kids can be picked up only by the person you select? Do strangers have access to the center? (No)
- Are there adequate safety measures to keep children away from windows, fences, electrical outlets, kitchen appliances, and utensils (knives, ovens, stoves, household chemicals, and so forth)?
- Are the kitchen, tabletops, floors, and sleep areas kept clean, and are garbage cans, diaper pails, bathrooms, and toys that could end up in toddlers' mouths cleaned thoroughly and regularly disinfected?
- Is there an emergency plan, including regular fire drills? Are fire extinguishers available and easily accessible to adults?

ABOUT THE PROGRAM

- Is there a daily balance of playtime, story time, and nap time?
- Are the activities right for each age group?
- Are there enough toys and learning materials for the number of children?
- Are the toys clean, safe, and within reach of the children?
- If the school provides meals and/or snacks, are they varied, wholesome, and nutritious? Are menus available in advance?
- Are rest and nap times scheduled so each child has a clean, individual place to sleep? Are there special quiet activities for kids who don't nap?
- Do teachers wear disposable gloves and wash hands with soap and water whenever changing diapers? Do they wash their hands after helping a child go to the bathroom and before touching food?
- Are hot running water, soap, and paper towels available—at kid level—to be used after going to the bathroom and before all meals and snacks?
- Are parents notified immediately of any accident or contagious illness? Is there

a clear policy for what to do (isolation, to start) with kids who get sick while at school?

♦ Does the school have a plan for dealing with violent children? While some hitting, pushing, and biting is pretty normal for young kids, anything more serious (stabbing, hitting with large objects, or repeated, unprovoked attacks) is not.

♦ Do children have to ride in car seats on field trips? (As required by law in your state.)

ABOUT OTHER THINGS

♦ Do you agree with the discipline practices and philosophy?

♦ Do you hear the sounds of happy children?

♦ Is the program licensed or regulated? By whom?

♦ Are surprise visits by parents encouraged?

♦ Will your child be happy there?

Try to visit each facility more than once, and after you've made your final decision, make a few unannounced visits — just to see what goes on when there aren't any parents around. And finally, ask yourself whether the day-care facility you're choosing is the kind of place you wish you had gone to when you were a kid.

A FEW DAY-CARE/PRESCHOOL RED FLAGS

As far as I'm concerned, any day-care center or preschool that doesn't satisfy *all* the qualifications listed on these pages should be viewed with suspicion. Beyond that, though, here are a few things that should make you take a prospective preschool off your list completely and run the other way.

A Few Words about Accreditation and Licensing

Every state has established certain guidelines for licensing group day-care centers and preschools. These guidelines, which you can get from your state's day-care licensing agency, are an important first step. But standards vary wildly from state to state, so licensing and accreditation are not necessarily the guarantees of quality that they ought to be.

On the national level, however, the NAEYC accredits programs that meet their extremely high standards. They'll send you info on finding accredited providers in your area. Call (800) 424-2460, extension 601, or write to NAEYC, 1509 16th Street NW, Washington, D.C. 20036-1426. But be careful: in most states family-day-care facilities aren't regulated at all, so you'll have to be especially vigilant when checking them out. Finally, never rely on accreditation as a substitute for thoroughly checking out potential day-care centers and preschools yourself.

Know Your Child

Perhaps the most important factor to consider when evaluating child-care options is your child himself—his energy level, sensitivity to his environment, attention span, whether or not he adapts well to new situations, and so on. These and other factors make up your child's temperament, which we don't have the space to analyze in detail here. (We do, however, cover it quite thoroughly in *The New Father: A Dad's Guide to the Toddler Years*). Here's how temperament should play into your child-care selection process:

TRAIT	SPECIAL CONSIDERATIONS
ENERGY LEVEL	
♦ High	♦ Your child will need lots of room to run around, plenty of indoor activities for rainy days, lots of ways to burn off excess energy. He will, however, need some moderately structured activities. Look for a program that has lots of kids his age or older: he'll admire their skills and want to emulate them. And make sure the teachers' energy level is high enough to cope with your child's.
♦ Low	♦ This child needs a quieter, smaller setting, and small groups.
♦ Moderate (especially those who take a while to get used to new situations)	♦ Your child will probably stick to the sidelines for a few days, watching and learning. He'll jump in after about a week. He likes more structure and predictability, and doesn't do well in large pre-schools, especially if there are a lot of more active kids his age—they can be frightening.
SENSITIVITY If your child is extremely sensitive to light, sound, or noise . . .	♦ Look for a fairly calm, subdued, relaxed environment. Lots of noise, colors, and activity can frighten your child.

♦ Parents are not allowed to drop in unannounced. You need to call before visiting or coming to pick up your child, or you're not allowed into the care-giving areas.
♦ Your child is unhappy or scared after more than a few months.
♦ The staff seems to change every day.
♦ The staff ignores any of your concerns.
♦ You child reports being hit or mistreated, or you hear similar reports from other parents. Check this one out thoroughly, though. Kids have been known to fabricate stories.

TRAIT	SPECIAL CONSIDERATIONS
ATTENTION SPAN	
♦ Short	♦ This child will need a constantly changing array of things to do and play with. Look for a staff that is large enough so that a teacher can spend some extra time with your child to expose him to new things.
PREDICTABILITY	
♦ High	♦ This child will need a regular schedule, regular meal and nap times, and so forth.
♦ Low	♦ This child doesn't need much in the way of schedule, but should have some anyway.
ADAPTABILITY	
♦ Slow	♦ Avoid day-care settings with rigid schedules and highly structured activities. Also avoid unstructured programs. Look for caregivers and teachers who will make a special effort to involve your child and introduce him to new materials slowly. Make sure you'll be allowed to stay with your child for a few minutes each morning (for at least the first week or so) to help ease his transition.
♦ Moderately slow to adapt	♦ This child may occasionally bite or hit other children. This will fade as he becomes more articulate. He may be upset when you drop him off at school and just as upset when you come to pick him up

Finding a good child-care provider is a lengthy, agonizing process, and it's important not to give up until you're satisfied. "Half to three-quarters of parents who use daycare feel they have no choices and must settle for what they can find," writes Sue Shellenbarger. The result? Most infants get mediocre care. A recent study by the Work and Families Institute (WFI) found that only 8 percent of child-care facilities were considered "good quality," and 40 percent were rated "less than minimal." According to WFI's president, Ellen Galinsky, 10 to 20 percent of children "get care so poor that it risks damaging their development." So be careful.

"I wish you'd try harder to like school, Jeremy. It's costing Daddy a bundle."

Passing the Buck

Coincidentally, the same week that my older daughter was admitted to preschool, a friend of mine was admitted to the University of California at San Francisco's medical school. My friend was griping about how much her tuition cost and was surprised when I wasn't more sympathetic. But when I told her that my daughter's preschool was more expensive than med school, she stopped. Naturally, not all preschools cost as much as medical schools, but it's not going to be cheap. If you have the money, great. But most of us could use (or wouldn't turn down) a little financial assistance. And asking your employer to help out a little may be your best bet. Here are a few alternatives:

♦ Direct financial assistance. Your employer pays for all or part of your expenses at the preschool of your choice.

♦ Negotiated discounts. Your employer—maybe in conjunction with other local employers—can negotiate group rates or discounts with a nearby preschool.

♦ Employee salary reductions or set-asides. You can have your employer put up to $5,000 of your pretax salary into a Dependent Care Assistance Plan (DCAP). This will enable you to reduce your preschool expenses by paying for them with before-tax dollars instead of after-tax ones. Your employer will save money too, since he or she won't have to pay social security tax or unemployment insurance on your DCAP money. (If your employee benefits department requests a reference, it's Section 129 of the 1981 Economic Recovery Tax Act.)

Of course, asking your boss for help—or anyone else, for that matter—isn't easy. In fact, the reason employees most often give for not asking their bosses to get involved in employee day-care problems is fear of losing their jobs. This may explain why fewer than six thousand of the nation's six million employers offer some kind of child-care assistance to their employees. Nevertheless, it's worth a try. The first thing to do is to remind him or her that some assistance programs won't cost the company a cent (see above). Then read your employer this quote from the Child Care Action Campaign (CCAC): "Studies have shown that working parents' anxiety about their child care arrangements erodes their productivity—and directly affects employers' profit lines." If those approaches don't work, follow the CCAC's advice and:

- Talk to other employees. Do any of them have trouble finding or paying for a good preschool? How do their worries affect their productivity?
- Find out what other employers in your field are doing about preschool. Some prospective employees are making decisions on which companies to work for based on benefits, and if the competition offers a more family-friendly environment, your company will have to follow suit.
- If you're in a union, speak to your union rep. Have other employers bargained for family-friendly benefits? You may be able to include some in the next contract negotiation.
- Encourage other employees to let management know about child-care problems.

The CCAC produces a variety of pamphlets that can help you approach your employer with your preschool questions and suggestions. Contact them for a catalog at 330 Seventh Ave, 17th floor, New York, NY 10001, or by calling (212) 239-0138.

Notes:

Setting up Your New Home

If you're a widower or the primary caretaker, you won't have to worry about setting up a new home, especially your kids' rooms—everything is probably already in place. But if you're like many newly single fathers and you've found yourself standing in a nearly empty apartment, you may be feeling a little lost. And if *you're* feeling that way, just imagine how your kids are feeling.

In general, your home should be as welcoming and familiar as possible. If your kids walk into a completely new place they're likely to feel a little like intruders. This is all the more true if you've moved in with a girlfriend, especially if she has kids of her own, with whom your kids will probably feel very competitive.

If at all possible, have your new place set up before the kids arrive. Decorate it with lots of comforting touches: family photos, the kids' drawings, a familiar painting, some of their books, a favorite chair or couch or even a set of candlesticks from the old home. The object is to let them know immediately that although it's a new place, they're *not* guests: it's their home.

And don't consign the kids' creations to out-of-the-way places. Hanging the papier-mâché mask your child made at school right next to your signed Picasso reinforces the message that your child's creations really matter, says design consultant Ro Logrippo.

Kids' Rooms

If you don't have custody, you might be thinking that having less kids' furniture and toys around will help to keep away the painful memories of your old life. And even if you do have custody, in your rush to get everything set up in your new place it's easy to give short shrift to your child's room. Don't make this mistake. Moving back and forth between two houses can be frustrating and confusing for children, especially young ones. For this reason, it's extremely important that your child's living space have as many comforting touches as you can manage. Coming into a room filled with (or at least containing) familiar toys, games, books, and clothes can lessen the anxiety caused by the transition between homes.

In this aspect of their lives, as in every other, kids need a sense of continuity. If possible, then, make sure you take some of your child's favorite items from her old room to your new home. If that doesn't work out, try to talk with your ex about selecting some common themes to unite the child's two rooms. Having the same rug, wallpaper, dresser, or bedspread can go a long way toward making your child feel at home in both places, suggests Ro Logrippo. If you can't match an item or pattern exactly, at least try to match the color. You're probably going to have to buy new sheets and blankets anyway, so let your child pick the ones she likes best. If neither of these alternatives is workable in your case, ask your child what she'd like to have in her room at your house (or have her name a few of her favorite things from her room at her mom's house); you might even offer to repaint her new room and let her pick the color.

How you outfit your child's room depends on what you already have and what you can afford. You can get most of the things listed below pretty cheaply at used-furniture stores or garage sales.

The Basics

♦ **Beds.** Regular or bunk, depending on the number of kids you have and on the size of the space you have for them. If your kids are very young or very active, though, bunk beds might be dangerous, so consider a trundle bed instead. If at all possible, let the kids "try on" their new beds before you buy them. And stay away from fold-up couches, inflatable mattresses, or sleeping bags because they may make the kids feel like visitors and they're also bad for young backs. Your kids need to know that your house is also their house and not just a temporary residence. It's also not a good idea to let your kids spend the night in your bed, especially if someone else is already sharing it with you.

♦ **Storage space.** It's important to give your kids someplace to store their toys and other supplies—and to get them into the habit of picking up after themselves. (There's nothing like having to clean up their room to make them feel that they're living at home.) If you have closets or shelves, great, if not, you can get stacking boxes at a hardware store. Smaller boxes—about shoe-box size—are better than larger ones because they increase the chances that the contents will actually get used. Be sure the boxes you get are transparent so your kids can see what's inside them. And label each one clearly to help in the clean up process. If your kids are too young to read, you can glue a Lego piece to the box where the Legos go, for example, or you can color-code the boxes.

The object here is to make your kids' belongings accessible and easy to keep track of. It's not an attempt to keep everything they own out of sight. Doing so would only make them feel unwelcome. After all, if your things aren't all hidden away why should theirs be?

♦ **Study/work area.** A desk, chair, and lamp are essential. Your kids need to have someplace private where they can go to read, do their homework, or write letters. Be sure to get the kids involved in selecting any office furniture you buy. If the chair is too hard or the desk too low they won't get used. And try to get furniture—especially chairs—that can "grow" with your child.

♦ **A calendar** with a complete schedule of where the kids will be and when. Knowing this makes them feel a lot more in control of their lives. You might also want to get some maps so the kids can see where you live, where their mother lives, where their school is, and so on. "Their space should support learning," says Logrippo, "not just be a fluffy place to play or sleep."

♦ **A photo album.** If you're widowed, this is especially important. Your children will be looking for every possible way to remember their mother and pay tribute to her (for more on this see pages 124–26). If you're not a widower, a photo album is still important. Unless your relationship with your children's mother was violent or abusive, your kids will probably want to remember the way things were. So stock their album with pictures of them alone, with you, and together with your ex. Encourage them to add to the album by putting in photos of their new family. And if your kids want to, let them frame and hang some of their favorites.

If you've got the skills or at least the desire to build your own furniture, do so with caution: unless your kids are older (say, over ten), they probably won't appreciate what you've done and you could end up feeling underappreciated and resentful. Finding a good-quality, safe bargain could be a lot more fulfilling.

Finally, when you've got everything you need, be sure to give your kids a lot of leeway organizing their space. Let them arrange their furniture and decide which drawers to put their underwear in. And don't forget to lower the rods in their closets so they can have easy access to their clothes.

Toys

Toys are an important part of every child's life and must be a part of every child's living space. You undoubtedly know the toys your child loves, and the ones he hates. You should have at least some of his favorites with you, no matter where you are.

Besides the old favorites, there are some generic toys and other playthings that you'll probably want to have around, depending, of course, on your children's ages:

♦ A dress-up box: If you don't already have one, you can scour garage sales, thrift

shops, and flea markets for funky, old clothes, wigs, shoes, garish jewelry, and anything else the kids might want to dress up in. The period following their parents' breakup is a particularly important time for them to be able to flex their imagination.

♦ Bookshelves and books.
♦ A piano or other musical instrument.
♦ Board games and card games.
♦ Art supplies: Markers, crayons, paints, and lots and lots of paper are essential.
♦ Tools, blocks, dolls, and action figures.
♦ Sports equipment (balls, bats, mitts).
♦ Stuffed animals.

Clothing

If someone else did all the clothes shopping in your family before your breakup, you were one lucky guy. But now that you're on your own, you're, well, on your own. And even if you're tempted, don't rely on your ex or anyone else to shop for your children's clothes. The whole idea may seem a little daunting, but don't worry, it's really not all that hard.

The first thing to do is to go through your kids' current wardrobe and write down the sizes of everything that fits—shoes, socks, underwear, pants, shirts, dresses, jackets, hats, mittens, and so on. You should also write down the kinds of clothes

A Special Note about Socks

Plan on restocking your kids' supply every six months or so. My younger daughter dutifully puts on a pair of clean socks every morning before heading off to school, but comes back barefoot every afternoon. Her excuses have ranged from "Two robbers took them" to "They were on fire so I took them off," but the bottom line is her socks are gone. All I can figure out is that there's apparently some special chemical in socks that causes them to dissolve into thin air. In the past year alone I've bought each of my kids twenty-four pairs of socks, and all I have left to show for it are three pairs each and a fifty-five-gallon trash bag full of sock widows.

One thing that might help stem the sock problem in your home (this really does work) is to buy sock clips and insist that your kids clip each pair together before tossing it into the laundry hamper. The clips aren't expensive and they'll probably pay for themselves within a few months.

your kids like best. My younger daughter, for example, loves pants made out of soft material but absolutely refuses to wear jeans. The older one won't wear anything green. It's good to know these things.

Once you've got your list of sizes and preferred styles, you can hit the stores. You might also want to give a copy to your parents or anyone else who's likely to want to buy your kids something to wear.

Beware: brand-new kids clothes are phenomenally expensive. I personally have never seen the sense in spending $25 on a pair of name-brand tennis shoes for a kid to wear out in three months when you can get the same pair, in great shape, for a quarter of the price at a thrift shop, used clothing store, or yard sale. Your kids may well get plenty of new clothes from the grandparents or other relatives. Understandably, though, your pride may not allow you to go this route.

Wherever you get your children's clothes, just be certain they're of good quality. Kids are usually a lot harder on clothes than adults are, so if you don't want to have to go shopping every month, make sure that what you're buying will last. Another way to make clothes last a little longer is to buy sizes that allow for a little—but not too much—growing room (shoes that are too big, for example, can cause blisters).

After quality, the very next consideration is quantity. Even if your kids are with you only for a weekend a month, you'll need to provide them with a wardrobe that's at least half the size of the one they have at their mother's, not including boots, jackets, swimsuits, and other seasonal clothes that you'll have to acquire as well. There will be a lot of duplication between what you have at your house and what they have at their mother's, but there's really no avoiding it.

In the long run, having a complete wardrobe for your child will save you all a lot of trouble. You won't have to run around borrowing clothes from your ex. And the kids will be able to come to (and leave) your house with only the clothes on their back instead of having to worry about schlepping things back and forth. Not only is that a convenience, it will also reinforce their sense of belonging when they're with you. There's something about a suitcase that makes people feel like they're only visiting.

If your kids are with you 50 percent of the time or less, here's the barest minimum you'll need. If you have them for a greater amount of time, adjust accordingly.

- 6 pairs of socks and underwear
- 4 pairs of pants
- 4 pairs of shorts
- 4 blouses or shirts
- 3 dresses or skirts
- 2 sweaters
- 1 warm jacket
- 1 raincoat
- 2 pairs of shoes (1 pair for sports, 1 for everyday use)
- 1 pair of walking boots
- 1 pair of rain boots (can double as snow boots)
- 1 umbrella

If You Don't Have the Space for a Separate Kids' Room

Having a separate room or rooms for the kids is wonderful, but not every father has the space or the resources for it. This doesn't mean that your kids can't feel completely at home, however. What's most important is for your child to feel that he belongs in your home and that he's a part of your life. Here are a few things you can do to accomplish this:

- Set aside a shelf or an area of a room as your child's special private place and tell him that *no one* will ever go into it and that he can store anything he wants in it. Stock this special area with as many toys, games, puzzles, books, sports equipment, stuffed animals, and art supplies as you can.
- Try to have at least one or two items that are similar or identical to things your child has at his mother's house (assuming, of course, that he *likes* those things). If you can, let the child pick the items and the colors. And be flexible. If your child has a favorite bedspread at his mother's, you might be able to get a curtain or a towel with the same pattern. If he doesn't like the bedspread—or anything else—at his mother's, he'll appreciate your asking for his opinion all the more.
- Make your child's presence felt. Put up photos of your child, his artwork, and all his notes to you. He needs to know that even though you don't have a lot of space, you're always thinking of him.

Toys and Clothes That Travel

No matter how many duplicate items your kids have in their two homes, one of the hazards of moving back and forth is that they're going to want to take a favorite toy, book, or article of clothing that "lives" at one house to the other. If your kids are good about bringing things back and forth, this won't be a big deal. But if they aren't, it could cause some problems.

With clothing, some of this "traveling" is, of course, unavoidable. When your kids leave your house to go to their mother's they have to be wearing something, right? But be careful. I've heard several friends complain that their kids show up at their house wearing old, ratty clothes, get sent back to their exes' in a nice outfit, and reappear the next time in more rags. This may also upset the people who bought all those pricey little Christian Dior outfits for your kids; they may resent your ex-wife's profiting from their largesse. In this type of situation, the only real solution is simply to send the kids back to their mother's in whatever they were wearing when they arrived. And keep careful track of the dates this happens.

The weather can exacerbate the traveling-clothes problem. What if your kids show up at your house on a warm, sunny day dressed in T-shirts and shorts and the day they leave it's hailing? Are you really going to let them out of the house without a jacket or raincoat? All you can do is ask your ex—and your kids—to make an effort to get things back to where they're supposed to be.

Toys are more complicated. The best way to handle wandering toys is to establish some ground rules for removing them from your house and put together a list of items (or categories of items) that simply can't leave the house. Be sure to include gifts the kids receive from your parents and relatives. My mother, for example, was livid when she found out that a rather expensive Barbie she'd given to one of my daughters had somehow moved to my ex's house. And for a while my other daughter would spend the allowance money I'd given her on porcelain dolls that she would immediately take to her mother's house.

When you're putting your list together don't be spiteful—you're not trying to hurt your kids or your ex. The purpose of restricting toy and clothing migration is to make sure that you don't wake up one morning and find that your kids' closets and toy baskets are nearly empty. There are also several benefits to being flexible: first, your kids will know that you respect them and trust them to bring things back; second, chances are that they'll be thinking of you when they're playing with the toy they took from your house.

Be especially flexible if your kids are under five. Having a small book or toy or some other object to which they're emotionally attached when they're shuttled back and forth can reduce their stress and make them feel more secure.

Of course if your child is involved in any kind of sports activity (gymnastics, soccer, baseball) or goes camping, you'll need the appropriate extra clothing and equipment. And if you live in a part of the country with severe winters, you'll need to add a full set of winter clothes as well.

Hopefully this won't come as much of a shock, but kids' clothing gets torn, stained, lost, loaned to friends, and sometimes even thrown away, not to mention outgrown. So don't be surprised if you have to replace articles of clothing every six months or so. And because you're going to have a tough time controlling the flow of clothes between your house and your ex's, it's natural for clothes to suddenly disappear and then mysteriously resurface a few weeks later. The less upset you let this get you, the better (see page 218 for more on this). Your ex, however, many not be nearly as flexible about these things as you are and may demand that certain items of clothing be returned to her house. If she insists, go along with her. Hopefully, she'll do the same if the situation is ever reversed.

A Final Note

Whether your kids have separate rooms, share one room, or have only a corner of the dining room to call their own, don't do anything too permanent. They're changing every day and so are their needs, wants, and favorite colors. So be as flexible and as accommodating as reason—and your budget—will allow.

Notes:

Setting up a Kitchen

If you're a widower, you probably have a fully outfitted kitchen and pantry. But if you're a divorced or never-married father, your kitchen shelves and cupboards may be pretty bare. Here's what you'll need in the way of equipment and food to get yourself set up.

Equipment

Items with an ○ at the beginning are optional, but may make your kitchen life a lot easier.

- ♦ Knives. You should have at least two: a chef's knife (8–10 inches long, with a wide blade) and one with a serrated (scalloped) edge for cutting breads, tomatoes, and other soft things, which a regular blade mushes instead of cuts.
- ♦ Cutting board. It's better than slicing up your kitchen table or countertops.
- ♦ Pans. Two: one 10–12 inches across and another 6–8 inches across. You don't want to cook tiny batches of sauce or anything else in a pan that's too large— it will burn. A nonstick coating is a good idea.
- ♦ Pots. Two or three of different sizes. Be sure to include an 8- to 10-quart stock pot for making large batches of soup, chili, and so forth, that you can freeze for later.
- ♦ Baking dishes. Two or three of differents sizes (9 × 9 inches and 9 × 13 inches are good to start with), for brownies, lasagna, bread, fish, or anything else that needs to be prepared in the oven. Metal is best—and less likely to break than glass.

- Mixing bowls. Several of different sizes (they generally come in 4-cup, 8-cup, and 12-cup); plastic is fine. You can also use these for serving.
- Wooden spoons and scrapers. They won't scratch the nonstick coating off your pans.
- Slotted spoon. So you can scoop solid things (like dumplings) out of liquid without dripping all over the place.
- Ladle.
- Spatula (sometimes called rubber scraper). For squeegeeing out the inside of jars, pots, or pans.
- The other kind of spatula. For flipping pancakes or burgers.
- Vegetable peeler.
- Measuring cups and spoons. A glass one (2-cup size) for measuring liquids (don't get plastic—it will crack if you put anything hot into it); a set of cups (1 cup, ½ cup, ⅓ cup, ¼ cup) for solids or dry ingredients; a set of spoons for smaller amounts (1 tablespoon, 1 teaspoon, ½ teaspoon, ¼ teaspoon).
- Cheese grater. Get the kind that has four sides, each one for grating food into different-size pieces.
- Colander. For draining pasta and washing fruits and vegetables.
- Corkscrew, bottle opener, can opener. How else are you going to get into those bottles and cans?
- Plastic wrap and aluminum foil. For wrapping and storing leftovers. Using foil to line your baking pans will also cut your clean-up time way down.
- Reclosable food-storage bags—regular and freezer types. Essential for storing leftovers.
- Dishes, silverware, and cups. Two or three times as many settings as you have people in your family. There's no sense washing dishes after every meal and who knows, you might want to have guests over.
- Dishwashing stuff. Sponges, scouring pads, detergent, soap, dish towels.
- Oven mitt. Do not use dish towels for this purpose—they can hang down and touch a heater coil or flame and catch on fire. Believe me.
- ○ Large stock pot (12 quarts or so). For larger batches of soup, stew, and chili. Get a good-quality one with a thick bottom so you don't burn anything. And stay away from any kind of enamel lining, which has a tendency to chip off and get into whatever you're cooking (none too tasty or healthy). And, according to my cooking guru friend Janice Tannin, enamel pots often "cook food unevenly, have hot spots, burn, and are a bitch to clean."
- ○ Crock pot. You can throw in a bunch of vegetables and other ingredients in the morning and come home from work to a delicious stew.
- ○ Muffin tin. For cupcakes too.
- ○ Timer.
- ○ Tea kettle.
- ○ Rice cooker. Lets you make perfect rice while you run around doing other things. And given that rice often accounts for more than half of what children

eat, this is a good investment. Many rice cookers come with attachments for steaming vegetables, fish, and other foods at the same time.
- ♦ ○ Salad spinner. A faster, easier way to wash and dry lettuce and other leafy vegetables. Kids love to play with this.
- ♦ ○ Hot pads (trivets) for resting hot things on so you don't ruin your table or countertops.
- ♦ ○ Vegetable steamer.
- ♦ ○ Microwave oven. This is almost an essential.
- ♦ ○ Food processor. A handy appliance to have around, but unless you use it a lot, you'll spend more time washing the blades than slicing vegetables.

A few things to keep in mind when outfitting your kitchen:
1. Get the best equipment you can comfortably afford. Pot handles that melt, cheapo nonstick coating that bubbles off, knives that don't cut, and peelers that don't peel will make your cooking experience miserable and can be dangerous.
2. Shop around. Department stores, hardware stores, and specialty shops often have sales. You do not need to buy prepackaged sets (except for measuring cups and spoons); if you need only one pot, buy it separately. And if you're on a tight budget, check out local garage sales, flea markets, and thrift shops.

Food

Now that you've got your kitchen properly outfitted, the only thing left to do is eat. Below you'll find a pretty comprehensive list of the foods you should have in your house at all times. But before you head out to the store, keep the following in mind:
- ♦ Eat healthy. Eating nothing but canned tuna and potato chips (which I'm perfectly happy to do) may be okay for you, but it's rotten for your kids. Get the freshest, least-prepared food you can. A balanced diet, low in sodium, sugars, and saturated fats is the best thing for your kids and you.
- ♦ Give yourself a break. An occasional high-fat, high-sugar snack is just fine and so is an occasional TV dinner or pre-prepared meal. Just don't make it a habit.
- ♦ Buy in bulk. If you've got the space, cases or large-size packages of canned, frozen, or dried items are almost always cheaper. If you don't have the space, consider splitting your bulk purchases with someone else.
- ♦ Don't overbuy fresh ingredients.
- ♦ Think big. It's just as easy to make three times more soup or stew or chili or sauce than you need as it is to make enough for one meal. In most cases, you can freeze the rest for later.
- ♦ Keep an inventory of what you have and a running shopping list of what you need. When you use something, write it down for replacement.

"Can I have that with a twist?"

Fresh Things

- Dairy. Milk, cheese, string cheese, yogurt, butter, margarine.
- Eggs. Hard-boil some to have around for quick snacks.
- Produce. Whatever's in season. Absolutely essential year-round: peeled baby carrots, broccoli, cherry tomatoes, lettuce, apples, oranges.
- Potatoes (yams and sweet potatoes too), onions, garlic.
- Juice.
- Bread.

Canned and Bottled Things

- Tomato products. Truly essential for so many dishes. Keep three or four cans of tomato paste, stewed tomatoes, and tomato sauce around at all times. Also get pizza sauce and salsa.
- Soups. Your kids' and your favorites. Also keep on hand a few cans of broth (it comes in chicken, beef, or vegetable).

♦ Fruits (for when the fresh stuff isn't in season). Pineapple chunks and mandarin oranges (preferably packed in water rather than in syrup) are big favorites.
♦ Vegetables. Creamed corn, peas, mushrooms, and so on.
♦ Beans. Garbanzo, black, pinto, refried, and prepared chili (vegetarian or with meat).
♦ Peanut butter (all-natural is better than the sugar-packed kind), jams, jellies, preserves.
♦ Condiments. Mustard, ketchup, mayonnaise.
♦ Miscellaneous. Tuna (in water rather than in oil), olives.

Dry Things
♦ Split peas and lentils. For soups.
♦ Grains. Couscous (comes in boxes too), rice (any kind), cornmeal, popcorn (bulk or microwavable).
♦ Nuts. Almonds, cashews, sesame seeds, peanuts.
♦ Pasta. Spaghetti, lasagna, elbow macaroni, stars, and dozens of other fun shapes.
♦ For baking. Flour (white or whole wheat, but that's harder to work with), baking power, baking soda, biscuit mix, cake and muffin mixes, brownie mix.
♦ Bouillon cubes. A higher-sodium alternative to canned broth.
♦ Sweet stuff. Sugar (brown and/or white), honey.
♦ Seasonings and spices. Salt and pepper as a minimum. But if you ever plan on following a recipe, you'll probably need at least some of the following: garlic powder, minced garlic (comes in a jar you keep in the fridge), basil, bay leaves, cayenne, cinammon, cloves, cumin, dill, curry powder, allspice, nutmeg, oregano, paprika, tarragon, turmeric, parsley, chili powder, ground ginger.
♦ Miscellaneous. Crackers (your kids' favorite snacking options), granola bars, dry soup mixes (including ramen noodles), macaroni and cheese.

Frozen Things
♦ Vegetables. Peas, corn, green beans, carrots (but try to use these only when the real thing is out of season).
♦ Fruits. Again, when the fresh stuff is out of season. Great for adding to pancakes and muffins.
♦ Juices.
♦ Chopped onion. Great for cooking and you'll save youself a lot of tears slicing the fresh ones.
♦ Grated cheese. For a quick pizza.
♦ Miscellaneous easy-to-prepare foods. French fries, tater tots, fish sticks, waffles, TV dinners.
♦ Ice cream and/or frozen yogurt.

Wet Things

♦ Oils. For dressings and for cooking, vegetable oil is healthier than other oils.

♦ Vinegars. Plain (white) and balsamic (tastes better in dressings).

♦ Other condiments. Soy sauce, Tabasco sauce, Worcestershire sauce, sesame oil, hot chili oil.

♦ Miscellaneous. Vanilla extract, food coloring.

Notes:

Giving Yourself a Financial Tune-up

Of the many, many things single fathers worry about, most of the men I've interviewed—whether they were divorced, never-married, or widowed—put finances close to the top of the list. Only a few said they were better off financially than they had been when they were together with their partners.

Whether your financial situation is worse or better than it was before, you fit into one of the following three categories:

♦ You spend less than you bring in and are saving the difference.
♦ You spend exactly what you earn and have nothing left over.
♦ You spend more than you earn and are getting deeper and deeper in debt.

If you're in the first category, congratulations! According to some studies, fewer than 20 percent of baby boomers are saving enough for their retirement, and 25 percent of adults ages 35–54 haven't even started saving at all. If you're in either of the other two categories (or if you're in the first and want to make your financial situation even better), you're going to have to get under your financial hood and do a little tinkering. It's a simple process, really, with only two deceptively simple steps:

♦ Reduce your expenses (and your debts).
♦ Increase your savings.

Reducing Expenses and Getting out of Debt on the Way

Although starting a savings or investment plan sounds like a lot more fun than going on a financial diet, the truth is that you can't save money until you've got a good handle on your expenses. The first step is to take a hard look at your current spending. It may be a little scary, but trust me, it's important.

Gather together every money-related scrap of paper that's crossed your hands in the past five or six months. At a minimum you'll need all your credit card statements and canceled checks. Categorize them by type of expense (housing, insurance, medical, child support, alimony, food, recreation, and so forth). Using several months' worth of expenses will help you average variable expenses, such as gas and clothes, and include irregular expenses, such as auto repairs or major appliance purchases. Be sure to include the money—especially cash—you spend on lunch, dry cleaning, gifts, and the like.

Once you've got this done, go over each of the expense categories to see whether you can do some cutting. Here are a few areas in which you can produce almost immediate, and often painless, returns:

♦ Food. Buy in bulk from Costco or other discount outlets, use coupons, and eat out less.

♦ Comparison shop. Prices vary widely on everything from refrigerators to long distance carriers, so check three or four places before you buy anything. And don't forget to check out mail-order prices—they're often cheaper and tax-free (if you and the mail-order company are in different states).

♦ Make a sensible tax plan (for more on this see pages 232–33).

♦ Car pool. This can help you reduce many auto-related expenses, such as gas and oil, repairs, and insurance rates.

♦ Auto insurance. If your car is more than five years old, you can probably save some money by getting rid of your collision and comprehensive coverages. Check with your insurance agent.

♦ Health insurance. If you're self-employed and paying for your own plan, consider increasing your deductible or putting your child(ren) on a separate plan. Sometimes "family" coverage is much more than two separate policies—one for you, one for the kids.

♦ Use savings to pay off your debts. If you have $1,000 invested at 10 percent, you're earning $100 a year, which gets reduced to $72 if you're in the 28 percent tax bracket. If you owe $1,000 on a 20 percent credit card, your interest payment is $200 a year, which, since you're using after-tax dollars to pay it off, is really $278 if you're in the 28 percent tax bracket. Get the point? In this scenario, taking the money out of savings would save you more than $200 a year. That may not sound like a lot, but it's enough to pay for most of the clothes a child will go through in a year, or a good chunk of your annual health club membership, or a few sessions with your therapist. You'd have to earn roughly 30 percent (before taxes) on your investment to justify not using your savings to pay off your debt. And if some emergency comes up and you really, really need the money again, you can always get a cash advance on your credit card and start all over.

◆ Stop charging. Especially for things that lose their value, such as gas, clothing, cars, furniture, and meals out. If you can't afford to pay cash for these things, maybe you can't afford them at all. Making only the minimum payment pays off your balance in no less than three years. But if you keep buying stuff, you'll never get clean. If you still insist on charging, at least try to pay off your balance in full every month.

◆ Use a debit card instead. These cards look just like credit cards but take the money directly out of your checking account. Keeping that in mind might just scare you out of using the card altogether.

◆ Take charge of your credit cards. Get credit cards that charge low interest rates and no annual fees. A few years ago I called my own credit card company (which had been charging me $50 a year and over 20 percent interest) and told them I'd take my business elsewhere if they didn't do something about their excessive rates. After working my way through several layers of "supervisors," I now pay no annual fee and about 9 percent interest. And pay the bills on time. Many card companies charge as much as $25 for late payments.

◆ Take out a consolidation loan. Chances are that your bank or credit union offers loans at lower interest rates than those you're paying now. In many cases the lender may want you to cancel your credit cards (or at least turn the cards over to them). If you own your own home, consider taking out a home equity loan. The interest you pay on these loans may be tax deductible. Either way, you'll be able to pay off your bills faster and at far lower cost. If you transfer your balance to a new low-interest card, watch out: those low rates are often teasers that last only a few months and then shoot way up. So if you aren't careful, you could be right back where you started.

If Things Get Really, Really out of Control

Of course you want to take care of your debt; just about everyone does. But sometimes, despite your best intentions, things just get to the point where they're no longer manageable. Fortunately, debtors' prisons went out with the nineteenth century. But that probably won't keep you from feeling helpless, humiliated, infuriated, frustrated, and, often, somehow less than a man. After all, men are supposed to know how to handle money. If you've gotten to this point and you're feeling completely overwhelmed by your debts and you're being hounded by creditors and collection agencies, you have three basic options.

◆ **Keep on doing what you've been doing.** But since that hasn't worked up to this point, why keep making yourself miserable?

◆ **Get some professional help.** A far more sensible approach. The Consumer Credit Counseling Service (CCCS) is a nonprofit group that helps people avoid bankruptcy and restructure their debts. They also have free workshops and seminars on debt management. You can find a local CCCS office by calling

"I've called you kids in here today in order to explain to you why I will no longer be able to make good on my pledge to raise your allowances by 25% over the next four years."

(800) 388-2227. You might also want to contact your local chapter of Debtors' Anonymous; check your white pages.

♦ **File for bankruptcy.** Truly the option of last resort. Bankruptcy can essentially wipe out all debts from credit cards, auto loans, medical bills, utilities, and a few others. On the downside, though, it'll screw up your credit report for at

The Best Investment

After paying off your credit cards, one of the most important—and safest— investments you can make is in yourself. If you never finished high school or college or grad school, get it done now. Enrolling in a local junior college, for example, is cheap, easy, and usually has no prerequisites. Over the course of your life, the increased salary you'll command and your increased self-esteem, confidence, and general level of happiness will more than pay for the cost of the increased education.

Be sure to let your employer know about your plans. Many companies offer tuition reimbursement or low-interest loans to employees.

least seven years. And even after you're done, you'll still owe any debts related to alimony and child support, taxes (in most cases), and student loans. Bankruptcy isn't for everyone. So if you're even considering it, get some sound advice first. *How to File for Bankruptcy* by attorneys Stephen Elias, Albin Renauer, and Robin Leonard is a good place to start.

Boosting Your Savings

Now that you've done everything you can to cut your expenses, you're ready for the fun stuff.

For most people, the first big question is, How much should I try to save? Well, the answer depends on your goals. Many experts feel that you should shoot for an income at retirement that's about 70 percent of your current income. If you're in your twenties and just starting to save, you'll be able to accomplish this goal if you sock away 4 to 6 percent of your take-home pay. If you're in your thirties, that goes up to 7 to 12 percent, and if you're in your forties, it's 15 percent or more.

Whatever your situation, the most important thing is to save as much as you can as regularly as you can. Here are some things to keep in mind as you're getting started.

- **Out of sight, out of mind.** This means trying to have money taken out of your paycheck automatically—that way you'll miss it less than if you had to write a check out every month, and you'll be more inclined to do it regularly. Most employers have direct deposit and most financial institutions are more than glad to help you set up regular electronic withdrawals to a savings account of some kind.
- **Regularity.** Make your savings plan a habit for life. Making investments of the same amount each month is called "dollar cost averaging" and has some great benefits: when prices are up, you're buying a smaller number of shares. When prices are down, you're buying more. On average, then, you'll be fine. This strategy also keeps you from falling into the trap of buying high (just to get on the bandwagon) and selling low (when the bottom has fallen out of the market).
- **Avoid temptation.** Don't put your long-term-savings money in any kind of account that has check-writing privileges. Making your money hard to get may increase the chances of your having it for a while.
- **Reinvest any interest and dividends.** It's almost like free money, so why take it out? Leaving earnings in the account also helps your balance grow faster.
- **Make a good tax plan** (see pages 232–33 for more on this).
- **Get an ESOP.** No, it's not a fable, it's an Employee Stock Ownership Plan, and it's offered by more than ten thousand employers across the country. Basically, these plans allow employees to purchase stock in their company without paying commission. Sometimes you can make your purchases with pretax dollars, sometimes with after-tax dollars. Some employers let you buy at below-market prices,

Special Financial Issues for Widowers

Like divorced and never-married fathers, newly widowed men—especially those whose wives worked outside the home—often find themselves in a financial squeeze. Because of what you're going through emotionally, it's very important that you put off making major financial decisions for a while. Turn as much of this over to your accountant or trusted financial advisor as you can.

There are, however, a few financial matters you'll need to address if you haven't done so already. You may not want to deal with these things right now, but it's important to take care of them sooner rather than later:

♦ Tell anyone who needs to know about your wife's death. This includes creditors (anyone you or she owes money to), her insurance agent, her lawyer, her accountant, your bank, your stockbroker, Social Security (the number's in the white pages of your phone book), the IRS, and your state's tax agency.

♦ Get certified copies of your wife's death certificate. Ten is probably enough.

♦ Find her will (if you don't already know where it is).

♦ Get all her financial papers together. Thinking about money at a time like this may sound absolutely ghoulish and mercenary, but it really has to be done—if not for you then for your children. Be sure to check the safety deposit boxes and watch the mail for statements from financial institutions you might not have known your wife was dealing with.

♦ Find her life insurance policies—another uncomfortable but important task. You may not know about all the life insurance she had, so be sure to check with her health insurer, union, and/or employer to see whether they may have provided some coverage that you were unaware of. In addition, some credit card issuers give automatic flight or accident insurance, and they and mortgage companies often provide insurance that pays off their balances in case of death. And she may have had other coverage through organizations you didn't even know she belonged to.

♦ Find out about death benefits. Talk to her employer's personnel office to see whether they provide burial coverage for employees. If she was a veteran, there's almost surely some coverage (check with the Veterans' Administration; their number is in the government pages of your phone book).

and some even contribute extra money to your account, which vests (becomes yours) over time, usually five to seven years.

The next big question is, So what do I do with all the money I'm going to be saving? Again, there's no magic formula. Whether you put your money in government bonds or short the pork belly futures market will depend on your individual and family goals

> ## DRIP a Little Savings into This
>
> If you're going the do-it-yourself route and you're thinking about investing in stocks, here's a way to save some real money. Hundreds of companies now offer current shareholders dividend reinvestment plans (DRIPs) that allow them to buy stock directly from the company without having to pay a broker. Some make this service available to new investors as well. These plans almost always allow investors to reinvest dividends without commission. Many allow for automatic electronic purchases direct from your checking account, and several dozen actually allow DRIP participants to buy stock at a below-market rate. Finally, most plans will also let you sell your stock at rates far under what even a discount broker would charge. So how can you find out about DRIPs? The hard way is to contact individual companies directly to find out whether they offer such programs. A much easier way is to check out the Direct Stock Purchase Plan Clearinghouse. Their phone number and Web address are in the Resources section at the end of this book.

and how you feel about risk. Correctly analyzing these things is a process that's far too complicated to cover here in a way that would be at all helpful. So unless you're already sophisticated financially, get some help. It is, of course, possible to do it yourself, and if you think you want to try, Eric Tyson's *Personal Finance for Dummies* will walk you through the whole process. If you want a more personal touch, you'll need to get yourself a financial planner (see pages 238–39).

A Couple of Things about Tax Planning

Before (or at least at the same time as) you make any real changes to any part of your financial picture, you should be sure to talk to someone knowledgeable about the tax consequences. Becoming a single father can have a major impact on your tax situation. Your alimony is tax deductible, for example, but child support is not. And if you're a widower you may have some inheritance issues to deal with. Your financial planner may be able to offer some help, but a good accountant would be a lot better.

One of the most important things to keep in mind is the changes in tax rates on capital gains (increase in an asset's value). As of July 1997, for example, if you've owned an asset (including shares of stock and mutual funds) for more than eighteen months, any capital gains are taxed at 20 percent, down from 28 percent under the old laws. If your taxable income is about $41,000 or less, your rate may be as low as 10 percent. So why am I telling you this? Because it may have an effect on the way you invest your money. Because the capital gains tax rate is so much lower than regular income tax rates, you're probably going to want to move your high-yielding assets into something that allows you to defer your income for at least eighteen months (your IRA or other tax-deferred accounts, for example). Keep any lower-earning investments in your taxable accounts (checking or money market, for example). Of course, before you start moving things around, check with your accountant.

Here are a few other critical ways to save on your taxes:

♦ Immediately start a 401(k) if you're eligible for one through your employer. These plans offer participants a series of great benefits. First, since your contributions are taken out of your paycheck before you pay taxes, you reduce your taxable income. Second, the balance of the account grows tax-deferred until you start making withdrawals—sometime after age 59½ or so. Sometimes there's a third benefit: your employer may match at least a portion of your contribution, giving you some free money that will also grow tax-deferred. Remember, though, that 401(k)s are not savings accounts. If you make withdrawals before age 59½, you'll have to pay at least a 10 percent penalty to the Feds and a smaller percentage, penalty to your state. And then you'll get hit with a bill for income tax on the full amount withdrawn. That could eat up 50 percent of what you've saved—not the kind of return you were hoping for.

♦ Start an IRA. As with a 401(k), your taxable income is reduced by the amount you contribute to your IRA, and the earnings grow tax-deferred until you start withdrawing them. One exception: if you're eligible for a company-sponsored retirement plan, your IRA contribution won't be deductible. But make the contributions anyway; the earnings are still tax-deferred.

♦ Consider a Roth IRA. Your contributions to these new IRAs aren't deductible from your income, but the earnings accumulate tax-*free*, unlike the regular IRA, which just puts off the bite until you retire. You might also consider rolling some or all of your existing IRA money into a Roth. But be careful: Roths aren't for everyone, so check with your accountant before you open one.

♦ If you're self-employed, start a KEOGH or SEP plan and put as much into it as you can. These plans sometimes have special requirements and are often complicated, so have your accountant give you a hand.

♦ Consider selling your house. For a single person, the first $250,000 in gain from the sale of your principal residence is now exempt from tax. You can repeat the process every two years.

Other Big Financial Concerns

Now that you've got your own financial situation in order, you can start worrying about everyone else's.

Getting Your Kids into Good Money Habits

As an adult, you know that there are four things you can do with money: get it, spend it, save it, and give it away. (The first one, of course, has to happen before any of the others can.) But your kids may not be completely clear on these concepts for quite a while. One of the best ways to teach your kids about money is to give them some of their own. And that, says Neale Godfrey, author of *A Penny Saved . . . : Teaching Your Children the Values and Life-Skills They Will Need in the Real World,* means putting them on the family payroll by giving them an allowance.

Starting on their third birthdays, I gave each of my daughters an allowance of three dollars every other week—a veritable fortune to those of us who had to make do on an extremely sporadic fifty cents a week—and have gradually increased that amount as they've gotten older. But don't worry, it didn't all go straight into their pockets.

Here's how it works: You pay out the three dollars as ten quarters and ten nickels (as your kids get older, add ten pennies, ten dimes, ten more dimes, and so forth—but be sure to keep any increases in increments of ten). The first thing your child does is take 10 percent of her money (one of each kind of coin) and put it into a jar marked "Charity." She gets to decide what to do with this money (either give it directly to a homeless person or combine it with some of

"It's called a coin. It's not made out of paper—but it's considered money all the same."

your money and send it by check to a deserving organization). She then divides the remaining nine coins into thirds and drops one third into each of the following jars:

- The instant gratification jar. Bite your tongue. It's her money, so let her spend it however she wants—even if it's on candy. She'll learn awfully quickly that once it's gone, it's gone.
- The medium-term jar. This one gets saved up for a week or two and can then be cashed in for a larger toy or expense.
- The long-term jar. Basically, she'll never see this money again. Let it accumulate in the jar for a while, then take it (and your child) down to the bank and open up a savings account.

As wacky as this whole allowance scheme sounds, the opportunities for learning are amazing: counting, percentages, division, categorizing, the importance of helping others, the value of patience, the benefits of saving, and so much more.

Oh, and since you may have been wondering, no, don't attach too many strings to your kids' allowances. You can (and probably should) take it away if they wise off too much or punch each other or do some other horrible thing, but don't make it dependent on their doing chores. Children should pull their own age-appropriate weight at home because they're part of the family and not because they're paid to do so.

"I kept a small percentage of your allowance for administrative costs."

Life Insurance

Becoming a single parent does some interesting things to your mind and to your outlook on life. On the one hand, it makes you treasure each second with your child more than ever, especially if you're not a custodial father. On the other hand, the dramatic upheaval in your life can make you painfully aware of how quickly—and often unpredictably—life can change. Simply put, the purpose of life insurance is to reduce (at least to the extent that money can) the unpredictability your children would experience if you died unexpectedly.

That sound like a simple enough goal, but according to the National Insurance Consumer Organization, more than 90 percent of Americans have the wrong kind of insurance coverage and in the wrong amounts. There really aren't any hard-and-fast rules or secret formulas to help you determine how much insurance you need. But spending some time thinking about the following questions will put you in the top 10 percent (it's really not that hard) of insurance consumers:

- ♦ Do you need or want to pay off your mortgage? If your kids are young (any age under thirty-five counts as young here) and you intend to leave them your house, the answer to this question is yes.
- ♦ Do you have a lot of debts you want to pay off?
- ♦ Do you need or want to leave an estate large enough to pay fully for your kids' college education?
- ♦ Do you want to leave an estate large enough to pay for all of your children's living expenses until they're old enough to take care of themselves? You can't—and shouldn't—count on your ex or anyone else to take care of this one.
- ♦ What do you expect your tax situation to be? If you have a huge estate, your children will have to come up with a tidy sum to cover inheritance taxes.

There are two basic ways to make sure your insurance needs are properly taken care of:

- ♦ Read a few good personal finance guides (or at least sections of them). Despite what you might think, it's not all that complicated. Eric Tyson's *Personal Finance for Dummies* is one of the best.
- ♦ Get yourself a financial planner (see pages 238–39 for some helpful tips).

Either way, you should at least be aware of your insurance options. Basically, there are two types of life insurance on the market: term and cash value; each is further divided into several subcategories. Here's a brief overview:

TERM

There are three types of term insurance, and they all share these features:

- ♦ Fairly low cost, especially in the early years.
- ♦ Premiums increase over time as your odds of dying go up.

♦ Policies are in effect only for a specified period of time.
♦ No cash value accumulation.

Here are your basic term insurance choices:
♦ Renewable term. You can renew the policy annually. Death benefit generally remains level, while premiums increase over time. (But watch out: if you develop a health problem, you may not be able to renew.)
♦ Level term. The death benefit and the premium remain the same for a specified period of time, usually five, ten, twenty, or more years.
♦ Decreasing term. The death benefit decreases each year, while premiums remain the same.

CASH VALUE

There are an increasing number of cash value insurance products available. Despite their differences, they all share the following features:
♦ These policies are essentially a combination of term insurance and a savings plan. A portion of your premium pays for pure term insurance. The balance is deposited into some kind of side fund on which you can earn interest or dividends.
♦ These policies tend to offer—initially—very competitive interest rates. The rate is usually guaranteed for a year, but then drops to whatever the market is paying.
♦ You can pay pretty much whatever you want to. But if your payment isn't enough to cover the insurance cost, the balance is taken out of your side fund, reducing your cash value.
♦ The cash benefit accumulates tax-free, and you can borrow against it or withdraw from it during your lifetime.
♦ If properly placed in trust, the entire cash and accumulated savings can go to your heirs free of income tax.

Here are your cash value choices.
♦ Whole life. Locks in a death benefit, cash values, and premium. The side fund is invested by the insurance company.
♦ Universal life. Similar to whole life, except that you can change the premium payment and death benefits anytime. And since the side fund is invested in fixed-income home securities (bonds and so forth), your cash values can fluctuate.
♦ Variable life. Similar to universal, except that you have a bit more input into how your side fund is invested. Your choices usually include money markets, government securities, corporate bonds, and growth, fixed-income, or mutual fund portfolios.

So how can you possibly make a choice between term and cash value? Financial author and counselor Eric Tyson has some fairly strong views on the subject: "Cash value insurance is the most oversold insurance and financial product in the history

Picking a Financial Planner

Since most states don't have laws regulating or accrediting financial planners (who may also call themselves "advisors," "consultants," or "managers"), just about anyone can set up shop to dole out financial advice and sell products. Most financial planners are paid on a commission basis, meaning that there's always at least the possibility of a conflict of interest. (In other words, whether or not your investments do well, the financial planner is assured his commission.) Commissions typically range from as low as 4 percent on some mutual funds to the entire first year's premium on a cash value life insurance policy. Others are paid on a fee basis and typically charge from $50 to $250 per hour.

This doesn't mean, of course, that fee-based planners are inherently better than their commission-based colleagues (although many experts believe that you'll be happier, and possibly richer, with someone who charges a fee). Your goal is to find someone you like and who you believe will have your best interests at heart. Here are a few things you can do to help you weed out the losers:

♦ Get references from friends, business associates, and other people whose opinions you trust. Alternatively, the Institute of Certified Financial Planners, (800) 282-7526, will give you some local references, and the National Association of Personal Financial Advisors, (800) 366-2732, makes referrals only of fee-based (as opposed to commission-based) planners.

♦ Select at least three potential candidates and set up initial consultations (which shouldn't cost you anything). Then conduct tough interviews. Here's what you want to know:

of the industry," he writes. His solution? Unless you have a high net worth, get yourself a term insurance policy with the following features:

♦ Guaranteed renewable (you don't want to be canceled if you get sick).

♦ Level premiums for five to ten years (that way you won't need to get a physical exam every year).

♦ A price you can live with. Costs for the very same policy can vary by as much as 200 to 300 percent, so shop around. (Since a rather big chunk of your premium is going to some agent in the form of commission, you can cut your costs way down by buying a "no-load" or "low-load" policy.)

WHEN YOU REALLY NEED TO BUY CASH VALUE INSURANCE

♦ Currently, an individual can leave up to $600,000, and a couple can leave up to $1,200,000 to beneficiaries without having to pay federal estate taxes. If you aren't worth this much, or don't expect to be when you die, stick with term.

♦ If you own a small business that's worth more than $1 million, cash value insur-

- ◆ Educational background. Not to be snobby here, but the more formal the education—especially in financial management—the better. Watch out for fancy initials: many planners prominently display the letters CFP (for Certified Financial Planner) after their names. *Forbes* magazine recently called the CFP credential "meaningless."
- ◆ Level of experience. Unless you've got money to burn, let your niece break in her MBA on someone else. Stick to experienced professionals with at least three years in the business.
- ◆ Profile of the typical client. What you're looking for is a planner who has experience working with people whose income level and family situation are similar to yours.
- ◆ Compensation. If fee-based, how is the fee calculated? If commission, what are the percentages on each product offered? Any hesitation to show you a commission schedule is a red flag.
- ◆ Get a sample financial plan. You want to see what you're going to be getting for your money. Be careful, though: fancy graphics, incomprehensible boilerplate language, and expensive leather binders are often used to distract you from the report's lack of substance.
- ◆ References. How long have customers been with the planner? Are they happy? Better off? Any complaints or weaknesses?
- ◆ Check your prospective planner's record with state and federal regulators. You can call the federal Securities and Exchange Commission, (202) 272-7450, or your state's equivalent to check on disciplinary action and to see whether your candidates have ever been sued.

ance makes sense, unless you have enough in liquid assets to pay off the estate taxes your heirs will owe.

Paying for Your Kids' Education

We all know it's going to cost a ton of money to send a child to college (realistic projections often exceed $200,000 for four years at a good private school). But too many of us look at all those zeros and panic, thinking we're going to have to write a check to pay for the whole thing. My ex and I bought our house for about that amount (in California, where $200,000 doesn't buy much) and never thought for a second of paying for the whole thing in cash.

So how do you finance your kid's education? Traditionally, parents have opened savings accounts in their children's names as a way of putting money aside for the child's education. This, however, is "usually a financial mistake of major proportions in the short- and long-term," writes Eric Tyson. The solution? Start socking away money—*into your own retirement account.* If that sounds a little counterintuitive (it did to me when I first heard it), consider this wonderful analogy Tyson told me:

If you were paying attention to the flight attendant before taking off on your last airplane trip, you'll remember that if those oxygen masks drop from the ceiling, you're supposed to put *yours* on first, *then* your child's, right? The idea is that if *you* can't breathe, you certainly won't be able to help anyone else. Tyson makes the same basic point about money: take care of *your* finances first—especially your IRA, 401(k), Keogh, or company-sponsored retirement—and your whole family will be better off.

But that still doesn't clear up the problem of how feathering your own personal retirement account instead of starting a college fund in your child's name will help put her through college. Well, here's how it works:

- Money you invest in your retirement accounts is often at least partially tax-deductible and always grows tax-free until you start withdrawing it. The dollars you invest in an account in your child's name are after-tax dollars and any interest and dividends may be taxable as income or capital gains.
- At the present time, financial-aid departments usually count just about everything you own as an asset—except your retirement accounts. They assume that 35 percent of all the money held in your child's name will be available for educational purposes each year. Only about 6 percent of the money held in your name is considered available for education, and funds in your retirement accounts are not counted at all. Therefore, the less money you have in your child's name, the more financial aid you'll qualify for.
- Plenty of financial-aid options are available: student loans (usually available at below-market rates), grants, fellowships, work-study programs, and so forth.
- You can always borrow against the equity in your home.
- If you'll be over 59½ by the time your child starts college, you may be able to withdraw money from your IRA or other retirement account without incurring any penalties.

Another option to consider is to prepay your child's college expenses. Currently fourteen states offer plans that let you pay in advance for your child's tuition (plus room, board, and books, in some cases) at state schools. Seven more states will be instituting these plans soon.

But investigate this option carefully. If your child doesn't end up going to a state school, you'll get your principal back plus a rather paltry return of about 3 to 5 percent. And even if she's going to take advantage of the plan, you might be better off investing this prepaid tuition money in the stock market, which has grown some 10 percent a year for at least the past fifty years.

WHAT ABOUT THOSE EDUCATION IRAS?

If you make less than $95,000 per year, you can put away $500 each year into a special account for each of your children. Although your contributions to these

"Dad, I need to dip into my college fund."

special Education IRAs aren't deductible from your income like regular IRAs, they grow tax-free if the money is used to pay for education, room, board, books, and related expenses.

While tax-free accumulation is always a good thing, there may be some drawbacks to these accounts, so you'd be wise to check with your accountant to make sure it's the right strategy for you. First, you won't be able to take advantage of some of the other education tax breaks (such as a credit for tuition) in the same year as you make an Education IRA contribution. And if you put money into a prepaid tuition plan and an Ed IRA in the same year you'll have to pay a major penalty. Second, if you're thinking you'll need financial aid, this account will be considered an asset and will reduce the amount of aid your child is eligible for.

Finally, if you're considering one of these accounts, keep in mind that there can be only one contribution to it per year. This means that you and your ex might have to coordinate things so that both of you (or either of your parents) don't contribute money in the same year.

IF YOU'RE PLANNING TO PAY 100 PERCENT OF YOUR CHILD'S COLLEGE EXPENSES

Despite all this sound financial advice, you may still be intent on paying cash for college. If you've got the money—and the desire—to do so, immediately disregard the above advice and start socking money away into an account in your child's name (with you as custodian). That way, you'll be able to save at least a little on taxes: until she's fourteen, the first $1,400 or so of your child's interest and dividends will be taxed at the (presumably lower) child's rate; the rest gets taxed at your rate. After age fourteen, however, all her income gets taxed at the rate for a single adult.

One important warning: do not retain any joint accounts with your ex, particularly accounts for which the two of you are joint custodians of money held in your children's names. You and you alone should be the custodian for any money put aside by you or anyone else in your family. If your ex is also saving money for them, great, but she should do so on her own.

Wills and Trusts

By this time, hopefully, you've got your life insurance situation under control. If not, put this book down right now and call your insurance agent. And while you're waiting for him to call back, you might want to review pages 236–38.

Knowing that your kids will be financially secure in the event of your death should make you breathe a little easier. But don't relax completely—there are a few other things you have to worry about. For example, if, God forbid, you're killed tomorrow,

---

Wills

ADVANTAGES

- You can distribute your assets exactly as you want.
- There is an automatic limit on how long someone has to challenge the terms of your will (varies from state to state). According to some estimates, one in three wills is contested, so this limit could be a very good thing.
- Creditors must make claims within a certain amount of time (again, varies from state to state).
- The activities of your executors, guardians, and trustees are supervised by the court.

DISADVANTAGES

- Probate. This is the name for the process through which everything in a will must go before it is completely straightened out. Probate can easily last as long as eighteen months. And until it's over, your heirs won't have access to most of the assets of your estate.
- Court fees, attorneys' fees, executor fees, accounting fees, and so forth can eat up 3 to 7 percent (or more) of the estate.
- In most cases, probate files are public records. This means that anyone can go down to the courthouse and take a peek at your will.

Living Trusts

ADVANTAGES

♦ The costs and time delays of probate are largely avoided. After your death, your survivors should have control over your assets without involving the courts.

♦ The trust document is not public, so no one can see it unless you show it to them.

♦ Assets are distributed as you wish —either directly to your heirs upon your death or gradually over time.

♦ A living trust "not only allows your continued total control over your affairs during your lifetime, but provides a continuity in management and supervision in the event of your incapacity," says attorney Harvey J. Platt.

DISADVANTAGES

♦ Trusts generally cost more and take longer to set up than wills. It will also probably cost you a few dollars to transfer ownership of your assets from you personally to the trust. However, all the probate-related expenses that wills require can come to about the same amount as the cost of setting up a trust.

♦ Improperly prepared, a living trust can cause some serious problems. If the IRS feels that your trust was not properly executed, your estate could wind up in probate—the very situation you were hoping to avoid.

♦ Since all your assets are transferred during your lifetime from your name into the name of the trust, you are giving up personal ownership in a lot of what you own. This can be tough psychologically.

♦ Trusts may not reduce your tax liability.

who's going to take care of your kids? Who's going to make sure they get the kind of education and upbringing you want them to have?

If you're divorced or were never married, the answers to these questions are pretty straightforward: custody (if you have it now) and absolute responsibility for the children and the right to determine their future will automatically go to your ex unless she refuses the job, abandons the children, or is legally unfit to handle things.

If you're a widower, things are somewhat more complicated. You'll have to spend some time thinking about who you'd like to be your children's guardian—the person who will take physical and financial care of them if you die. It's a big decision, and it should not be taken lightly.

Whether you're divorced, widowed, or have never been married, you still have a lot of control over who gets your property and, if it goes to your kids, how that property (and money) will be managed after you're gone. In most states, kids can't legally own property or manage any amount of money greater than about $2,000, so you'll have to appoint someone to manage anything you leave to them until they're at an age you think is old enough for them to squander it. Pick only one person to manage your children's inheritance. Two might disagree, and if the two you're thinking about are a couple whose relationship happens to break up, things will get awfully complicated—and that will only hurt your child. Appoint the same person to handle the financial affairs of all your children, no matter how many you have.

All of these instructions will be outlined in a will or a trust, or both. But about half of all parents with young children don't have either one. Don't allow yourself to belong to that half.

If you die *intestate* (meaning without a will, trust, or other document that tells how you want your assets distributed), the details will be handled according to the laws of your state. In most cases, this means that a judge will appoint a guardian for your estate and another one for your children. Chances are, neither of these guardians will be the one you would have chosen.

So which is better? A will? A trust? Actually, the answer may be both. As soon as you become a parent, you absolutely, positively need a will to designate a guardian for your child. You can also use a will to distribute your assets, but many experts feel that setting up a *revocable living trust* is a better alternative. However, because of the time and expense involved, many decline to take advantage of the living trust alternative. Some of the advantages and disadvantages of both are listed on pages 242 and 243.

As Long as You're Thinking about Depressing Things . . .

♦ Consider a *durable power of attorney.* This document (which you'll need an attorney to help you prepare) gives someone you designate the power to manage your affairs if you become incapacitated. You can include a health-care directive, which covers such topics as whether or not you want to be kept on life support if things ever come to that.

♦ Consider making some gifts. You (and your parents, for that matter) can each transfer up to $10,000 per year to each of your children, thereby reducing the size of your estate as well as the amount of estate taxes that the children will have to come up with later. (Estate taxes, by the way, are usually due and payable within nine months of death.)

New Relationships

Dating for (Single) Daddies

Some newly single fathers have no problem moving from one relationship to the next. But the majority—whether they're widowed or divorced, or have never been married at all—are too sad, depressed, or angry even to think about the possibility of getting involved with anyone new. Chances are, though, that no matter how bad you feel right now, you'll change your mind fairly soon.

For a lot of men, starting a new relationship, with all the dating and extra showers and being on your best behavior, can be a traumatic and frightening experience, especially after a bad breakup or a partner's death. For that reason, don't start dating before you truly feel ready. Your friends and family will probably try to fix you up, especially if you're a widower, but there's absolutely nothing wrong with being by yourself or with people you have no romantic interest in. No matter how tough you think you are, you've been through a rough time and a break will do you good.

While you're waiting, consider getting some therapy. At the very least, a professional will probably be able to help you avoid dragging your old emotional and psychological baggage into your new relationships.

But whether you get therapy or not, you should spend a lot of time thinking about what you want from a new relationship and why you want it. For most men, fatherhood and fathering are inextricably linked with marriage (or at least with being in a committed relationship), says researcher Shirley Feldman. And if they aren't in a relationship, a lot of men think that they aren't capable of being good fathers and that their children will suffer. The truth is that even if you're a widower, you do not need a woman to make you whole again, to make you a good father, or to give your children a real family. Sadly, too many fathers don't know this and get remarried or involved in long-term relationships way too soon. Perhaps that's one of the reasons that, while about half of all first marriages end in divorce, the odds are even worse (more than 60 percent) the second time around.

Once you've made the decision that you're really ready to start dating, start slow; Parents Without Partners (see the Resources section for contact information) and a variety of community and church groups organize picnics and other events for single parents on a regular basis. This is a great way to meet people who know exactly what you've been through.

In addition, here are some important dating dos and don'ts:

♦ **Keep your kids and your dates separate.** Try to do your dating when you don't have the kids or at least meet your dates somewhere else besides your house. The idea here is not to introduce your kids and your dates unless it's clear that you're starting a long-term relationship. If you're going out with a lot of different people and you introduce your kids to every one, they'll get confused. If you absolutely can't avoid having your children meet one of your dates, introduce her only as a friend. Be sure to read the section on making introductions, pages 252–53.

♦ **Go for some variety.** The last thing you want to do right now is get into a long-term relationship with the first woman you go out with. She may make you feel loved and needed, perhaps for the first time in a long time, but chances are you're nowhere near ready yet. It took me over a year after my divorce even to consider anything other than a casual relationship.

♦ **Be up front with your dates.** I never really got around to mentioning my kids to the first few women I went out with after my divorce. The problem with this omission is, if it turns out that the woman you're seeing doesn't like kids she's bound to be pretty pissed when she finds out your little secret. And if she does like kids, she's going to wonder what kind of father you are if you don't care enough about your children even to mention them. Don't underestimate the importance of this issue: a lot of women tend to think that the way you relate to your children is the way you'll relate to them. So do everyone a favor and tell your dates you have kids. And talk about them—but not too much. Your dates want to know that you're interested in them too.

♦ **Don't talk about the other women in your life.** If you're widowed, your dates and prospective girlfriends have a right to know. But if you talk about your deceased wife constantly, they'll feel intimidated. And if you have an ex, talking about how wonderfully the two of you are getting along will make your date think you're headed for a reconciliation. On the other hand, don't spend the evening bad-mouthing her. A new girlfriend is naturally going to side with you against your ex but your relationship should be built on something more than a mutual dislike for someone else.

For Gay Dads Only

PROBLEMS YOU MAY FACE WITHIN THE GAY COMMUNITY

Because gay culture tends to be oriented around singles or couples without children, you may not get a huge amount of support from your other gay friends. "[Many] people who don't have children have a low tolerance for them," writes researcher Frederick Bozett. "Gays are no exception, and often they do not comprehend how important children are to the father." And because the gay world values youth and independence perhaps even more than the straight world does, gay fathers sometimes find that having children may make it harder for them to get into long-term relationships, adds Bozett.

As a result, many gay fathers find themselves living in what one researcher calls the "double closet"—the heterosexual closet they get out of by disclosing their gay identity to nongays, and the paternal closet they exit by disclosing their father identity to gays.

Interestingly, there's a bit of evidence that this may be changing, although very slowly. Kelley Taylor recently started publishing *Alternative Family* magazine (see the Resources section), which includes articles on gay-specific parenting issues, activities, and a good list of appropriate books, videos, and family organizations.

Some Situations You May Find Yourself Dealing with Soon

VERY SHORT-TERM RELATIONSHIPS

There's nothing wrong with having a lot of sex with a lot of different people without the commitment of a long-term relationship (if, of course, you're practicing safe sex). In fact, short-term relationships—even one-night stands—can often be good, giving you time to rediscover yourself and helping you to regain some of your lost or damaged self-confidence. But keep these short relationships as far away from your kids as possible—especially if you're seeing more than one woman at a time.

Bringing home every woman you date can only make your kids uncomfortable. They might be angry at you for dating in the first place. Or, if they really want you to get remarried, their hopes will be dashed when the woman from last Thursday doesn't show up again. Your children need consistency and security in their lives; exposing them to a lot of different women gives them just the opposite. In addition, while having a revolving door installed in your bedroom may have seemed like a great idea when you were younger, now it will only give your children the idea that women are interchangeable and that relationships aren't meant to last—ideas that can become self-fulfilling prophecies for both boys and girls.

SLIGHTLY LONGER, BUT STILL CASUAL RELATIONSHIPS

After you've gotten the one-night-stand thing out of your system (if it was ever there), you may find yourself in a relationship that's a lot of fun but that you know full well won't work out in the long run. You might have just one of these casual relationships or several in a row. Again, it's important to think long and hard before introducing a casual girlfriend to your kids. If they like her and see the two of you together a lot, they'll start forming a strong attachment to her. Then they'll be devastated when the inevitable breakup happens. And believe me, they've already had enough devastation and emotional upheaval to last them quite a while.

If you do end up introducing your kids to someone who will be in their lives only temporarily, be sure that they understand the difference between being a good friend and a part of the family, says Mary Mattis, author of *Sex and the Single Parent*. "Friends can visit," she says. "Family lives there."

SLEEPING ARRANGEMENTS

Sex is a wonderful thing. And you should do it wherever and whenever you can, whether it's in a hotel, at your date's house, in the back seat of your car, or in a crowded elevator. But try to resist the temptation in your own home—at least when your kids are there—until you're in a serious relationship. (This, of course, could get a little complicated if the woman you're going out with has kids of her own; she probably won't want you staying at her place either.) Be prepared, though. Kids have an incredible knack for figuring out exactly what their parents are up to. You should also be sensitive to your girlfriend's feelings. If you don't explain why you never invite her to spend the night at your house she may start questioning whether you like her or whether you've got body parts hidden in your refrigerator.

It goes without saying that your kids should never have their first introduction to a woman you're involved with while you and she are in bed. So if you and your date do decide to sleep together at your house, try to bring her home after your kids are asleep and ask her to leave before they're likely to wake up in the morning. All this sneaking around may make you and your date feel either very cheap or like you're back in high school, but the less your children have to deal with your sex life, the better. Seeing you in bed with someone else, whether they know her or not, may bring up a lot of difficult issues for them, including the irrational fear that since you love someone else (and you wouldn't be in bed with her if you didn't, right?), you won't love them anymore. So if you think there's any possibility that your kids will walk into your room in the middle of the night, lock your door.

And finally, if it looks like your relationship is getting serious and the kids have already met your girlfriend, tell them in advance that she'll be sleeping over. If they haven't met her, read pages 252–53 and make sure they do first.

GETTING CAUGHT WITH YOUR PANTS DOWN

You read the kids their bedtime story and put them to sleep a few hours ago, and now you and your girlfriend are enjoying a little adult time together—naked. It's tender, it's wonderful, it feels fantastic, but all of a sudden you become aware that you've got an audience. So what do you do?

The first step is to deal with it immediately, even if you think the child didn't see much. Experts agree that even brief exposure to intercourse can be confusing and sometimes harmful to children. Very young kids can misinterpret entangled bodies and cries and moans of pleasure as a fight and worry that someone is getting hurt. Older kids—especially teens—who know something about sex may be put off by the idea that you're a sexual being or may be aroused by what they've seen and take it as encouragement to do some experimenting of their own. They also might get the idea that bringing home a lover is okay for them to do as well.

If your child walks in on you, here's what to do:

- **Don't get angry.** Tell him calmly yet firmly to leave, close the door, and go back to his own room. Yelling at him could scare him and make him think that what he saw was wrong.

- **If your child won't go, lead him.** And if you scared him off or if he bolted on his own, follow him back to his room.

- **Reassure your child.** When he's back in his bed, sit by his side and tell him that everything is fine and that no one was hurting anyone else. Mary Mattis suggests telling very young children (under six) that you and your lover were just playing together, and that grown-ups kiss and hug to be close to each other. But be prepared: even little kids know a lot more about sex than we did when we were their age and they may not be satisfied with a short answer.

- **Children older than six might need a somewhat sophisticated explanation of what they saw.** They probably already know that sex involves putting a penis inside a vagina and that that's how babies are made. Answer their questions simply and honestly, using the correct terminology. But don't offer any more information than they ask for.

- **Make sure they know they can always ask you more later.** You may be trying to keep sex a secret from your children, but doing so can inadvertently give them the impression that it's dirty or wrong—precisely the wrong message if you want them to have a healthy attitude toward sex when they're older.

- **Don't act embarrassed or ashamed, even if you are.** Kids need to know that having sex is a normal, healthy thing for adults to do. And don't apologize unless you bit your child's head off for walking in on you.

- **Take some precautions that this won't happen again,** such as putting a lock on your door or using the one you have.

SOOTHING YOUR GIRLFRIEND

Your first obligation is to your kids, so you'll need to explain to your lover that you'll be back as soon as you make sure the kids are okay. Don't ask her to leave, and if she starts to go, try to convince her to wait for you.

When you're through with the kids, you and your lover need to talk. As a parent you may already have had the experience of a child interrupting your lovemaking. And if your girlfriend has kids of her own, the same thing may have happened to

Problems in Bed

Most newly single fathers—especially the divorced and never-married ones—probably weren't having much sex during the last months (or years) of their relationships. As a result, the prospect of getting some again can be pretty exciting. And downright stressful.

Psychologists generally agree that a lot of what happens during sex takes place inside our heads. And given that you're still in the midst of recovering from a psychological blow, don't be surprised if you experience some sexual performance problems in the early stages of starting a new relationship. These include premature ejaculation or the inability to get or keep an erection.

If either or both of these things happens, don't panic. If you've never had any sexual difficulties before, they're almost surely a completely normal (though admittedly unpleasant) reaction to what's going on in your life. You may, for example, be feeling guilty; after spending years being with one woman the idea of sleeping with someone else—even if you're divorced—may subconsciously seem like a betrayal. Or, having been rejected by the last woman in your life, you may want so much to please your new lover that you're trying too hard. Or you may be so overwhelmed with your new responsibilities as a single father that you can't concentrate on anything else, even a naked woman in your bed.

Whatever the reason, be assured that this type of sexual dysfunction doesn't mean that there's anything wrong with you, that you aren't a real man, or that you secretly don't find your lover attractive. And remember, it's almost always temporary. In the meantime, though, here are four things that will help:

♦ **Slow down.** At the first sign that something is "wrong," many men's first reaction is to thrash around looking for a quick solution. You may rush off to your doctor, hoping he'll prescribe Viagra or some other drug, which you don't need unless your problem is physical—and yours most likely isn't. Or you may spend hundreds of dollars on absolutely useless "cures" advertised in magazines or on the Internet. Please don't do this. It just puts more pressure on you and that's the last thing you need right now.

♦ **Try something else.** One of the things that makes sexual dysfunction devastating for men is that we're so focused on orgasms—usually our partners'. Too many of us worry that we can't get them to climax without a well-functioning penis. Well, that's wrong. First of all, not every sexual encounter has to end in an orgasm. And second, not every orgasm has to be reached by penetration. If you make it clear to your partner that whatever problem you're experiencing has nothing to do with her, she'll more than likely be extremely supportive and quite willing to explore other ways that you and she can satisfy each other sexually. So don't be afraid to use your hands, your tongue, or even a vibrator or other fun toy. It will make your sex life more interesting and will make you feel a lot less inadequate.

♦ **Take care of yourself.** Having a sexual problem can be so depressing and consuming that it's hard to think of anything else—including what's good for you. Eating badly and not exercising will reduce your energy and ability to concentrate, which will make you even more anxious than you were before. "If it's good for the heart, it's good for the penis," says urologist E. Douglas Whitehead.

♦ **Meditate.** This may sound absolutely spacy, but it works wonders, enabling you to relax and take your mind off your problems. It's also very easy. Simply close your eyes and concentrate on your breathing—in, out, in, out. You'll be able to do that for about eight seconds before your mind wanders off to something else, like an image of you not performing in bed. When you become aware that you're no longer concentrating on your breathing, gently steer yourself back. Two twenty-minute meditation sessions a day is ideal, but even ten minutes a day will help a lot. After you do it for a few weeks you'll find that your mind is flitting around less and less. Two more hints: Don't meditate when you're exhausted or when you're lying down—you don't want to fall asleep. Instead, sit up in a reasonably comfortable chair. And don't check the clock every minute—you can't possibly hurt yourself by meditating too long. If you need to, set a timer.

"When you get a chance, son, I'd like to have a little talk about sex. . . . I could use a few pointers."

her. But if it hasn't, and especially if she doesn't have kids, she may be freaked out by the whole experience. So talk about what you're both feeling. Really and truly, there's no reason why this little episode should have any impact on your relationship, says Mattis, although it may affect your girlfriend's desire to spend the night at your house again.

When Things Get Serious

Making Introductions

There aren't any hard-and-fast rules about when to introduce your lover and your kids. Generally, though, most experts recommend waiting until you're "serious." That doesn't mean you have to be engaged, but as long as your relationship is exclusive and committed, the time is right. As simple as it sounds, making introductions is often very stressful for everyone involved and requires a lot of preparation. When, how, and where you set up the initial meeting is, of course, up to you. But here are a few pointers to keep in mind:

- **Later is better than sooner.** Make sure your children are ready—or at least as ready as they can be. If you're a widower, your kids may need longer to adjust to being without their mother. If you're divorced or separated, your kids may still be hoping you and your ex will get back together.
- **Shorter is better than longer.** A few hours is probably enough for a first meeting. You all need time to ease into things. A week camping in the wilderness is way too long and puts far too much pressure on everyone.
- **Have a plan.** Don't just arrange for everyone to get together and sit around. Plan some activities or a short outing. And what will you do afterward? Drop your lover off? Drop your kids off?
- **Prepare your children.** Tell them you want them to meet someone very special. But don't tell them how they're going to feel about her. Doing so puts too much pressure on them and can make them feel horribly guilty if they don't like her right away.
- **Tell your girlfriend about your kids and their quirks.** When she was three, my younger daughter expressed affection for people by making death threats—something I completely forgot to mention to my girlfriend. So you can imagine how taken aback she was when my daughter raised a thumb and forefinger, held them an inch apart, and shouted, "You only have this long to live!"
- **Go easy on the physical stuff.** You or your girlfriend may think that hugging and kissing each other in front of the kids will show them how much you love each other. It might, but it also might make the kids very uncomfortable, jealous, and resentful.
- **Warn her that you may be somewhat distracted.** Your kids may not be on

their best behavior and you may need to devote a lot of attention to them. As a result, your girlfriend may feel jealous and left out. She may want you to let her know everything is okay—even if that means holding her hand under the table—but you may not be able to.

♦ **Don't expect perfect behavior from everyone—including yourself.** Your kids may be anything from angelic to horrible and snotty. Your lover may be friendly or aloof. And you may find yourself snapping at everyone, especially if they aren't getting along as well as you'd hoped.

♦ **Don't set your expectations too high.** No matter how much you want it to happen, your new lover and your kids probably aren't going to be instant best friends. The purpose of the first meeting is simply to let them get to know each other a little. True friendships take time to develop.

If Your Girlfriend Has Kids of Her Own

Given how often marriages and other relationships break up, there's a pretty good chance that the woman you're going out with will have children of her own. If so, making introductions is going to be a little more complicated. To minimize complications, you should introduce the two families only after you and your girlfriend have met each other's kids alone. Give the children time to get a little bit used to the new adults before bringing anyone else into the picture. Once you've decided it's time to get everyone together, be sure to keep these things in mind:

♦ **Let the kids have some input.** The more fun everyone's having, the better the chances they'll want to get together again. So if the kids want to see a movie, go out for pizza, or do a picnic in the park, let them. It's better than a three-hour lecture on plant biology.

♦ **Keep the first few visits short.**

♦ **Don't put pressure on any of the kids.** Telling the kids that they're going to meet someone who is in the same grade or who also loves to draw is one thing. But telling them they'll be best friends is something else. Phrases like "new family," "new brother," and "new sister," also put a lot of unnecessary pressure on the kids.

♦ **Have reasonable expectations.** Your children may be very jealous of your girlfriend's kids and hers may be jealous of yours. So don't be surprised if they don't get along splendidly the first time out.

What You May Be Going Through

As we've discussed throughout this book, ending a relationship or losing a wife can bring up a variety of emotions and feelings. Interestingly, though, *starting* a relationship can be just as much of an emotional upheaval. Here are the most common feelings and emotions I've heard from single fathers across the country who are in the early stages of starting over:

- **Elation.** Isn't it wonderful to love and be loved again?
- **Relief.** Now there's someone to help take care of and discipline the children. While there's nothing wrong with getting some help now and then, resist the urge to dump all the child care on your girlfriend. She won't like it and neither will the kids.
- **More open emotionally.** My girlfriend once told me that she thought that ending a long-term relationship was like peeling away several layers of skin— it leaves you emotionally raw. The disadvantage of this rawness is that you feel more emotional pain than you ever have before. But there's an upside, too: you're probably a lot more in touch with positive emotions such as joy and empathy than you ever were before. In other words, while your lows will be lower, your highs will be higher.
- **Vulnerable.** If you're like most men, when you lost your wife or girlfriend you probably lost your closest confidante, one of the very few people you could be emotionally honest with. For the past few months or years you may not have been able to talk to anyone about how you're feeling. But now that there's a new woman in your life, you may find that you're able to discuss deep emotional issues for the first time in months or years. While this is a good thing, try not to become too dependent on her.
- **Conflicted.** Starting a relationship and being an active father isn't easy and you might sometimes feel as though you have to choose between your kids and your lover. You may, at the same time, resent your children for making things so hard for you (the logic being that if you didn't have kids you wouldn't be in this predicament).
- **Worried—about yourself.** You've worked hard to reestablish your independence and you know you can handle this parenting thing pretty well. But now that you're getting involved with someone else you're worried that you might lose your independence and your authority in your kids' lives.
- **Worried—about everyone else.** How are your kids going to react to your girlfriend? How's she going to react to them? How's your ex going to deal with things? All this worrying about everyone else is enough to drive you nuts. While it's good to be concerned about other people, spending too much time on it will make it impossible for you to take care of your own needs.
- **Guilty.** You may feel that you're placing your needs above those of your kids by spending time on your new relationship that should really be spent with them.
- **Trying too hard.** Some single fathers become so focused on their new girlfriend that they completely ignore what's going on with their kids, say Richard Gatley and David Koulack. This in an extremely easy trap to fall into, because "if you feel that you've 'failed' in one relationship, you may go overboard trying

to please your new companion in order to make a go of the new relationship," they write.

♦ **Overprotective.** Along similar lines, if you're worried that your "failure" in your previous relationship is a guarantee of failure in this one, you may be trying to spare your children another horrible breakup by doing things (subconsciously or overtly) to keep your girlfriend and your kids from getting too close.

What Your Children May Be Going Through

When confronted with your serious new relationship(s), your kids have some adapting to do as well. Most kids handle things pretty well and if you're lucky, they'll fall in love with your girlfriend right away and encourage your relationship with her. My girlfriend is a children's book illustrator who, coincidentally, had illustrated one of my daughters' favorite books and they were wild about her. Interestingly, in this regard you may have it easier than your ex. children are generally far more accepting of their fathers' new loves than their mothers'.

If your kids are supportive of the new woman (or women) in your life, you've got nothing to worry about. But in many cases, they won't be. The trauma of your breakup or the death of their mother may have brought you and your children closer than ever before. In their minds you belong to them and they may feel frightened of, threatened by, and even hostile toward anyone who seems like a possible threat to your relationship. They're afraid of being abandoned and worry that if you love someone else there won't be enough love left for them. And if you're a widower, they may take your getting involved with someone else as a sign of disrespect for their mother's memory.

If your kids aren't feeling secure about their place in your life and in your heart, they may come up with all sorts of creative ways of trying to undermine your relationships with women. Especially common are throwing huge tantrums just before you leave the house, excessive clinginess, "forgetting" to pass on phone messages from your dates, coming down with last-minute, usually imaginary illnesses, and making rude comments to your dates.

Helping Your Children Cope with Your Love Life and the Women in It

The more secure your children feel in their relationship with you, the fewer problems they'll have with your getting involved with women other than their mother. But even in the most secure relationships, children can be less-than-completely welcoming of your new girlfriends. Still, as their father, you have a great influence over how they'll adapt to the changes they're going through. Here are a few other things to help them cope:

*"Dad, when did you realize you weren't, you know,
exactly studly anymore?"*

- **Make sure they know you love them.** Men tend to express their love by doing (and buying) things. And while that's fine in most cases, working four hours of overtime every day and spending the extra money on presents isn't enough. Your kids need plenty of verbal and physical demonstrations of your love far more.
- **Don't start dating too soon.** Whether you're divorced, never-married, or widowed, your children are grieving and they need time to adjust to their new situation. Starting a new social life right away doesn't give them that buffer zone and can make them even more anxious and resentful.
- **Let them know you aren't trying to replace their mother.** Whether your children's mother is alive or not, no one can replace her, either in their lives or their memories. They need to know that the reasons you're going out with other women have to do with you and your needs, not them.
- **Encourage their input.** If they have questions, answer them, but don't go into a lot of detail, especially if they want to know something particularly personal. If they like or dislike a particular woman you're seeing, let them tell you. Overall, let them know that while their input is welcome, you'll be making the final decisions on your own.

- **Don't ask permission.** Although your social life may affect them in some way, it's really none of their business. Asking them whether they mind if you go out or whether they like a particular date of yours gives them the erroneous impression that they have the power to veto or approve of your relationships.
- **Be honest.** If you're going out, even with someone you know they don't like, let them know. And be sure they know how long you'll be gone. If you're staying the night someplace else, say so.
- **Listen to them.** Listen to why they say they don't like your date. You don't have to agree, but maybe they see something you don't.
- **Don't introduce them to your dates too soon.** See pages 252–53 for more on this. Before making your introduction, talk about the woman you're seeing, let them know how much you and she enjoy being with each other, and let them know you'd like to have everyone meet.
- **Don't tell them how to feel.** There's absolutely nothing you can say that's going to make your kids love your girlfriend. What they need is time. So leave them alone and let them establish their own relationship. And never, never encourage them to call anyone "Mom" but their real mother.
- **Don't make out in front of them.** They're already feeling as though they have to compete with your girlfriends for your love and attention.

What Your Girlfriend May Be Going Through

It's Not Always Easy Going out with a Single Father

I have a tremendous amount of respect and admiration for women who get involved with men who have children. And after talking with dozens of women who've done it, I can assure you that it's a lot harder than it seems. So just to give you an appreciation of what life is like on the other side, let's take a look—from your girlfriend's perspective—at why it's so difficult:

- **It takes guts.** Your children are constant, living reminders that you loved—and had a lot of sex with—another woman, a woman you're probably going to have an ongoing relationship with for many, many years to come.
- **She may love you but not be sure she really wants to be a (step)parent.** Watch out for this one. You know you can do a fine job taking care of your children by yourself and you (hopefully) didn't get involved with your girlfriend because you were looking for a mother for your kids. But the truth is that no matter how much of the child-related responsibilities you say you'll manage, your girlfriend/ prospective wife will have to take on at least some kind of parenting role. So if she's not all that hot about kids and is more or less ambivalent about possibly being a stepmother, you may be with the wrong woman.
- **It's hard to carve out a place for herself in your life.** She loves you and wants to be a part of your life, but she knows that your children are going to be

a priority. And if you're widowed and she moves into the house where you and your wife lived together, how will she fit in?

- **She may resent your children.** Kids have a way of distracting their parents, and the more time you spend with them, the less time you'll have available for your lover.
- **It's hard to figure out where she stands with your kids.** Is she going to try to be their mother? Their friend? Or something in between? If your ex is still alive, your kids already have a mother who loves them and your girlfriend may feel that the kids will never come to love her. If you're a widower, things can be even tougher: your girlfriend is going to have to assume a major maternal role, but she'll still have to compete with your children's memories of their mother, which is harder than competing with a living person. In addition, she may not know whether she's supposed to—or allowed to—discipline your children. And if you sometimes take the kids' side in an argument, she might feel like it is your "happy little family" against her.

Helping Her Cope

You are the single most important factor in determining how the new woman in your life will deal with her roles as your lover and possible stepmother to your children. You're the one who has to welcome her into your family and you're the one who has to make sure the children understand her role. Like just about anyone stepping into a preexisting family unit, your girlfriend is probably going to feel a little insecure. Here are some things you can do to help her feel more confident:

- **Let her know that she doesn't have to be your children's mother.** In most cases, in fact, she can't be—they already have one. What she can and should do, however, is treat your children with love and respect. After a while she'll get the same back from them.
- **Give her plenty of time to develop her own relationships with the children.** This means letting things happen at their own pace, not forcing her to take on more responsibility than she's able to.
- **Let her know how she's doing.** She may not say so, but she really wants to know that the kids like her and that she's doing a good job. So if they say something nice to you about her, pass it on. Compliment her when she does something great with the kids, and give her some gentle pointers if she does something wrong. Hovering over her shoulder puts way too much pressure on her. Instead, let her discover how to do most things for herself the same way you did—by making mistakes.
- **Talk to your kids.** Make sure they know what her authority is and that they know what's expected of them in relation to her.
- **Encourage her to tell you how she's feeling.** She may be having the time of her life, or she may be frustrated, exasperated, and annoyed. Help her celebrate the joys and be supportive when she needs to cry on your shoulder.

How Your Parents, In-laws, and Other People Might React to the New Women in Your Life

The fact that your social life is really none of their business probably won't keep your parents and your former in-laws from having—and sometimes even expressing—an opinion on the subject. If you're lucky, they'll all be delighted that you're moving on and support you every way they can, but don't hold your breath.

If you're divorced or unmarried, your parents may warn you that every woman you go out with is "just like her [your ex.]" Your ex's parents might question your morality if they find out that a girlfriend spent the night at your house. And if you're widowed, your former in-laws might see your dating and having fun as a betrayal of their daughter's memory.

In small doses, you can ignore these kinds of comments. But if they become too annoying you need to let the appropriate buttinsky know that your social life is your business and that you don't care to discuss it with anyone else. The big danger here is that they might express their dissatisfaction with your lifestyle to your children. If you think this is happening, it's essential that you stop it immediately. Grandparents and other relatives can alienate your children from you in essentially the same way that their mother can. Tell your in-laws that if they have something to say they should say it to you and only you, and that any future attempts to involve the kids in your private business or to alienate them from you may result in their not being able to see your children for a while—at least not when you have them. Be very firm on this. For more suggestions on handling alienation, see page 187.

Try to be patient, though. In many cases other people's less-than-tactful comments about your dating are really the result of fear; they're essentially afraid that if you get involved with someone else their relationship with your kids will suffer. If you can reassure them that it won't, you may be able to nearly eliminate any future problems.

♦ **Help her deal with your ex.** Your girlfriend and your ex probably won't have that much to do with each other. But they might bump into each other at family, school, or sporting events. You can help minimize potential conflicts by being balanced in the way you talk about your ex. If you've been saying nothing but bad things, your girlfriend is probably going to be somewhat hostile. But if you've been nothing but complimentary, she'll probably be jealous.

♦ **Set up some ground rules.** It's critical that you and any woman you're involved with on a long-term basis reach a clear understanding about the following issues:

◊ Discipline. Who will discipline your kids and how? This can be especially important if she has kids of her own and an established way of handling them. See pages 159–62 for more on discipline.

◊ Other involvement. To make her feel a part of your family you have to give her some authority over the kids and back her up when she uses it. At the same time, you don't want her stepping in and telling you how to run your (and your kids') life. Also, will she be expected to help the kids with their homework? Drive your car pool? Attend parent-teacher conferences?

◊ Money. How will you handle household finances? Will any of her income be used to pay child support for your children or, even worse, alimony? If she has kids of her own, will any of your income be used to pay for them?

◊ For more issues that may come up, be sure to read the section on step-parenting (pages 265–69)—just reverse the genders as you're reading.

Dealing with Your Ex's Reaction to Your Girlfriend

If you and your ex are best friends, she may be sincerely overjoyed when she finds out about the new woman in your life. But most ex-wives and girlfriends aren't nearly that open-minded. Even though your social life is no longer her concern she'll probably have a pretty strong reaction when she finds out about the new woman in your life—similar to the one you had (or will have) toward the new man in hers.

♦ She may be scared, thinking that your new girlfriend will somehow undermine her role as her children's mother.

♦ She may be angry and antagonistic, especially if you initiated the breakup or if your new girlfriend was already on the scene before your old relationship ended.

♦ She may be jealous if your girlfriend is smarter, prettier, richer, more talented, or whatever than she herself is.

♦ She may envy your new, happy, family situation—especially if she isn't in a new relationship.

♦ She may be depressed if she had been holding on to the fantasy that you and she would ever get back together.

Your ex will probably be able to get over her other-than-positive feelings about your new love. But if she accidentally lets her anger and resentment get the best of her, you could have some problems. The most common is that she'll put the kids in the middle. She might bad-mouth you or your girlfriend in front of them. Or she might try to undermine your new relationship by refusing to let the kids come to your house if "that woman" is there, or punish you by not letting you see them at all. If any of these things occur, try to talk to your ex as soon as possible. She needs to know that as angry as she is about you, getting the kids involved will only hurt them. If you can't talk to her or if you're afraid that she'll take other, more drastic steps to keep you away from your children, prepare yourself by reading the sections on pages 181–87.

The Big Commitment—Moving in or Getting Married

At the risk of sounding preachy, let me start off by saying this: don't move in with your girlfriend; marry her instead. Generally speaking, I have no real objection to couples living together and I've done it myself several times. But that was before I had kids.

Maybe it's from watching too many movies or reading too many fairy tales in which the prince and princess get married and live happily ever after, but even very young children equate marriage with a relationship that will last forever. If you and your children's mother split up, this belief has obviously been shaken somewhat. But deep down it's still there. If you move in with someone without getting married, then your kids will believe that the relationship is temporary. As we've talked about before, kids need security and consistency in their lives and their relationships and they're not going to get either one if they're worried about another big breakup.

Whether you get married or decide to live together, you must be very careful to give the kids as much warning as possible. They have a right to know about major events that affect them and you shouldn't spring your plans on them at the last minute.

What You Might Encounter If You're Divorced or Were Never Married

In most cases, your kids are going to be happy about the big change that's in the works. But even if everything has been going well and your children are getting along great with the woman you're marrying or moving in with, you should be prepared: kids sometimes react very badly. Whether they've told you or not, they may have been holding on to the dream that you and your ex would get back together; the closer your wedding or move-in date gets, the worse they may behave, trying to do everything they can to interfere.

You should also be prepared for a change in your ex's behavior toward you (see page 260). Adjusting to your going out with other women is one thing, adjusting to your being married to one of them is another.

What You Might Encounter If You're a Widower

Remarriage is usually a little easier on widowers than on divorced or never-married fathers. Although some children might still feel that you're trying to replace their mother, most are going to be happy for you and will get along very well with their new stepmother. You also have the advantage of being able to function as a single family unit—no going back and forth between your house and their mother's. Finally, while your new wife may still feel intimidated by the memory of your first wife, she won't actually have to deal with her. Given all that, it's no wonder that, overall, widowers are happier in second marriages than divorced fathers.

Dealing with Your Ex's Love Life

The New Guy

Like it or not, your ex is probably going to get involved with someone new before too long. And whenever and however it happens, you're in for quite a blow. (If your ex was having an affair before the two of you broke up, you've had a little time to adjust to the idea, but not everyone's going to be that "lucky.") Finding out that your ex is sleeping with someone else—even if you haven't been together for a while—can bring up all sorts of emotions.

♦ **Sadness and disbelief.** Your ex's love life sans you is glaring proof that your relationship with her is over and dashes any hopes you might have had (or not even known you had) for getting back together.

♦ **Curiosity.** Whether you hate her or still love her, you're probably going to be incredibly curious about who she's going out with, where they're going, what they're doing, and so on.

The most important thing to keep in mind about your ex's new relationships—even if she's going out with three complete idiots every week—is that they're none of your business and there's nothing you can do about it. (If you're still talking to each other, though, you should encourage her to at least keep her boyfriends away from the kids, but don't get your hopes up that she'll take your advice.)

♦ **Insecurity.** One of my first fears after my ex moved in with her boyfriend was that my position as my children's father would be undermined and that I'd end up becoming a distant presence in their lives. It just killed me to know that another man was playing with my kids, reading them bedtime stories, and teaching them right from wrong, and that my kids might run to *him* for comfort if they were hurt or needed a hug. Just about every single father I've ever met—especially the ones with limited access to their children—has had similar feelings. While it's natural to try to overcome your own insecurity by undermining the new guy's relationship with your kids, don't. Instead, read the next page.

♦ **Jealousy.** One of these days your kids are going to come home and tell you what a great time they have with the new guy and how much they like him. And they'll tell you all sorts of other things that will tear you apart, like how he's got more hair than you do or that he's taller than you are or that in one minute flat he fixed that toy that you'd been futzing around with for weeks. Try to remember that kids love to tell you about what's going on in their lives; they really aren't trying to hurt you by talking about the new guy. First, don't try to compete with the new guy—it shows your kids you're insecure. Second, as much as it hurts, encourage them to continue. They need to know that it's okay for them to develop their own relationships with people and that their liking someone you don't particularly care for doesn't have anything to do with your feelings for them. Finally, take refuge in the fact that they're telling him all sorts of things about how great you are and how he'll never be their daddy 'cause they already have one. Go ahead and smile to yourself as you imagine how painful it is for him to hear that.

♦ For some other possible reactions to her new relationships, take a look at the section on how she might react to *your* love life (pages 260–61) and reverse the genders.

Yuck!—Supporting the New Guy

Unless you have primary or sole custody, the sad truth is that your children are going to be spending at least as much time with the new guy as they are with you— maybe even more. And because you love your children more than anything and because you want only the best for them, it's up to you to make their relationship with the new guy as positive as possible. This, as you can imagine, puts you in the strange and often uncomfortable position of having to support your children's relationship with someone you may not like very much. It's one of the hardest—and most important—things you'll ever do as a single father.

The fact is that your children should be with people whom they love and who love them, including men who can provide positive male role models. You, of course, will give them those things when they're with you. But since you can't be with them all the time, the best wish you can make is that the new guy will love them and be a good example for them, and that—gag!—they'll come to love and respect him as well. Here's how you can foster the relationship between your kids and the new guy, even if you don't really want to:

♦ **Never call him names or criticize him in front of the kids and when they talk about him, respond positively.** The fact that they have a good relationship with him doesn't detract at all from their relationship with you.

♦ **Don't ask too many nosy questions about him.** All you need to know is that your kids are in good hands when they're not with you.

♦ **Don't tell your ex what a jerk the new guy is.** She obviously doesn't agree and won't take your advice anyway.

♦ **If you ever meet him, be nice.** If the kids have told you some nice things about him, tell him. And let him know that you'd be glad to help him out (at least with the kids) any way you can. Who knows, you might actually become friends. Stranger things have happened, but don't hold your breath.

♦ **Have faith.** Hopefully the new guy will be as supportive of your role in the kids' lives as you are of his. If he isn't, your kids will figure it out sooner or later and will resent him for trying to hurt you. And you can take comfort in the fact that you took the high road and did the right thing.

But What If the New Guy Really Is Bad News?

In some cases you may genuinely suspect the new guy of being a true danger to your children and you won't feel right about supporting his relationship with them. If this happens, the first thing to do is ask yourself why you suspect him. Is it because there's really something there to worry about or is it because you're jealous of him or you think he's a jerk? If it's jealousy, you're going to have to learn to deal with your feelings. But don't dismiss your suspicions completely.

According to Rutgers University sociologist David Popenoe, children are much more likely to be abused by their stepfathers than by their biological fathers. And in a study of abuse in single-mother homes, sociologist Leslie Margolin found that boyfriends were responsible for 64 percent of the abuse that wasn't committed by parents. So if your fears are legitimate, you must take immediate action:

- **Document your suspicions.** Keep detailed, written records of everything that has you worried: unusual bruises, blood in a child's underwear, overtly sexual behavior, your children's comments that the new guy hurt them or touched them "down there," or anything else. Write down the date you first noticed what you noticed, your children's actual words, what you said or did, and how your children reacted.
- **Stay calm.** When talking to your children about this, *never* accuse the new guy and *never* ask whether he did anything specific. Instead, ask in a matter-of-fact kind of way how that bruise got there or whether anyone has been touching them in their private place. If your kids see that you're all upset they may tell you what they think you want to hear instead of the truth. In many cases there's a perfectly reasonable explanation.
- **Raise your suspicions with your ex.** But be as nonaccusing and nonconfrontational as possible. Tell her what you've seen and why it should concern both of you.
- **Notify the police about your suspicions if you have to.** Be sure to bring your documentation with you.
- **Go to court to try to get a restraining order keeping the new guy away from your children.** But don't expect much.

When Your Ex Remarries

In a lot of people's minds there's not much difference between being married and just living together. But while we can debate the pros and cons of these two options all day (we won't), the fact is that your ex's getting married can involve certain consequences that wouldn't result if she were only living with her boyfriend:

- There may be some financial advantages for you. If you were paying alimony before, that might stop with your ex's new marriage. But watch out: in most cases, your child support obligation won't change—even if she marries a millionaire.
- The new guy isn't just the new guy anymore; he's your children's stepfather. In everyone's minds—yours and the kids' at least—that's a much more serious

relationship. And for that reason you may find yourself even more jealous of him than before and even more afraid that he'll edge you out of your children's lives.

♦ Your ex may actually try to cut you out. "Some ex-wives who remarry want to draw a tight circle around their new family (the wife, her husband, and her children) and exclude the biological father," writes therapist and sociologist David Knox. "One way they may try to accomplish this is by moving their children to another state to make it difficult for you to remain an active parent in the lives of your children." Knox suggests that the best ways of protecting yourself against this kind of behavior is a court-ordered agreement that prohibits either you or your ex from taking your children out of state.

A Final Warning

You may feel depressed and frustrated by the new guy's greater role in your children's lives; you may feel jealous that they like him. And you might even be convinced by your ex's insistence that the children would be better off being raised in a two-parent family. But no matter how bad you feel, *do not ever give in to a request to let the new guy adopt your children.* Stepping out of their lives is not only stupid, it's harmful.

In case you've forgotten, your children love you and need you. Yes, your relationship with them has changed now that they have a real live stepfather. But that doesn't mean that your role as real live father is any less important. Abandoning them now (and let's be honest, that's exactly what giving them up for adoption is) will be absolutely devastating to them—and to you.

If You Become a Stepfather

Within three years of their divorce, about 80 percent of men and 70 percent of women remarry. These already high percentages don't even include the widows and widowers who remarry, the formerly married people who live with their partners without getting married again, and the never-marrieds who start a new nonmarital relationship. When all is said and done, there aren't very many people who stay single for too long.

And given that a lot of these new families involve children from previous relationships, it really shouldn't come as much of a surprise that 35 percent of all children will spend at least five years before they're eighteen living in a stepfamily, according to the Step Family Association of America. And given that 65 percent of children living with a stepparent live with a stepfather, there's a pretty good chance that your next long-term partner will have children of her own and that, in addition to being a father, you'll find that you're a stepfather too.

On pages 257–60 we talked about some of the difficulties the new woman in your life may encounter as she settles into a new life with you and your children. Now that the situation is reversed, a lot of those issues and concerns apply to you as well, so you might want to go back and read (or reread) those pages, reversing the genders. But there are some additional difficulties that seem to be peculiar to stepfathers.

A lot of stepfathers erroneously think that they're going to ease into their new situation right away and that their new, blended family will behave just like a regular biological family would. In reality, this hardly ever happens. The truth is that stepfathers have a very difficult time figuring out just where they fit into the new family structure. It's not easy trying to mold relationships with children who already have a father somewhere else. They also rarely have any kind of legally established authority—that stays with the biological father. And even if their place were clearly prescribed and protected by law, most men, even if they're fathers themselves, don't have much practice or training in parenting other people's kids and often don't know what to do.

A lot of stepfathers are also surprised when the love they expected to feel for and from their stepchildren doesn't materialize—either as soon as they'd hoped or at all. In one important study of stepfamilies, researcher Lucile Duberman found that only 53 percent of stepfathers reported that they had "parental" feelings about their stepchildren. And only 45 percent of them said that they felt "mutual love" between themselves and the stepchildren.

If you already are a stepfather or are about to become one, there are a number of important issues that you may find yourself dealing with. Ignored, these issues can get out of control and interfere with your relationship with your new partner, her kids, and even your own kids. While an in-depth discussion is beyond the scope of this book, simply being aware that these potential problem areas exist will go a long way toward helping you and your new partner stay out of the traps that too many stepfamilies fall into.

Your New Partner

♦ She may resent the time you spend with your children, feeling that it's time that won't be available to be spent on her, her children, or any children the two of you have together. Or you may resent the time she spends with her kids instead of with you or your children.

♦ If your own children don't live with you, you may feel guilty about spending more time with her kids than your own.

Her Kids

♦ When it comes to setting limits and enforcing them for your own children, you're in charge. But what about disciplining your stepchildren? Most stepfathers are unsure about where they stand on this issue. And if you haven't had a lot of time to get to know your stepchildren and earn their respect, disciplining them may be difficult.

♦ You may not know exactly how much affection to show your stepchildren (assuming you want to show them any at all). Too much would be insincere, too little isn't a good idea either.

♦ And what if you feel some sexual attraction for your stepdaughter? This is perfectly natural but extremely disconcerting when it happens. And yes, we all know what happened with Woody Allen.

♦ Her children may be angry and resentful that you're taking their mother away from them. The longer she's been a single parent, the more covetous the kids will be of their mother and the more true this will be.

♦ At the same time, you may resent her kids for cutting into your time with their mother.

Your Kids

♦ Because your ex probably has more time with your kids than you do, and because your new partner has more custody of her kids than her ex does, you'll undoubtedly be spending more time with your new partner's children than with your own. Your children, especially if they aren't living with you, may feel that since you have "new" kids you don't or won't love them anymore. As a result, they may develop a strong rivalry with or even dislike for their stepsiblings.

♦ And how will you handle any sexual attraction that might develop between your kids and hers? They need to know—in no uncertain terms—that even though they aren't related by blood, it's simply not okay for them to get involved.

♦ Your kids may be extremely reluctant to start a new family. This is especially true if you've been a single father for a long time or if you're barely out of your relationship with their mother.

♦ In some cases, you may be so scarred by your relationship with your ex that you feel as though you'd be better off starting a completely new life, without anything—kids included—to remind you of the past.

♦ If you're starting to get close to your new partner's children you might be feeling as though you're betraying your own kids and that there won't be enough love to go around.

Finances

♦ The issue of who pays for what (or for whom) is a frequent source of trouble in stepfamilies. How are you and your new partner going to arrange the finances of supporting two families?

♦ If you're paying child support, will your new partner resent that all of your income isn't available to your new family? And if your kids are living with you,

how will she feel about the money you spend on their private school tuition or other expenses that neither she nor her children derive any benefit from?
- How are you going to feel about spending your money on things for her children? And will she resent spending her money on yours?

Her Ex

- We all secretly want the women we get involved with to have been virgins before we met them, but the existence of her kids can make it kind of hard to keep that fantasy alive. And the existence of her ex-husband—especially if he wants to be as involved with his kids as you want to be with yours—makes it impossible.
- If he is involved with his kids, will you be able to handle seeing him all the time and hearing what a great guy he is?
- What if he's a jerk and starts a custody fight as a weapon to hurt his former wife?
- Remember that it's pretty hard for you not to be affected in some way, real or imaginary, by your partner's ex. You may wish he'd disappear but that would only hurt his kids. And by the way, it's perfectly normal for you to hate him (whether you've met is completely irrelevant).

Society as a Whole

- Whether you're a brand new stepfather or have been one for years, you'll have to deal with people's suspicions that you're a child abuser, especially if one (or more) of your stepchildren is a girl. The truth is that while stepfathers are more likely to abuse their children than biological fathers, *neither* is as likely to harm their children as the children's own mothers.
- Besides this unfortunate and inaccurate suspicion, society seems to have even worse stereotypes about stepmothers than stepfathers. Just think of *Cinderella, Hansel and Gretel,* and a host of other fairy tales.

Tips for Stepfathering Success

According to researcher Kay Pasely, researchers have identified three factors that accurately predict whether a stepfather will be satisfied with his role:
1. The level of communication with his stepchildren. The more the better.
2. The amount of time he spends with the stepchildren. Again, the more the better.
3. The support he gets from his new partner for his involvement in the discipline of the stepchildren. What a surprise: the more the better.

Clearly, communicating well and spending lots of time with your stepkids and getting lots of support from their mother will help ease you into your new role. Here are some other very important steps you can take to make your stepfathering a more enjoyable experience for everyone:

♦ Have realistic expectations. The idea that her kids and you are going to fall instantly in love with one another and that you're now one perfect, happy little family is just a fantasy. Relying on it too much will only set you up for failure.

♦ Don't try to get too attached too fast. Doing so makes you vulnerable to rejection, which you're probably going to get a lot of for some time.

♦ Don't let the stepkids get to you, or at least don't let them see that they did; it will make them use the same hurtful tactics over and over.

♦ Be a grown-up. If they do hurt your feelings, don't try to get even by rejecting them.

♦ Establish some new family traditions. Rituals and traditions help families bond. You have some from your family, your partner has some from hers. Neither is better or worse than the others, they're just different. Coming up with something new can make all of you feel that you're working together to create something.

♦ Work with your new partner to determine your long-term role in the structure of your new blended family. And pay special attention to the role you'll be playing in limit setting and enforcement.

♦ Be patient. According to researchers, it can take from eighteen to twenty-four months for newly formed stepfamilies to work out all the kinks. Others say it takes even longer—perhaps as many years as the age of the oldest child in the new family.

♦ Take a stepparenting class at your local community center. These classes have been shown to help new stepfamilies "develop more realistic expectations of stepfamily life, reducing conflict over failure to meet unrealistic expectations and increasing interest in intellectual and cultural matters," writes Pasely. Also, couples gain a "greater clarity about their new roles and feelings about the stepfamily experience and [learn] ways to resolve issues of daily living." You might also check out Carl Pickhardt's *Keys to Successful Stepfathering*, or contact the Stepfamily Association of America (see the Resources section, page 290).

Conclusion

As you probably figured out a long time ago, being a single father—whether it was your choice or not—is a hard, hard job. It can be frustrating and annoying; it can make you feel lost, alone, helpless, confused, and like running away as fast as you can. But it's also one of the most rewarding—and important—jobs you'll ever have. Nothing can compare to the pride you'll feel when you see that your child has learned a lesson that only you could have taught him. One hug, one kiss, one letter, one "I love you, Daddy" from your child, and all the hard stuff will suddenly seem insignificant. Being a father teaches you about life, about joy, about happiness. Most important, it teaches you about love. But you can't get any of that if you aren't there.

Single fatherhood can also be a little lonely at times. If you need some help along the way, reread the appropriate parts of this book and check out some of the resources on the following pages. Above all, be there for your kids as much as you possibly can. It's the best thing you'll ever do for them. And the best thing you'll ever do for yourself.

Good luck.

Notes:

Preparing Your Own Parenting Agreement

Whether you're divorced or never married, one of the most important things you and your ex can do for yourselves and your children is to put together a shared parenting agreement. If you're getting along, you can start the process by yourselves and you'll probably be able to put together a pretty good draft in a few hours. When you're done, give it to your respective lawyers for final approval.

Because this agreement will set the tone for your relationship with your child for years to come (and, to some extent, your relationship with your ex as well), it's important that you keep the following in mind:

- Make sure it's in writing. The fewer chances for misinterpretation, the better.
- Keep it flexible. Your ex's, your child's, and your own circumstances will change over time, and your agreement will have to allow for change.
- Make it as comprehensive as possible. Paper is cheap, so don't skip anything that seems even remotely important to either one of you.

The checklist that follows contains just about everything you'll want to cover in your parenting agreement, regardless of your custody situation. I used Elizabeth Hickey's and Elizabeth Dalton's Parenting Plan Worksheet as a jumping-off point but added quite a lot of additional information. This checklist may seem rather daunting, but you'll be happy you used it. Feel free to edit, but think more about adding points than deleting.

Appendix

1. Physical-custody arrangements
   A. Week-to-week or month-to-month schedules
   B. Schedules for holidays or other special days (birthdays, parents' birthdays, Father's Day, Mother's Day), and for special occasions (weddings, funerals, graduations)
   C. Arrangements for school, sports, church/synagogue, or community events (back-to-school night, parent-teacher conferences, school programs, sporting events, church programs)
   D. Vacations
      ◊ Changes in custody schedules
      ◊ Summer camps and other activities
      ◊ Decision making
      ◊ Payment arrangements
      ◊ Adult vacations—with and without the children
   E. Emergencies (parents', children's, or family illness or injury)
   F. Child-care arrangements for when the custodial parent is at work
   G. Grandparents' and other relatives' visitation rights

2. Long-distance parenting arrangements (if one parent lives more than 100 miles away from the other)
   A. Yearly time-sharing schedule
   B. Transportation details (including allocation of transportation costs)
   C. Logistics of sharing information
   D. Communication with the children

3. Transportation details
   A. How do the kids get from one home to the other?
   B. Where, when, and how are transitions handled?

4. Parent contact with kids when they're at the other parent's home
   A. Are drop-in visits allowed?
   B. Can parents call anytime or is there a set schedule?
   C. Are there limits or restrictions on fax, e-mail, or written communication?

5. Procedure for sharing information
   A. Parenting meetings
      ◊ Agenda
      ◊ Scheduling (weekly, monthly, quarterly)
   B. Types of information that it's important to communicate to the other parent and how to share it
      ◊ School-related, extracurricular, health-related, and so forth

6. Procedures for making decisions
   A. What kind of decisions do the parents make individually, and what kind require notification of the other parent (education, day care, medical and dental treatment, therapy)?
   B. How are these decisions to be made?
   C. Procedure for resolving stalemates and for handling disagreements

7. Education
   A. Access to school records (report cards and the like)
   B. Changes in schooling
      ◊ Public to private, private to public
      ◊ Special needs schooling
   C. Attendance at parent-teacher conferences and other school events
   D. Financial aid
      ◊ Cooperation in applying for
      ◊ Tuition split
   E. Higher education
      ◊ Minimum educational guarantee?
      ◊ Who pays for college?
      ◊ College savings plans or financial-aid options

8. Health care
   A. Medical/dental/psychological coverage
      ◊ Whose policy covers the children?
      ◊ Who pays the premiums?
      ◊ Who picks the doctors/dentists?
   B. Payment of deductibles and uncovered medical expenses
   C. Scheduling of well-child medical and dental appointments
   D. Access to medical records
   E. Informing the other parent of medical needs and treatment
      ◊ Elective surgeries or optional treatments
   F. Procedure for taking care of medical and dental emergencies
   G. Health and life insurance for parents
      ◊ You both must get and maintain health and life insurance
   H. Basic health and hygiene standards for both homes
      ◊ Brushing after meals and so on

9. Child support
   A. Amount to be paid
      ◊ Method of calculation
      ◊ Payment schedule

◊ Provisions for changing payments
◊ If custody arrangements change
◊ If financial circumstances change

B. Itemization of what child support covers and how it is to be spent
◊ Agreement to pay extra support if extraordinary expenses come up
◊ Provision of itemized statement detailing how the money is being spent

10. Other financial issues
    A. Payment of other, non-child-support expenses
       ◊ Braces, car payments, auto insurance for teen drivers (God forbid)
    B. Income tax issues
       ◊ If only one child, who takes him as the deduction?
       ◊ If more than one, who deducts which one(s)?

11. Lifestyle issues
    A. Can you agree to maintain consistent house rules?
       ◊ Bedtimes, chores, homework, TV watching, personal use of the telephone
    B. Religion
       ◊ Religious observance
       ◊ Religious education and training
       ◊ Celebration of holidays
       ◊ Agreement to respect religious differences
    C. Agreement to respect the children's respect and love for the other parent
    D. Guidelines for participation of new boy- or girlfriends in school and family functions

12. Adjustments to the plan
    A. Resolving disputes
       ◊ With the plan itself
       ◊ With the items covered in the plan
       ◊ Agree to rely on mediation or arbitration and to stay out of court
    B. An annual review of the plan relative to the children's and parents' needs and circumstances
    C. Procedure for modifying the plan
    D. Impact on the plan of changes in employment, residence, and marital status

Selected Bibliography

Books

Adler, Robert. *Sharing the Children: How to Resolve Custody Problems and Get on with Your Life.* Bethesda, Md.: Adler & Adler, 1988.

Ahrons, Constance R., and Roy H. Rodgers. *Divorced Familes: A Multidisciplinary Developmental View.* New York: Norton, 1987.

Barret, Robert, and Bryan Robinson. *Gay Fathers.* New York: Lexington Books (Simon and Schuster), 1990.

Beal, Carole. *Boys and Girls: The Development of Gender Roles.* New York: McGraw-Hill, 1994.

Beech Acres' Aring Institute. *Helping Children Cope with Divorce.* Cincinnati, Ohio: Beech Acres, n.d.

Bensen, Peter L., Judy Galbraith, and Pamela Espeland. *What Kids Need to Succeed: Proven, Practical Ways to Raise Good Kids,* rev. ed. Minneapolis, Minn.: Free Spirit Publishing, 1998.

Berman, Claire, *Making It as a Stepparent: New Roles/New Rules,* rev. ed. New York: Harper and Row, 1986.

Biller, Henry, and Robert Trotter. *The Father Factor: What You Need to Know to Make a Difference.* New York: Pocket Books, 1994.

Blankenhorn, David. *Fatherless America: Confronting Our Most Urgent Social Problem.* New York: Basic Books, 1995.

Blau, Melinda. *Families Apart: Ten Keys to Successful Co-Parenting.* New York: Berkley Publishing Group/Perigee, 1993.

Bray, James, and John Kelly. *Step Families: Love, Marriage, and Parenting in the First Decade*. New York: Broadway Books, 1998.

Brott, Armin. *The New Father: A Dad's Guide to the First Year*. New York: Abbeville Press, 1997.

———. *The New Father: A Dad's Guide to the Toddler Years*. New York: Abbeville Press, 1998.

Bryan, Mark. *The Prodigal Father: Reuniting Fathers and Their Children*. New York: Random House, 1997.

Clawar, Stanley, and Brynne Rivlin. *Children Held Hostage: Dealing with Programmed and Brainwashed Children*. Chicago: American Bar Association Press, 1991.

Corn, Elaine. *Now You're Cooking*. Emeryville, Calif.: Harlow and Ratner, 1994.

Curry, Hayden, Denis Clifford, and Robin Leonard. *A Legal Guide for Lesbian and Gay Couples*. Berkeley, Calif.: Nolo Press, 1996.

Dalton, Elizabeth, and Elizabeth Hickey. *Healing Hearts: Helping Children and Adults Recover from Divorce*. Carson City, Nev.: Gold Leaf Press, 1994.

De Freitas, Crystal. *Keys to Your Child's Healthy Sexuality*. New York: Barron's, 1997.

Dowd, Nancy E. *In Defense of Single-Parent Families*. New York: New York University Press, 1997.

Duberman, Lucile. *The Reconstituted Family: A Study of Remarried Couples and Their Children*. Chicago: Nelson-Hall, 1975.

Elias, Steven, Albin Renauer, and Robin Leonard. *How to File for Bankruptcy*. Berkeley, Calif.: Nolo Press, 1997.

Elium, Don, and Jeanne Elium. *Raising a Son: Parents and the Making of a Healthy Man*. Berkeley, Calif.: Celestial Arts, 1997.

Elium, Jeanne, and Don Elium. *Raising a Daughter: Parents and the Awakening of a Healthy Woman*. Berkeley, Calif.: Celestial Arts, 1994.

Emery, Robert. *Renegotiating Family Relationships: Divorce, Child Custody and Mediation*. New York: Guilford Press, 1994.

Erickson, Donna. *Donna's Day: Fun Activities That Bring the Family Together*. New York: HarperCollins, 1998.

Erickson, Erik H. *Childhood and Society*. New York: W. W. Norton, 1964.

Fagerstrom, Karen, Rodney Nurse, Peggy Thompson, et al. *Divorce: A Problem to Be Solved, Not a Battle to Be Fought*. Orinda, Calif.: Brookwood Publishing, 1997.

Fitzgerald, Helen. *The Grieving Child: A Parent's Guide*. New York: Fireside, 1992.

Ford, Judy, and Anna Chase. *Wonderful Ways to Be a Stepparent*. Berkeley, Calif.: Conari Press, 1999.

Furstenberg, Frank, and Andrew Cherlin. *Divided Families*. Cambridge, Mass.: Harvard University Press, 1991.

Gardner, Richard A. *The Parental Alienation Syndrome*, 2d ed. Cresskill, N.J.: Creative Therapeutics, 1998.

Gatley, Richard H., and David Koulack. *Single Father's Handbook: A Guide for Separated and Divorced Fathers*. Garden City, N.Y.: Anchor Press, 1979.

Giannetti, Charlene, and Margaret Sagarese. *The Roller-Coaster Years: Raising Your Child Through the Maddening Yet Magical Middle School Years*. New York: Broadway Books, 1997.

Glennon, Will. *Fathering: Strengthening Connection with Your Children No Matter Where You Are*. Berkeley, Calif.: Conari Press, 1995.

Gonsiorek, John, and J. D. Weinrich, eds., *Homosexuality: Research Implications for Public Policy*. Beverly Hills, Calif.: Sage Publications, 1991.

Gottman, John. *The Heart of Parenting: Raising an Emotionally Intelligent Child*. New York: Simon and Schuster, 1997.

Green, Maureen. *Fathering*. New York: McGraw Hill, 1976.

Greenspan, Stanley, and Nancy Thorndike Greenspan. *First Feelings: Milestones in the Emotional Development of Your Baby and Child*. New York: Penguin, 1985.

Hanson, Shirley M. H., and Frederick W. Bozett. *Dimensions of Fatherhood*. Beverly Hills, Calif.: Sage Publications, 1985.

Hardwick, Charlotte. *Win Your Child Custody War*, rev. ed. Livingston, Tex.: Pale Horse Publishing, 1998.

Heatherington, E. Mavis. *Long-Term Impact of Divorce on Children's Marital Stability*. Charlottesville, Va.: University of Virginia, 1987.

Horgan, Timothy J. *Winning Your Divorce: A Man's Survival Guide*. New York: Dutton, 1994.

Jensen, Amy Hillyard. *Healing Grief*. Redmond, Wash.: Medic Publishing, 1995.

Kahan, Stuart. *For Divorced Fathers Only*. New York: Simon and Schuster, 1978.

Knox, David. *The Divorced Dad's Survival Book: How to Stay Connected with Your Kids*. New York: Plenum Press, 1998.

Krane, Gary. *Simple Fun for Busy People: 333 Free Ways to Enjoy Your Loved Ones More in the Time You Have*. Berkeley, Calif.: Conari Press, 1998.

Kushner, Harold S. *When Bad Things Happen to Good People*. New York: Avon Books, 1983.

Kutner, Lawrence. *Your School-Age Child*. New York: William Morrow, 1996.

Kvols, Kathryn. *Redirecting Children's Behavior*. Seattle, Wash.: Parenting Press, 1997.

Larson, Reed, and Maryse Richards. *Divergent Realities: The Emotional Lives of Mothers, Fathers, and Adolescents*. New York: Basic Books, 1994.

Levine, James, and Todd Pittinsky. *Working Fathers: New Strategies for Balancing Work and Family*. Reading, Mass.: Addison-Wesley, 1997.

Leving, Jeffrey M. *Fathers' Rights: Hard-Hitting and Fair Advice for Every Father Involved in a Custody Dispute*. New York: Dutton, 1997.

Logrippo, Ro. *In My Room: Designing Living and Learning Environments for the Young.* New York: John Wiley & Sons, 1995.

Ludtke, Melissa. *On Our Own: Unmarried Motherhood in America.* New York: Random House, 1997.

Mattis, Mary. *Sex and the Single Parent: How to Have Happy and Healthy Kids—and an Active Social Life.* New York: Henry Holt, 1986.

Moir, Anne, and David Jessel. *Brain Sex: The Real Difference Between Men and Women.* New York: Lyle Stuart, 1991.

Nelsen, Jane, Cheryl Erwin, and Carol Delzer. *Positive Discipline for Single Parents.* Rocklin, Calif.: Prima Publishing, 1994.

Neuman, Gary M., with Patricia Romanowsky. *Helping Your Kids Cope with Divorce the Sandcastles Way.* New York: Times Books, 1998.

Oddenino, Michael L. *Putting Kids First: Walking Away from a Marriage Without Walking Over the Kids.* Salt Lake City: Family Connections Publishing, 1995.

Parke, Ross. *Fatherhood.* Cambridge, Mass.: Harvard University Press, 1996.

Pickhardt, Carl. *Keys to Successful Stepfathering.* New York: Barron's, 1997.

Platt, Harvey J. *Your Living Trust and Estate Plan: How to Maximize Your Family's Assets and Protect Your Loved Ones.* New York: Allworth Press, 1995.

Popenoe, David. *Life Without Father: Compelling New Evidence that Fatherhood and Marriage Are Indispensible for the Good of Children and Society.* New York: Free Press, 1996.

Ricker, Audrey, and Carolyn Crowder. *Backtalk: Four Steps to Ending Rude Behavior in Your Kids.* New York: Simon and Schuster, 1998.

Schatz, William. *Healing a Father's Grief.* Redmond, Wash.: Medic Publishing, 1984.

Shapiro, Jerrold Lee. *The Measure of a Man: Becoming the Father You Wish Your Father Had Been.* New York: Delacorte, 1993.

Silberg, Jackie. *300 Three-Minute Games: Quick and Easy Activities for 2–5 Year Olds.* Beltsville, Md.: Gryphon House, 1997.

Snarey, John. *How Fathers Care for the Next Generation: A Four-Decade Study.* Cambridge, Mass.: Harvard University Press, 1993.

Spangler, Doug. *Fatherhood: An Owner's Manual.* Richmond, Calif.: Fabus, 1994.

Steinberg, Laurence, and Ann Levine. *You and Your Adolescent: A Parent's Guide for Ages 10–20.* New York: HarperPerennial, 1997.

Stevens, Joseph H., Jr., and Marilyn Matthews, eds. *Mother-Child, Father-Child Relations.* Washington, D.C.: National Association for the Education of Young Children, 1978.

Thomas, Shirley. *Parents Are Forever.* Longmont, Col.: Springboard Publications, 1995.

Thorndike, John. *Another Way Home: A Single Father's Story.* New York: Crown Publishers, 1996.

Twilley, Dwight. *Questions from Dad: A Very Cool Way to Communicate with Kids.* Boston: Charles E. Tuttle Company, 1994.

Tyson, Eric. *Personal Finances for Dummies.* Foster City, Calif., IDG Books Worldwide, 1996.

Wallerstein, J. S., and Joan B. Kelly. *Surviving the Breakup: How Children Actually Cope with Divorce.* New York: Basic Books, 1980.

Wallerstein, Judith, and S. Blakeslee. *Second Chances: Men, Women, and Children a Decade after Divorce.* New York: Ticknor and Fields, 1989.

Warshak, Richard A. *The Custody Revolution: The Father Factor and the Motherhood Mystique.* New York: Poseidon Press, 1992.

Articles

Amaral, Edward, Jr. "Memorandum to Clients on Children's Concerns and Behavior during the Divorce Process—Re: Divorce Practice and Procedures Concerning Children and Behavior." Undated manuscript downloaded from the Internet, 1998.

Bigner, J., and Frederick Bozett. "Parenting by Gay Fathers." *Marriage and Family Review* 14 (1989): 166–68.

Bigner, J. J., and R. B. Jacobsen. "Parenting Behaviors of Homosexual and Heterosexual Fathers." *Journal of Homosexuality* 18 (1989): 173–86.

Blush, Gordon J., and Karol L. Ross. "Sexual Allegations in Divorce: The SAID Syndrome." *Conciliation Courts Review* 25, no. 1 (June 1987).

Bozett, Frederick W. "Gay Men as Fathers." In Shirley M. H. Hanson and Frederick W. Bozett. *Dimensions of Fatherhood.* Beverly Hills, Calif.: Sage Publications, 1985.

Buchanan, C. M., E. E. Maccoby, and S. M. Dornbusch. "Caught Between Parents: Adolescents' Experience in Divorced Families." *Child Development* 62 (1991): 1008–29.

Burgess, Jane K. "Widowers as Fathers." In Shirley M. H. Hanson and Frederick W. Bozett. *Dimensions of Fatherhood.* Beverly Hills, Calif.: Sage Publications, 1985.

Cowan, Philip A., et al. "Mothers, Fathers, Sons, and Daughters: Gender Differences in Famly Formation and Parenting Style." In Philip A. Cowan, Dorothy Field, and Donald A. Hansen, eds. *Family, Self, and Society: Toward a New Agenda for Family Research.* Hillsdale, N.J.: Erlbaum, 1993.

Dawson, Debra. "Family Structure and Children's Well-being: Data from the 1988 National Health Interview Survey." *Journal of Marriage and Family* 53 (1991): 573–84.

Duncan, Greg, Jeanne Brooks-Gunn, and Pamela Kato Klebanov. "Economic Deprivation in Early Childhood Development." *Child Development* 65 (1994): 296–318.

Selected Bibliography

Erwin, Cheryl. "The Family Meeting." *Nevada Parent.* Undated article downloaded from the Internet.

Fay, Robert. "Joint Custody in Infants and Toddlers: Theoretical and Practical Aspects," 1995.

Feldman, Shirley S., S. C. Nash, and B. G. Aschenbrenner, "Antecedents of Fathering." *Child Development* 54 (1983): 1628–36.

Fergusson, David, John Horwood, and Michael Tynsky. "Parental Separation, Adolescent Psychopathology, Problem Behaviors." *Journal of the American Academy of Child and Adolescent Psychiatry* 33 (1994): 1122–31.

Franz, Carol E., David C. McClelland, and Joel Weinberger. "Childhood Antecedents of Conventional Social Accomplishment in Midlife Adults: A 36-Year Prospective Study." *Journal of Personality and Social Psychology* 60 (1991): 586–95.

Friedman, Howard, et al. "Psychological and Behavioral Predictors of Longevity." *American Psychologist* 50 (1995): 69–78.

Furstenberg, Frank, and Paul Allison. "How Marital Dissolution Affects Children: Variations by Age and Sex." *Developmental Psychology* 25 (July 1989): 540–49.

Gross, Julien, and Harlene Hayne. "Drawing Facilitates Children's Verbal Reports of Emotionally Laden Events." *Journal of Experimental Psychology: Applied* 4, no. 2 (June 1998): 1–17.

Henry, Ron. "'Primary Caretaker': Is It a Ruse?" *Family Advocate* (American Bar Association, Summer 1994): 53–56.

Heatherington, E. Mavis. "Coping with Marital Transitions: A Family Systems Perspective." *Monographs of the Society for Research in Child Development* 57 (1992): 1–242.

Heatherington, E. Mavis, Martha Cox, and Roger Cox. "The Aftermath of Divorce." In Joseph H. Stevens, Jr., and Marilyn Matthews, eds. *Mother-Child, Father-Child Relationships.* Washington, D.C.: National Association for the Education of Young Children, 1978.

Green, G. Dorsey, and Frederick W. Bozett. "Lesbian Mothers and Gay Fathers." In J. C. Gonsiorek, and J. D. Weinrich, eds. *Homosexuality: Research Implications for Public Policy.* Beverly Hills, Calif.: Sage Publications, 1991.

Jenny, Carole, et al. "Are Children at Risk for Sexual Abuse by Homosexuals?" *Pediatrics* 94 (July 1994): 41–44.

Kalter, Neil. "Long-Term Effects of Divorce on Children: A Developmental Vulnerability Model." *American Journal of Orthopsychiatry* 57 (1987): 587–600.

Kiedrowski, John, C.H.S. Jayewardene, Ph.D, et al. "Parental Abduction of Children: An Overview and Profile of the Abductor." Paper written for the Missing Children's Registry, Ontario, Canada, August 19, 1994.

Little, Margaret A. "The Impact of the Custody Plan on the Family: A Five-Year

Follow-Up." *Family and Conciliation Courts Review* 30, no. 2 (April 1992): 243–51.

Lund, M. "The Non-Custodial Father: Common Challenges in Parenting after Divorces." In C. Lewis and M. O'Brien, eds. *Reassessing Fatherhood: New Observations of Fathers and the Modern Family.* Beverly Hills, Calif.: Sage Publications, 1987.

McLanahan, S., and L. Bumpass. "Intergenerational Consequences of Marital Disruption." *American Journal of Sociology* 84 (1988): 130–52.

Margolin, Leslie. "Child Abuse by Mothers' Boyfriends: Why the Overrepresentation?" *Child Abuse and Neglect* 16, no. 4 (July–August 1992): 541–51.

Pasley, Kay. "Stepfathers." In Shirley M. H. Hanson and Frederick W. Bozett. *Dimensions of Fatherhood.* Beverly Hills, Calif.: Sage Publications, 1985.

Patterson, Charlotte. "Children of Lesbian and Gay Parents." *Advances in Clinical Child Psychology* 19 (1997): 235–82.

Pearson, Jessica, and Nancy Thoennes. "Mediating and Litigating Custody Disputes: A Longitudinal Evaluation." *Family Law Quarterly* 17 (1984): 497–517.

Riley, Tom. "Where Are All the Missing Children?" Washington, D.C.: Statistical Assessment Service, May 1995.

Rodgers, Fran Sussner, and Charles Rodgers. "Business and the Facts of Family Life." *Harvard Business Review* 67 (November–December 1989): 121–29.

Santrock, J., and R. Warshak. "Father Custody and Social Development in Boys and Girls." *Journal of Social Issues* 35 (1979): 112.

Singer, Jerome L. "Television, Imaginative Play, and Cognitive Develpment: Some Problems and Possibilities." Paper presented at the meeting of the American Psychological Association, San Francisco, September, 1977. Cited in Ross Parke. *Fatherhood.* Cambridge, Mass.: Harvard University Press, 1966, p. 300.

Stanton, Warren, Tian Oci, and Phil Silva. "Sociodemographic Characteristics of Adolescent Smokers." *International Journal of the Addictions* 7 (1994): 912–25.

Teachman, J. D. "Intergenerational Resources Transfers Across Disrupted Households: Absent Fathers' Contribution to the Well-Being of Their Children." In S. J. South and S. E. Tolnay, eds. *The Changing American Family: Sociological and Demographic Perspectives.* Boulder, Col.: Westview Press, 1992, p. 226.

Thomas, Susan L. "From the Culture of Poverty to the Culture of Single Motherhood: The New Poverty Paridigm." *Woman and Politics* 14, no. 65 (1994): 65–98.

Wakefield, H., and R. Underwager. "Personality Characteristics of Parents Making False Accusations of Sexual Abuse in Custody Cases." *Issues in Child Abuse Accusations* 2 (1990): 121–36.

Ward, Peggie. "Family Wars: The Alienation of Children." *Custody Newsletter,* no. 9, 1993.

Wattenberg, Esther. "Paternity Actions and Young Fathers." In Robert Lerman and Theodora Ooms, eds. *Young Unwed Fathers: Changing Roles and Emerging Policies.* Philadelphia: Temple University Press, 1993.

Williams, Victoria Schwartz, and Robert G. Williams. "Identifying Daddy: The Role of the Court in Establishing Paternity." *Judges' Journal* 28, no 2 (1989).

Zill, Nicholas, Donna Ruane Morrison, and Mary Jo Coiro. "Long-Term Effects of Parental Divorce on Parent-Child Relationships, Adjustment, and Achievement in Young Adulthood." *Journal of Family Psychology* 7 (1993): 91–103.

Resources

This list of resources is by no means a complete or comprehensive guide. It is designed to offer some immediate answers to your questions and to steer you in the right direction.

Many of the resources listed here have e-mail addresses or Internet Web sites. If you don't have a computer or access to one, don't worry. Your public library probably does and you can tap into many of these valuable resources there.

Activities and Advice, General

BABYCENTER.COM has a huge selection of resources for parents of infants, babies, and toddlers. I write a regular column for them on fatherhood issues.
www.babycenter.com/

FAMILY.COM has a number of columnists who dispense advice on just about every topic you can imagine. It's a Disney property so expect more than a little advertising, but it's a great source of information and support.
www.family.com/

PARENTSPLACE.COM has one of the largest clearinghouses of parenting advice on the Net. Their bulletin boards are especially interesting and offer answers from other parents on just about any aspect of parenting.
parentsplace.com/

Resources

PARENTSOUP is run by the same people who own ParentsPlace.com. There's some overlap, but this is still another great source of valuable info.
www.parentsoup.com/

POSITIVEPARENTING.COM offers on-line parenting classes and links to other good parenting sites.
www.positiveparenting.com/

Erickson, Donna. *Donna's Day: Fun Activities that Bring the Family Together.* New York: HarperCollins, 1998.

Krane, Gary. *Simple Fun for Busy People: 333 Free Ways to Enjoy Your Loved Ones More in the Time You Have.* Berkeley, Calif.: Conari Press, 1998.

Child Care

CHILD CARE ACTION CAMPAIGN produces a variety of pamphlets that can help you approach your employer with your preschool questions and suggestions. They'll be glad to send you a complete catalog.
330 Seventh Avenue, 17th floor
New York, NY 10001
Tel.: (212) 239-0138
e-mail: hn5746@handsnet.org
www.usakids.org/sites/ccac.html

CHILD CARE AWARE is a nonprofit initiative whose mission is to ensure that all parents have access to good information about finding quality child care and resources in their community.
Tel.: (800) 424-2246
www.naccrra.net or www.naccrra.net/childcareaware/index.htm

NATIONAL ASSOCIATION FOR THE EDUCATION OF YOUNG CHILDREN administers an accreditation system to which nearly 6,000 preschools, kindergartens, and child-care centers conform.
www.naeyc.org (for general information)
www.naeyc.org/accreditation/accred_index.htm (to find an accredited center on line)

THE NATIONAL SCHOOL-AGE CARE ALLIANCE supports and accredits quality programs for school-age children and youth in their out-of-school hours.
1137 Washington Street
Boston, MA 02124

Tel.: (617) 298-5012
Fax: (617) 298-5022
e-mail: staff@nsaca.org
www.nsaca.org

Pardini, Jane Crowley. *The Babysitter Book: Everything You and Your Babyistter Need to Know Before You Leave the House.* Chicago: Contemporary Books, 1996.

Shatoff, Debra K. *In-Home Child Care: A Step-by-Step Guide to Quality, Affordable Care.* St. Louis: Family CareWare, 1998.

Discipline

Jane Nelsen's Positive Discipline series of books is great for all ages and stages. You can pick them up in just about any book store, or order them from:
Prima Publishing
P.O. Box 1260
Rocklin, CA 95677-1260
Tel.: (800) 632-8676

Fatherhood, General

FATHER'S WORLD is an on-line community for men who want to learn more about fatherhood. The focus is on balancing work and family, health and fitness, and making fatherhood fun.
www.fathersworld.com

FATHER'S RESOURCE CENTER offers parenting classes, support groups, and workshops geared toward helping fathers become more capable and involved parents so that fathers, mothers, children, and subsequently all society will benefit.
5701 Shingle Creek Parkway, Suite 500
Brooklyn Center, MN 55430
Tel.: (612) 560-8656

FATHERWORK is a Web site designed to encourage good fathering. The folks at FatherWork view fathering not so much as a social role men play, but as the work they do each day to care for the next generation.
fatherwork.byu.edu

NATIONAL CENTER FOR FATHERING offers resources designed to help men become more aware of their own fathering style and then work toward improving their skills. Call for a free issue of NCF's quarterly magazine, *Today's Father.*

10200 West 75th Street, Suite 267
Shawnee Mission, KS 66204-2223
Tel.: (800) 593-DADS
e-mail: ncf@aol.com
www.fathers.com

NATIONAL FATHERHOOD INITIATIVE conducts public awareness campaigns promoting responsible fatherhood, organizes conferences and community fatherhood forums, provides resource material to organizations seeking to establish support programs for fathers, publishes a quarterly newsletter, and disseminates information material to men seeking to become more effective fathers.

1 Bank Street, Suite 160
Gaithersburg, MD 20878
Tel.: (800) 790-DADS (3237) for recorded information or (301) 948-0599
for a real person
www. fatherhood.org

Fathers, Divorced

AMERICAN COALITION FOR FATHERS AND CHILDREN works to create a family law system and educate the public on issues that promote equal rights for all parties affected by divorce or the breakup a family, with the goal of improving the emotional and psychological well-being of children.

1718 M Street NW, Suite 187
Washington, DC 20036
Tel.: (800) 978-3237

BEECH ACRES' ARING INSTITUTE puts out an information-packed, wisdom-filled booklet called "Helping Children Cope with Divorce," which is available from:

6881 Beechmont, Avenue
Cincinnati, OH 45230
Tel.: (513) 231-6630

CHILDREN'S RIGHTS COUNCIL has a well-stocked catalog of resources, including great books on the subject for kids and their parents.

www.vix.com/crc/catalog.htm

DADS & DIVORCE: AN INTERNET RESOURCE GUIDE provides a thorough listing of Internet resources for divorced fathers.

www.digitalfx.com/dads/

THE DIVORCE SURVIVAL GUIDE is a free monthly e-mail newsletter intended for people going through a separation or divorce. You can sign up at their web site:

www.divorcesurvivalguide.com

FATHERS' RIGHTS & EQUALITY EXCHANGE is a not-for-profit organization dedicated to the premise that both fathers and mothers should share equally in the parenting and support of their children.

3140 de la Cruz Avenue, Suite 200
Santa Clara, CA 95054
Tel.: (500) FOR-DADS
e-mail: free@vix.com
www.vix.com/free

NATIONAL CENTER FOR FATHERS AND CHILDREN is a civil-rights organization for fathers and children offering resources, attorney referrals, support and help dealing with custody issues, false allegations of abuse, and much more. Information is available for married, divorced, and never-married fathers.

9454 Wilshire Boulevard, Suite 207
Beverly Hills, CA 90212
Tel.: (800) SEE-DADS
e-mail: nc@ncfc.net
www.dadnkids.com/ncfc

Adler, Robert. *Sharing the Children: How to Resolve Custody Problems and Get on with Your Life.* Bethesda, Md.: Adler and Adler, 1988.

Braver, Sanford, with Diane O'Connell. *Divorced Dads: Shattering the Myths.* New York: Tarcher/Putnam, 1998.

Leving, Jeffery M. *Fathers' Rights: Hard-Hitting and Fair Advice for Every Father Involved in a Custody Dispute.* New York: Basic Books, 1997.

Fathers, Gay

ALTERNATIVE FAMILY MAGAZINE is a wonderful new magazine filled with great information for gay parents of both genders.

P.O. Box 7179
Van Nuys, CA 91409
Tel.: (818) 909-0314
e-mail: altfammag@aol.com

COLAGE (Children of Lesbians and Gays Everywhere) is a support and advocacy organization for children of gay and bisexual parents.

www.colage.org/

Resources

FAMILY PRIDE COALITION (formerly the Gay and Lesbian Parents Coalition) provides resources and support to gay and lesbian parents and has extensive links to other resources, including several excellent Web-based mailing lists that provide help geared to the specific concerns of gay fathers.

    P.O. Box 34337
    San Diego, CA 92163
    Tel.: (619) 296-0199
    www.familypride.org

GAY DAD MAILING LIST offers support to all dads for the ups, downs, issues, and fun of being a gay/bi father. Sign up through their Web site:

    www.milepost1.com/mailing/lists/dadmail.html

LAMBDA LEGAL DEFENSE AND EDUCATION FUND may be able to provide assistance and guidance with severe legal problems.

    666 Broadway
    New York, NY 10012
    Tel.: (212) 995-8585

NATIONAL GAY AND LESBIAN TASK FORCE offers general help and can hook you up with a support group in your area.

    2320 17th Street NW
    Washington, DC 20009
    Tel.: (202) 332-6483

Curry, Hayden, Denis Clifford, and Robin Leonard. *A Legal Guide for Lesbian and Gay Couples.* Berkeley, Calif.: Nolo Press, 1996.

Martin, April. *The Lesbian and Gay Parenting Handbook: Creating and Raising Our Families.* New York: HarperPerennial, 1993.

Fathers, Long-Distance

THE WRITE CONNECTION is especially for fathers with kids 4 to 12. Includes helpful information and guidance on writing letters that will keep the child entertained, hints on kids' interests at various ages, and some suggestions about what to write about. Also available on videotape.

    P.O. Box 293
    Lake Forest, CA 92630
    Tel.: (800) 334-3143

Newman, George. *101 Ways to Be a Long-Distance Super Dad . . . or Mom, Too.* Tucson, Ariz.: Blossom Valley Press, 1996.

Fathers, Never-Married

See AMERICAN COALITION FOR FATHERS AND CHILDREN, NATIONAL CENTER FOR FATHERS AND CHILDREN, and FATHERS' RIGHTS EQUALITY EXCHANGE, in Fathers, Divorced, or the appropriate resource in Problems, Fatherhood, General, or Advice, General

Fathers, Primary or Sole Caretaker

AT-HOME DAD NEWSLETTER offers just about everything a stay-at-home dad could want to know. The quarterly newsletter also includes in each issue the At-Home Dad Network, a listing of more than 300 dads across the country looking to connect their families through playgroups.

Peter Baylies
Publisher
61 Brightwood Ave.
North Andover, MA 01845
(508) 685 7981
e-mail: athomedad@aol.com
www.athomedad.com

SINGLE AND CUSTODIAL FATHERS NETWORK is a member-supported organization dedicated to helping fathers meet the challenge of being custodial parents. SCFN seeks to provide informational and supportive resources to custodial fathers and their families.

1700 E. Carson Street
Pittsburgh, PA 15203
Tel.: (412) 381-4800
www.single-fathers.org/index.html

SINGLE FATHER MAILING LIST is for single fathers who are solely responsible for raising their children. To subscribe, send the message *subscribe single-father* to Majordomo@list.pitt.edu.

Fathers, Single (General)

PARENTS WITHOUT PARTNERS
401 N. Michigan Avenue
Chicago, IL 60611
Tel.: (800) 637-7974 or (312) 644-6610
www.parentswithoutpartners.org/

Resources

SOLO is a reasonably father-friendly magazine for single parents.
   c/o Hall/Sloane Publishing
   10840 Camarillo Street, Suite 10
   Toluca Lake, CA 91602
   Tel.: (800) 477-5877
   http://pages.prodigy.com/Solo/guide.htm

Fathers, Step

STEPFAMILY ASSOCIATION OF AMERICA
   Tel.: (800) 735-0329
   www.stepfam.org/

Bray, James, and John Kelly. *Step Families: Love, Marriage, and Parenting in the First Decade.* New York: Broadway Books, 1998.

Ford, Judy, and Anna Chase. *Wonderful Ways to Be a Stepparent.* Berkeley, Calif.: Conari Press, 1999.

Pickhardt, Carl. Keys to Successful Stepfathering. New York: Barron's, 1997.

Fathers, Widowed

NEW HOPE FOR WIDOW/ERS AND THEIR FAMILIES is a newsletter addressing the needs of widows and widowers raising children at home; it has special sections for widowers. For a free sample issue, contact:
   Grace Lacoursiere
   New Hope Newsletter
   Box 20031
   Vernon, BC V1T 9L4 Canada
   e-mail: lacoursi@bc.sympatico.ca
   www.geocities.com/Heartland/Hills/2015/
   or
   www3.bc.sympatico.ca/NewHope/

WIDOWNET is a great source of information and self-help resources for widows and widowers on a wide variety of topics. It also includes links to other related and helpful Web sites.
   www.fortnet.org/WidowNet

Kushner, Harold S. *When Bad Things Happen to Good People.* New York: Avon Books, 1983.

Finances (College Savings, Estate Planning)

COLLEGE SAVINGS PLAN NETWORK
P.O. Box 11910
Lexington, KY 40578-1910
Tel.: (606) 244-8175
Fax: (606) 244-8053
www.collegesavings.org

DRIP Investor
www.dripinvestor.com/

NETSTOCK DIRECT
www.netstockdirect.com

Monroe, Paula Ann. *Left-Brain Finance for Right-Brain People: A Money Guide for the Creatively Inclined.* Naperville, Ill.: Sourcebooks, 1996.

Platt, Harvey J. *Your Living Trust and Estate Plan: How to Maximize Your Family's Assets and Protect Your Loved Ones.* New York: Allworth Press, 1995.

Tyson, Eric. *Personal Finance for Dummies.* Foster City, Calif.: IDG Books, 1995.

Mediation

ACADEMY OF FAMILY MEDIATORS can give you a referral to a certified family mediator in your area.
5 Militia Drive
Lexington, MA 02173
Tel.: (781) 674-2663
e-mail: afmoffice@mediators.org
www.mediators.org

Problems

If your child is being alienated from you, consult *The Parental Alienation Syndrome,* by Richard Gardner, the most comprehensive look at the problem available. You can order it from the publisher:
Creative Therapeutics
155 County Road
P.O. Box 522
Cresskill, NJ 07626-0317
Tel.: (800) 544-6162

Resources

CHILD SUPPORT ENFORCEMENT is a private agency that tracks down delinquent parents if you need help collecting child support.
Tel.: (800) 801-KIDS

ACES offers a brochure on collecting child support (but don't expect much help from them otherwise).
Tel.: (800) 537-7072

FEDERAL OFFICE OF CHILD SUPPORT ENFORCEMENT in Washington, D.C., is required to assist you in collecting unpaid and delinquent support from your ex.
Tel.: (202) 401-9373
www.acf.dhhs.gov/programs/cse/

If you're having problems related to child custody, see AMERICAN COALITION FOR FATHERS AND CHILDREN, NATIONAL CENTER FOR FATHERS AND CHILDREN, FATHERS' RIGHTS EQUALITY EXCHANGE, and other resources in Fathers, Divorced.

Hardwick, Charlotte. *Win Your Child Custody War*, rev. ed. Livingston, Tex.: Pale Horse Publishing, 1998.
P.O. Box 1447
Livingston, TX 77360
Tel.: (409) 327-9666

PARENTAL ABDUCTION SEARCH SPECIALISTS can help if your child has been kidnapped.
3116 North Federal Highway, Suite 194
Pompano Beach, FL 33064
Tel.: (954) 783-2304
Fax: (954) 782-1947
e-mail: pass@parentalabduction.com
www.parentalabduction.com/

If you have any comments or suggestions about anything contained in this book, or resources you think should be included, please let me know. We'll try to include them in future printings.
Armin Brott
P.O. Box 2458
Berkeley, CA 94702
e-mail: armin@pacbell.net

Index

Index

Index

Index

National Center for Missing or Exploited Children (NCMEC), 193
National Gay and Lesbian Task Force, 55
Neely, Richard, 48
negative intimacy, 16
Nelsen, Jane, 152, 161, 162
Neuman, M. Gary, 44, 52, 56–57
Newman, Barbara and Philip, 141
nursery schools. *See* preschools, nursery schools, or day-care centers
nutrition, 22, 251

O

obedience, 112
Oddenino, Michael, 119
offers of help, 23
Oobleck, 139
overbooked children, 82

P

paralysis: father's feelings of, 18
Parental Alienation Syndrome (PAS), 57, 74, 81, 88, 183, 184–87, 291; levels of, 185–86; what to do about, 187
parenting advice, 283–84
parenting agreements, 44, 47–51, 172; preparing your own, 271–74
"parenting" behaviors: in children, 85, 113
parenting skills, 75
parenting styles, 152; differences in, 44; of fathers vs. mothers, 130–31
parents (of single father): breaking news of breakup to, 102–3; reactions of, to your love life, 259. *See also* grandparents
Parents Without Partners, 246
Parke, Ross, 112, 122, 132
part-time work, 196
Pasely, Kay, 268, 269
passports, 192
patience: and evolution of feelings, 22–23
Patterson, Charlotte, 61
Pearson, Jessica, 35, 42
Petronio, Sandra, 155, 156
phone calls: between visits, 74, 79–80, 92; children allowed to make, 114; kidnapping risk and, 193; long-distance dads and, 154–55
photo albums, 214
Pickhardt, Carl, 269

play, 130–34; cognitive development and, 132–33; with fathers vs. mothers, 130–31; imaginative, 112–13, 137, 139–40; with infants, 130–31, 135, 136–37; with peers, 111, 139; of toddlers, 111, 138, 139–41
Popenoe, David, 264
preschoolers (3–5 years), 97; access schedules for, 79, 81; adjustment problems of, 80–81; feelings of, 111–13; interpersonal problems of, 122; involving yourself with, 142–44
preschools, nursery schools, or day-care centers, 200, 204–9; accreditation and licensing of, 207; evaluating caregivers in, 205–6; evaluating facilities of, 206; evaluating programs of, 206–7; red flags for, 207–8
preteens (10–12 years): access schedules for, 79–80, 81; adjustment problems of, 80–81; feelings of, 115–16; phone calls to, 154; staying involved with, 147–49
pretend play, 137, 139–40
primary custody. *See* sole custody
privacy, 44, 149
probate, 242, 243
property settlements, 26, 34, 72
psychological problems: in children, 128–29
puberty, 150–53
public assistance, 71
punishment, 160, 161–62; corporal, 163

Q

Questions from Dad (Twilley), 156, 158

R

Radin, Norma, 131–32
Railsback, Tom, 54
reaching games, 135
reading, 147–48; to children, 135, 137, 139, 141, 142, 145
reconciliation fantasies, 43, 113, 119, 125
regressions, 80, 111, 112, 121
rejection: father's feelings of, 19
relatives, 174–78; breaking news about breakup to, 102–3; as day-care providers, 205; ex's side of family, 174–75; of widowed fathers, 175; your side of family, 176–78. *See also* grandparents

CARTOON CREDITS

About the Author

Armin Brott, author of *The Expectant Father: Facts, Tips, and Advice for Dads-to-Be, The New Father: A Dad's Guide to the First Year,* and *The New Father: A Dad's Guide to the Toddler Years,* has written extensively on parenting and fatherhood for such publications as *Newsweek,* the *New York Times Magazine,* the *Washington Post, Redbook, Parenting, Baby Talk, American Baby,* and *Child.* He is also the host of "Positive Parenting," a weekly talk show on one of San Francisco's top radio stations. A single father, Brott equally shares custody of his two young children.